THE
HUMAN
CULTURE
IMPERATIVE

THE LEADER'S PLAYBOOK
FOR INNOVATION AND
SUSTAINABLE GROWTH

Dr Linden R. Brown, Dr Chris L. Brown
and Sean Crichton-Browne

First published in 2025 by MarketCulture Pty Ltd
ABN 70673792197 | www.marketculture.com

External content:

Dr Linden R. Brown, Dr Chris L. Brown and Sean Crichton-Browne have no responsibility for the persistence or accuracy of URLs or QR codes for external or third-party Internet Websites referred to in this publication and do not guarantee that any content on such Websites is, or will remain, accurate or appropriate.

URLs and QR codes have been included to offer supplementary information or video content from the organisation or individual mentioned.

At the end of each chapter, you'll find a QR code linking to a podcast version of the chapter, created using Google NotebookLM.

Editor: The Editorial Collective – Fiona Crawford
Graphics: Corporate Identity Design – Andy Mathers
Typesetter: Pure Colours Digital Imaging – Ellie MacLulich

NATIONAL LIBRARY OF AUSTRALIA

A catalogue record for this book is available from the National Library of Australia

ISBN: 978-0-9943697-9-6 (hardback)
ISBN: 978-1-7642219-0-0 (paperback)
ISBN: 978-1-7642219-1-7 (ebook)

The team at MarketCulture dedicates this book to our partners, our customers, their employees, and the visionary leaders who have embraced our frameworks, methodologies, and measurement tools to build human-focused customer cultures and achieve remarkable success. This book would not exist without your commitment and collaboration. We extend our heartfelt thanks to Dr Stan Glaser and Jerker Fagerström for their invaluable guidance and insightful feedback throughout this journey. We are also deeply grateful to the organisations and individuals who generously gave their time for interviews and feedback. Your contributions shaped this book into what it is today.

ENDORSEMENTS

"This book reminded me of my days at Telstra, where we were committed to building a culture that put people and customers at the heart of everything. It's a powerful reminder, that I have been reminded of regularly, that true innovation and sustainable growth begin with a people-first mindset. Any leader serious about transformation should read this book and use the powerful tools it provides."

David Thodey OA—Chancellor University of Sydney,
Former Chair CSIRO, Former CEO Telstra

"As I travel the world working with organisations across the public and private sectors, one theme consistently stands out: culture or more accurately, the lack of it. Of all the capabilities needed to build a truly customer-centric organisation, culture is repeatedly cited by experience management practitioners and business leaders as the area most lacking in maturity. That's why The Human Culture Imperative is such an essential read. Written by some of the most knowledgeable minds in organisational culture, this book goes far beyond theory. It shows what it really takes to build businesses that are not only customer-led but genuinely HUMAN-led. For leaders determined to design organisations that endure in an increasingly unpredictable world, The Human Culture Imperative is the definitive playbook for sustainable growth."

Ian Golding—CCXP, Global CX Specialist

"I really do believe the MRI was a key contributor to driving our member focused culture which ultimately got us through a period of intense competition."

Linda Bostock GAICD—Former CEO & MD of StateCover Mutual Limited

"All the work we did globally at Wright Medical really moved the dial of change....it reminded me today of how satisfying the MRI process was as we saw the positive improvements to the business and culture. This will be a great practical guide for leaders."

Peter Cooke—Former International President Wright Medical Group

"This book is a game-changer for anyone looking to transform their organisation into an experience-led powerhouse. Through MarketCulture's proven framework, readers will gain actionable insights on how to embed experience-driven thinking into every level of their business. It shows how to create a culture that thrives on purpose, collaboration, and continuous improvement—empowering leaders and employees alike to make real-time, impactful decisions. The book doesn't just offer theory; it provides the structure, platform, practical tools and measurement techniques to ensure that every experience initiative aligns with your business goals and drives tangible, measurable success. When you're navigating cultural shifts, this book is critical to learn and leverage what has worked for other companies and will equip you with the strategies and execution tools to lead a truly experience-led transformation."

Diane Magers, CCXP, MS, MBA—Founder, CEO Experience Catalysts

"These authors have managed markets from pickled onions to AI and the experience shows. There are numerous ways to lead improvements in corporate performance and this book is replete with examples. Most importantly it shows how these changes can be measured, tracked and quantified. Do changes in your corporate culture have an impact on ROI? The Human Culture Imperative calculates the numbers and explains how the strategies work."

Dr Stan Glaser—Emeritus Professor Macquarie University,
Emeritus Professor Australian National Institute of Management and Commerce.

"*The Human Culture Imperative deserves its place among the most respected works in contemporary business thought. More than a theoretical discussion, it offers practical tools to measure and enhance both employee and customer centricity, while demonstrating a compelling link between human connectedness and business success. A must-read for any leader committed to building a business grounded in humanity.*"

Dr David Cooke—Author, *Kind Business: How Values Create Value*

"*The Human Culture Imperative is built on a human-first philosophy, offering leaders a practical framework to unite their leadership teams, inspire employees, and, most importantly, deeply connect with customers. The authors have transformed the often-intangible concepts of culture and engagement into something clear, actionable, and measurable. This is more than a book, it's a guide for any leader determined to create a lasting legacy that inspires people and drives meaningful impact.*"

Nicole Noye—Non Executive Director

"*Published in the Harvard Business Review in 1994, "Putting the Service-Profit Chain to Work" (Heskett et al.) highlighted the link between internal service quality and business performance. Few have advanced this thinking as effectively as the authors of The Human Culture Imperative, who offer a practical framework and tools for building a customer-centric culture that drives loyalty and profitable growth. From the 'Three Pillars of Human Engagement' to the 'Market Responsiveness Index', this book empowers readers to activate the service-profit chain in their own organisations.*"

Tom DeWitt—Executive Director of the XM Global Collaborative.

"Having used the MRI and worked with the MarketCulture team for many years, I was excited to read their new book. It brings the theory, and then adds examples from the real world, from around the world, large corporations, and small companies. This demonstrates the value of the process across geography, industry and business size."

Bryan Jago—Executive Manager Service, Canon Medical Systems ANZ Pty Limited

"The Human Culture Imperative offers a practical roadmap for leaders who understand that culture isn't a 'soft' thing - it's the main thing. It's a timely, thoughtful, and actionable guide that aligns beautifully with my belief that culture is not part of the game - it is the game."

Garry Ridge—Chairman Emeritus, WD-40 Company
USA Today Bestselling Author of *Any Dumb Ass Can Do It*

"This book has emphasised the very necessary element of humanity and connection to customer centricity and sets out many practical examples of the MRI in action with the human factors of strategic alignment, empowerment and collaboration and the power of a human centric customer culture imperative."

John Stanhope AM—Chancellor of Deakin University,
Former CFO of Telstra and Chairman of Australia Post

CONTENTS

INTRODUCTION
THE HUMAN CULTURE IMPERATIVE

The Leaders Playbook for Innovation and Sustainable Growth

Our Story

Sometimes the most profound insights emerge from unexpected places, from the intersections of different lives, different perspectives, and different dreams. Our story, the story of three individuals whose paths would converge around a revolutionary discovery, begins in three very different places.

Linden's Story: A Journey in Customer-Centric Leadership

Business was in my blood. Growing up in a family of entrepreneurs, I learned early on that success came from knowing your customers—not just their names, but their needs, frustrations, and preferences. My parents built two thriving businesses in different industries simply by putting people first.

That lesson stayed with me when, in our twenties, my cousin Ben and I bought Blue Banner Pickles. We took over a beloved Tasmanian brand with a 90% market share. But when we expanded interstate, we hit a wall. What worked locally didn't translate nationally. We realised that product alone wasn't enough. We had to understand and adapt to the needs of new customers. It was a crash course in the importance of customer focus.

My first corporate job at Cadbury taught me a different kind of lesson. In a rigid, hierarchical system, listening to the customer often took a back seat. I watched opportunities slip by simply because leaders didn't seek frontline feedback. That experience cemented what I already knew: business success is built on understanding people not just processes.

Later, I co-founded a removals company in Sydney, serving Greek immigrants moving back home. We succeeded by targeting a niche market, focusing relentlessly on the customer, and empowering staff to improve how we served them. The formula was clear: leadership, teamwork, and a customer-first mindset.

In time, I turned to academia and spent two decades researching marketing and corporate culture across Australia, Europe, and the US. I saw the same problems repeated: businesses cared about customers but lacked the culture to act on it. Leaders managed systems not relationships. Employees followed procedures not customer needs.

That realisation sparked a mission. I moved to Silicon Valley and spent 15 years consulting to US global firms. In the early years I led a research team with Chris to crack the customer centricity code. The result was the MRI, a system to measure, build, and sustain a strong customer culture. It's not just a theory. It's a proven, actionable model that helps companies unlock growth, gain competitive edge, and create workplaces where both customers and employees thrive.

From Tasmania to the world stage, one belief has shaped my journey: businesses that put people first win. This book is about building that kind of culture. One where listening, learning, and leading with empathy drive real, sustainable success.

Chris's Story: From Tech to Customer-Centric Leadership

My journey began in the high-pressure world of tech distribution at Tech Pacific (later Ingram Micro), where thin margins made every decision critical. In that environment, relationships were everything. The real value wasn't in the products, but in how we worked with dealers.

From there, I joined HP as a Product Manager in Imaging and Printing. HP's culture was a deeply human one, in which leaders were expected to stay connected, listen, and lead with purpose. I worked with engineers who were genuinely obsessed with how customers used our products. But over time, the culture shifted. The focus moved from people to performance, and the human element started to fade.

A turning point came when I began training HP Product Managers across the globe. I saw firsthand that even the best strategies collapse in cultures that aren't market focused. That insight lit a fire in me: culture either powers strategy or destroys it.

That passion led Linden and I to develop the MRI, a tool that measures the degree to which a company is truly customer-centric. I wanted to make culture more tangible by grounding it in behaviours that can be observed and measured. I saw how leaders reacted when faced with real employee feedback. Some denied it. The best? They listened, acted, and transformed.

One moment stands out. A senior executive challenged the MRI findings. I calmly pointed out, "This isn't my opinion. This is what your people are saying." Months later, I watched him host a customer event where genuine engagement replaced surface-level interaction. The change was real and powerful.

To dig deeper I conducted more research to find out what sets great, customer-centric leaders apart. The key? They don't just accept feedback, they seek it, even when it's uncomfortable.

That's what this book is about: helping leaders build cultures where feedback is fuel, employees are energised, and customers become advocates. Because success isn't just about results, it's about the journey you take to get there.

Sean's Story: From Sales to Culture Transformation

I spent 25 years at Konica Minolta, not just selling production print technology but helping businesses adapt and grow. The real key to success? Trust. Customers didn't just want products, they wanted partners who understood their world.

"I'll never buy a digital printer!" That's what the owner of one of Sydney's largest offset printing companies shouted while chasing me out of his warehouse with a wrench in his hand. His resistance wasn't just about technology; it was personal, emotional, and deeply rooted in decades of doing things a certain way. Fast forward a few years, and that same owner became one of my most loyal customers. What changed? Not the technology. The relationship. I took the time to listen, understand his concerns, and show him how digital print could complement, not replace, his world. By focusing on trust and delivering consistent value, we turned a staunch sceptic into a passionate advocate.

Customer-centricity is a team sport. Early in my career, I believed customer experience was my responsibility alone. I quickly came to understand that real impact is achieved when the entire organisation aligns around the customer. With support from a bold leader, we broke down silos. We even brought our accounts receivable team to meet clients, turning invoice numbers into real relationships. The result? Loyalty extended far beyond me. The results spoke for themselves.

When I left Konica Minolta, customers stayed not just because of me, but because they trusted the whole company. That's the power of a true customer-centric culture.

At MarketCulture, I've helped global businesses from large enterprise organisations like Deutsche Telekom to organisations of 15 employees like 3e Advantage create lasting change. This has proven to me that changing culture can happen in businesses of any size.

Changing culture isn't easy but it's possible. When companies truly listen and act on what customers and employees say, the results are extraordinary. Engagement rises. Loyalty deepens. Performance improves. That's what I help leaders do every day: turn customer-centricity from idea to action. Because when you shift mindsets, you transform outcomes.

And that's what our human-centred methodology is all about: a proven system, real-world experience, and a global network dedicated to making customer culture measurable, actionable, and unstoppable.

The Awakening

Our individual journeys were marked by moments of profound realisation—what we now call our "engagement epiphanies".

For Linden, this realisation came through years of observing the growing disconnect between academic theory and business reality. In a university classroom, Linden stood before his students, teaching the principles of business that he'd refined over decades in academia. "I remember the moment everything changed, he reflects now. A student raised her hand and asked, 'But Professor, if these principles work so well, why are so many businesses failing to connect with their people?' That question would trouble me for years, eventually leading me down a path I never expected."

His research kept pointing to a fundamental fact. The most successful organisations weren't necessarily those with the best strategies on paper, it was those that had mastered the art of human connection.

Across town, in the bustling offices of Konica Minolta, Sean was discovering something that would transform his understanding of business forever. "Every day, I watched brilliant sales strategies fall flat", he shares, leaning forward with the intensity that has become his trademark. "It wasn't about the products or the pricing; it was about something deeper, something human. I saw companies investing millions in technology while overlooking the fundamental power of genuine human connection."

Sean's revelation emerged from the trenches of sales and entrepreneurship. "I remember sitting in a client's office," he shares, "watching their employees shuffle past, eyes down, spirits low. The company had invested in cutting-edge technology and processes, but they'd forgotten about the hearts beating inside their walls. That's when I knew we weren't just facing a business problem, we were facing a human one."

Meanwhile, Chris was immersed in the digital world, orchestrating marketing campaigns that looked perfect on paper. "The metrics were beautiful", he recalls. "Click-through rates, engagement statistics, conversion funnels everything tracked perfectly. But something was missing. I could feel it in my gut, even if I couldn't name it yet."

For Chris, the awakening was sparked by technology itself. "The more I worked with marketing automation and AI, the more I realised that these tools were meant to enhance human connection, not replace it. But somewhere along the way, businesses got it backwards. They were using technology to create distance rather than bridge it. Yet, I've found that the more 'hi-tech' you have the more 'hi-touch' you need for success."

When our paths finally crossed, it wasn't just a meeting of minds it was a collision of perspectives that would spark something bigger than any of us could have imagined. Linden brought the academic rigour and theoretical foundation. Sean contributed the raw, real-world insights from the frontlines of business transformation. And Chris added the technological perspective that would help us translate human insights into actionable tools.

Together, we began to see patterns that none of us could have recognised alone. Through our work with the Market Responsiveness Index (MRI), we've had the privilege of witnessing transformations in over 1,000 organisations. Each company's story added another piece to the puzzle we were assembling, which, when our solution is applied, reveals the true nature of business growth in the modern age.

Perhaps the most beautiful irony we've discovered is that, in an era obsessed with digital transformation, the key to sustainable growth isn't technological at all; its fundamentally human. As Linden often says, "The greatest technological advancement in business history would be for leaders to truly listen to their people".

Sean adds, "Every successful sale I ever made came down to one thing: genuine human connection. When we scale that principle across an entire organisation, the results are extraordinary."

And Chris, with his technology background, puts it this way: "The best technology in the world is useless without human engagement. It's not about replacing human connection—it's about enabling it."

This Book—And Why It Matters

The world of work has changed and so have the rules for growth. Disengaged employees and disconnected cultures quietly drain performance, innovation, and customer loyalty. Over the past two decades, the MarketCulture team has partnered with organisations around the world, helping them pursue business excellence. Our first book, *The Customer Culture Imperative*, explored the seven disciplines that form the foundation of a truly customer-centric culture. Here, we go a step further, taking a more holistic approach to highlight *The Human Culture Imperative*, and offering a roadmap to put those disciplines into action.

This book introduces the Engagement Growth Engine a practical, proven framework to transform engagement into a competitive edge. It's not about theory. It's about action. Think of this book as like a coach's playbook essential for guiding the team, setting strategy, implementing structure, and staying aligned under pressure. That's exactly what we aim to achieve here. It's designed to inspire and equip you to build a culture that delivers exceptional results consistently, and at scale.

This isn't a book meant to gather dust on a shelf or be remembered simply as a good read. It's a tool to be used, revisited, and relied upon as a reference to steer leaders in the right direction, especially when the path forward isn't clear.

It also supports consistency, which is often lacking in many organisations. When leaders operate from the same principles and framework, alignment is created across the organisation. As the saying goes, "Let's all sing from the same song sheet". That's how strong cultures are built and sustained.

The following chapters will provide an in-depth look at a proven framework that helps leaders stay connected with both their employees and their customers and, just as importantly, ensures customers remain connected and loyal to the business. You'll find a clear methodology for embedding this approach into your organisation, supported by tools to measure progress and success.

Most importantly, you'll read stories from real companies that have applied this methodology to drive transformation and achieve sustainable growth.

Who This Book Is For

If you're ready to build a culture where people thrive and performance follows, you're in the right place. This book is for leaders who believe that thriving businesses begin with thriving people.

- CEOs, founders, and business owners who see engagement as a growth driver, not just a "nice-to-have".
- Customer experience leaders who know great customer outcomes start with empowered employees.
- People-first executives—CHROs, COOs, CFOs, CTOs, CIOs[1]—who want to align culture with performance.
- Risk leaders and CROs who recognise culture as a critical lens for managing risk and resilience.
- Investors and board members seeking to future-proof high-performing organisations.
- And anyone who believes success is built from the inside out.

Why This Book Will Benefit You

In today's fast-moving world where customer expectations are greater than ever, competition is fierce, and employee disengagement is a growing risk, businesses can no longer rely on strategy alone. The real differentiator? Human energy. Engaged people drive performance.

This book provides a practical, research-backed framework designed to turn employee engagement and customer engagement into a powerful growth strategy. You'll gain tools to measure, manage, and scale engagement to deliver stronger customer loyalty, deeper innovation, and lasting business results.

At the centre of this approach is the MRI, a proven diagnostic measurement tool that helps leaders identify and close the gaps between intention and impact.

Building on the foundation of *The Customer Culture Imperative*, this book takes the next step: from insight to implementation.[2]

If you're ready to turn culture into your competitive advantage, this is your playbook.

What You'll Gain from This Book

1. **Turn engagement into growth:** learn how to measure and manage engagement using the MRI by linking it directly to performance, loyalty, and profit.

2. **Build a high-performance culture:** create a culture where people are energised, collaborative, innovative, and committed to delivering results.

3. **Align employee and customer experience:** discover how internal engagement drives external customer loyalty and how to connect the two.

4. **Focus on what matters:** you can ditch vague surveys because the MRI gives you clear, actionable data to drive change, not just discussion.

5. **Apply what works:** get a practical playbook with real-world examples and proven tools to activate the Engagement Growth Engine in your business.

What Success Looks Like

"Great things in business are never done by one person; they're done by a team of people." Steve Jobs—Apple

- Continuous innovation
- Higher productivity, lower burnout
- Lower employee turnover, stronger teams
- More loyal customers and revenue growth
- Clear ROI and reduced risk
- Leadership alignment and culture that lasts

If you're ready to lead with purpose and a human-centric focus, this is your playbook.

Scan or click the QR code to learn more on our Podcasts

CHAPTER 1

THE ENGAGEMENT GROWTH ENGINE

Employees Are the Life Blood of Any Organisation

The Profit Equation: Happy Customers = Happy Culture

At first glance, you might think we've got this the wrong way around: doesn't a happy culture create happy customers?

Time and again, we've seen that focusing solely on employee engagement can fall short. Many well-intentioned companies become too inward-looking, creating workplaces where employees are happy with each other but disconnected from what really matters: the customer experience.

Our experience working with diverse organisations shows that it's often the other way around. When customers are genuinely delighted, employees feel proud, motivated, and connected to a purpose beyond themselves. Happy customers create a culture people want to be part of and that's where real profit begins.

This book is all about challenging assumptions and rethinking old ideas. It's inspired by the authors' experiences of what makes organisations truly successful. One insight stands out above all: in today's world of relentless disruption driven by rapid technological advancement and the powerful, often unchecked influence of social media, retaining customers and driving sustainable growth has never been more critical. This dynamic environment offers extraordinary opportunities but also serious risks. In the end, the ability for organisations to win and keep customers will be the defining factor between those that succeed and those that disappear.

Leaders often say that changing their organisational culture is the most difficult challenge they face. The solution to this problem is to have a clear methodology. Without a way to measure culture objectively, track progress, and connect it directly to business outcomes, it's hard to build the confidence needed to act.

What is Culture?

The word culture originates from the Latin "cultura", meaning "care". In a business context, culture is often summed up by the phrase, "It's what we do around here". But it goes deeper than that. Culture is the collective set of behaviours, values, attitudes, and unwritten rules that shape how people act and behave. It's reflected in how individuals in an organisation respond to challenges, make decisions, treat customers, and collaborate with colleagues. Ultimately, culture isn't what's written on the walls—it's the behaviours lived throughout the organisation.

Customer Culture and Business Performance

The customer culture pyramid illustrates a concept from two viewpoints. Starting from the base of the pyramid, a strong customer-centric culture is the foundation for creating a superior customer experience. This, in turn, fosters customer loyalty, ultimately driving sustainable revenue and profit growth. Alternatively, many leaders begin at the top, with financial targets. However, the figure emphasises that without customers, a business cannot survive. Customer loyalty, fuelled by advocacy, is essential for sustained financial performance. Achieving this loyalty requires delivering a superior customer experience, which is directly supported by a culture where leaders and employees consistently prioritise excellent service.

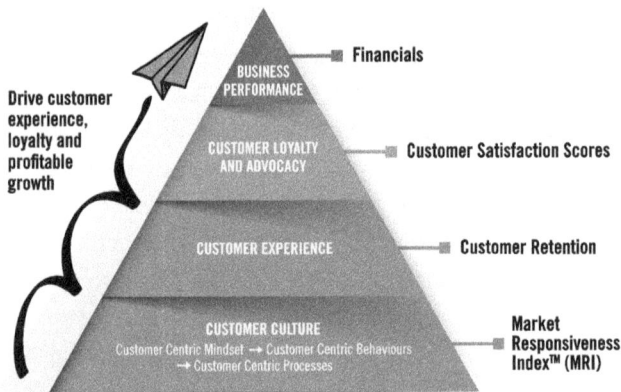

Linden

As a marketing professor working across the UK, Europe, and the Asia-Pacific, and through delivering marketing programs for major global organisations, I could see troubling gaps in our understanding of what drives sustained organisational success. I was frustrated at witnessing profitable companies operating in rigid silos, often to the detriment of their customers. My PhD research on competitive strategy, detailed in *Competitive Marketing Strategy*,[3] highlights how dominant firms in sectors like telecom and banking used resources, regulations, and defensive tactics to protect their market share. Yet, I also saw how internal inefficiencies, poor cross-functional alignment, and weak customer connections left them vulnerable to disruptive challengers. My passion for business and customer value has been a lifelong driver in exploring these issues. I've combined my research and experience to help more than 1,000 companies successfully transform their cultures using MarketCulture's proven methodology and measurement system.

Culture is the Foundation of Any Organisation—Especially for the Customer

Culture isn't just internal; it shapes how an organisation serves its customers. A company's values and behaviours directly impact the customer experience. When culture is aligned and customer-centric, it builds trust, loyalty, and long-term value.

A customer-focused culture empowers employees to act with empathy, responsiveness, and ownership. These traits should transcend from leadership to every level of the business. From product design to support, strong culture ensures decisions prioritise customer impact.

Customers notice culture. They feel it in engaged employees, clear communication, and kept promises. A fractured culture, by contrast, leads to missed expectations and weak connections. In today's competitive landscape, culture is an edge. It drives internal unity and external credibility. The most successful organisations make culture and customer focus inseparable. Ultimately, culture doesn't just support the customer experience. It *creates* it.

Chris

In the early 2000s, my work at Hewlett-Packard and as a marketing consultant in Silicon Valley uncovered a key insight: organisations that lost customer focus by turning inward were inevitably headed for acquisition or failure. This inability to maintain customer connection proved particularly problematic as technological advancements reshaped industries and redefined how businesses needed to engage with their clientele, leaving many incumbent market leaders struggling to adapt. Some of my marketing initiatives fell short, not due to poor strategy but because of a lack of customer focus and insufficient buy-in from key departments. This caused me immense frustration. But over time I began to understand why many of my marketing colleagues claimed they spent just 10% of their time focused on customers and 90% navigating internal dynamics and communications to secure buy-in from other leaders.

I realised that culture is the driving force behind an organisation's ability to consistently deliver customer value and adapt to changing market and competitive conditions and ultimately succeed.

I went on to earn a doctorate from Pepperdine University in California, focused on customer-centric leadership. My research uncovered the key traits and behaviours of leaders who consistently put customers at the centre of their decision-making and how these qualities contribute to organisational success. Importantly, my findings highlight how leadership styles vary depending on the business context.

A Tool for Transforming Culture—The Market Responsiveness Index

Undoubtedly, culture plays a vital role in organisations. But what type of culture truly matters? Can it be measured? Does it genuinely impact business performance? How does it drive growth and profitability?

In our ground-breaking research, outlined in *The Customer Culture Imperative*, we discovered that many leaders and employees have limited visibility into how their organisations engage with customers. This lack of insight leads to hidden barriers that prevent revenue and profit growth from reaching their full potential. We consistently found that leaders are hindered by blind spots, often failing to tap into the valuable insights of their next level leaders and employees who, in turn, feel ignored.

What was missing was a proven methodology that could be easily implemented. Moreover, we found an absence of tangible measurement tools with a clear link to business results. However, we also identified organisations like Amazon, Apple, and Lego, that had cracked the code by building a customer-centric culture that fuelled innovation and growth. Much like a skilled doctor uses precise tools to diagnose, effective leaders need accurate insights to make informed decisions.

Our research introduced a methodology that empowers leaders with a structured approach to create a culture that fosters employee engagement and delivers exceptional customer experiences. The MRI provides a diagnostic level of precision, uncovering hidden obstacles, risks, and opportunities within an organisation bringing the invisible into focus. It was developed to assess the key behaviours of leaders and employees that drive consistent growth and uncover potential risks. The eight behavioural disciplines measured by the MRI have been scientifically validated and are directly tied to critical business outcomes, including customer retention, innovation, new product success, sustainable revenue, and profit growth. A recent study conducted at Pepperdine University in Southern California confirmed that improvements across the eight disciplines also led to increased employee satisfaction and retention.

More Information: https://www.marketculture.com/product-page/pepperdine-university-mri-study

The MRI gives leaders a unique perspective on growth and the actions needed to achieve it. Once these insights are revealed, they are unforgettable. What's even more powerful is that over 1,000 organisations have used the MRI disciplines and measurement tools to benchmark themselves against other global organisations, with the majority taking meaningful action to accelerate their growth. Chapter 4 expands on how the MRI drives business performance and growth.

Sean

Chris and I forged a strong bond through a shared love of the Tour de France and years of competing in Ironman events around the world. From these experiences we learned endurance, focus, and resilience.

I had built a 25-year career as a top sales agent at Konica Minolta. When, looking for a new challenge, Linden gave me *The Customer Culture Imperative*, I was blown away. I said to Linden, 'That's me! You've written about what I do.' My work has been guided for years by a simple but powerful decision-making framework: Is it good for the customer? The company? And for me? If yes to all three, go ahead.

Linden, Chris, and I had found a new purpose. With the courage of our convictions and our longstanding experience in research and business, we launched a three-month global tour to engage partners focused on customer experience. A standout moment came during a highly engaged workshop at the Dubai Business Women's Council. Their insights on building a people first culture underscored the value of delivering exceptional customer experiences.

We saw the same energy in Singapore, meeting with leadership coaches and development experts. One breakfast with executives from SAP, Amazon, Google, and Wolters Kluwer was especially memorable. Just as we began, Peter Moore from Amazon Web Services pulled up an extra chair. I asked him, "Are we expecting someone else?" Peter replied, "That's for the customer".

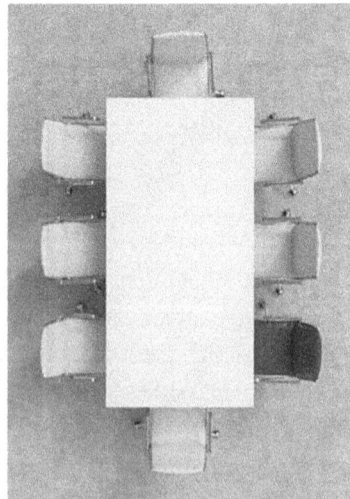

The MRI in Action

After the merger of Wright Medical (US) and Tornier (France), former International President Peter Cooke enlisted MarketCulture to help create a unified culture. We were introduced by Tara Kimbrell Cole, an MRI expert partner who leads a leadership coaching and development consultancy in Singapore. We shared stories with Peter from other companies, which immediately convinced him to implement the same approach within his organisation. Over the next three years, we worked closely with Peter and his country leadership teams, applying the MRI in various ways to embed a customer-centric culture. By the end of our engagement, Wright Medical was acquired by Stryker, with its share price having increased by an impressive 41% over the previous two years.

A Crisis of Culture in Businesses Today

Today, whether you're a leader or employee, you're expected to navigate shifts like changing customer expectations, emerging competitors, ongoing talent shortages, and sudden disruptions such as pandemics, geopolitical conflict, or shifting trade policies. Many of these forces are beyond your control. However, three tectonic shifts are reshaping the business landscape from within: the evolution of organisational culture, the transformation of the workplace, and a widespread erosion of trust.

Organisational Culture and Employee Engagement

Employees are the lifeblood of any organisation. They carry untapped insights into daily operations, hidden gems that often go unnoticed. Yet, companies frequently overlook these voices, leaving behind opportunities for innovation and growth. An example is this story about Colgate-Palmolive, which highlights the power of listening beyond the boardroom. During a late-night strategy session, the product and marketing teams wrestled with flatlining sales in the dental hygiene market. They debated costly strategies, including redesigning the toothpaste tube based on consumer complaints around the difficulty in removing the toothpaste. They also discussed launching new educational campaigns via pharmacists.

As the team mulled over ideas, a contract cleaner happened to walk by and overhear the conversation. Without breaking stride, he casually remarked,

"Why not just make the hole at the end of the tube bigger?"

That simple, offhand suggestion, landed with surprising force. The team acted on it and the result was a surge in toothpaste usage and customer satisfaction. A low-cost, high-impact innovation had come from the most unexpected place. Sometimes, the best ideas come from those not even in the meeting. All we have to do is listen.

And yet, as Gallup reports, employee engagement is at a 10-year low.[4] At one mid-sized tech firm, despite modern perks, morale was stagnant. A product manager summed it up: "How can I inspire them when I'm not inspired myself?" Disengaged managers often lead to disengaged teams.

If you're feeling emotionally stretched and underprepared, you're not alone. Nearly 60% of managers feel unequipped for the emotional and practical demands of leadership.[5] But there's hope: we have seen firsthand engagement rising more than 78% after prioritising manager development.

Struggling with clarity? Post-pandemic, role clarity has dropped from 56% to 46%, fuelling frustration and disengagement.[6] The fix starts at the top, engaged leaders empower inspired managers, and inspired managers drive engaged teams.

Workplace Transformation and Technology

The fall of industry giants like Kodak and the decline of many traditional retailers in the early internet era are stark reminders of business fragility. Workplace change is accelerating due to rapid technological disruption and shifting demographics. Automation brings both the promise of innovation and the threat of obsolescence. For instance, are Apple's low-cost EarPods disrupting the hearing aid industry despite their limited functionality, or are they adding value by offering an accessible early-adoption model?

The rise of AI presents a similar threat and opportunity for today's businesses. Its rapid rise brings the potential to significantly boost productivity across both organisations and individual roles. It has never been more important to understand the evolving needs of both the business and its customers. To successfully develop and implement AI, employees must be genuinely heard and actively involved in the process. Engaging them through education and clear communication is essential, not only to reduce fear of redundancy but to help them see how their roles can be enhanced. When employees feel supported and empowered, AI becomes a tool for growth rather than a threat, driving productivity and innovation throughout the organisation.

That is because AI is enhancing not replacing human capabilities. For example, firms are using AI to automate repetitive sales tasks, freeing up time to reintroduce phone support and improve customer engagement. This reflects a broader reality, while AI handles routine work, human skills like emotional intelligence and engagement grow in value. Organisations that integrate tech effectively understand this shift and history confirms it. From the printing press to electricity, the telephone, and mobile phones, every major innovation has been powered by human creativity. AI is no different; it's a tool for humans, not a replacement.

What really drives progress is people. Human engagement, judgment, and innovation is irreplaceable. This creates what we call the "engagement premium"—the rising value of distinctly human strengths like context, ethics, and relationship-building.

To thrive through disruption, adopt a reinvention mindset. Balance tech with human-centered leadership, and you'll position your organisation for future success.

Decline in Trust

Richard Branson's business philosophy is to enter industries with poor customer experiences like airlines, music, and banking and disrupt them with a customer-first approach, driven by empowered and engaged employees. What Branson has harnessed is a decline in trust that can have potentially catastrophic effects on business performance. It's likely pointing to a deeper issue, especially if it's reflected in rising customer complaints and eroding brand credibility.

Research shows a shift away from people-first leadership. Gallup warns that ignoring this erosion can stall innovation, increase attrition, and weaken culture.[7] Customers feel it too. Practices like prioritising new customers over loyal ones or offering indifferent service send a clear message: profit over people. While not always intentional, the impact is real and widespread.

Across industries, trust is declining. Over the past decade, sectors from banking to tech have lost public trust due to unethical or even illegal practices. Investigations have uncovered severe leadership failures, harmful incentive structures, and shocking examples like charging deceased customers.

This decline extends to public institutions and monopolies, where people feel ignored, and whistle-blowers punished. At the root of it all is a lack of humanity. What's missing is genuine care, authentic, human-centered leadership that values people both inside and outside the organisation.

The Lightbulb Moment That Led to a New Lens

A pivotal shift in our thinking occurred during the height of the COVID-19 pandemic as we presented an MRI report to Deutsche Telekom. Beatrix Kapitany, a seasoned CX executive, asked a critical question: "Some functional heads are saying, this is nice to know, but does it really matter?" Our response was clear and direct: "The blind spots we've uncovered are holding the organisation back affecting both revenue and profit". It was a scenario we had seen repeatedly in large organisations across the world where cultural misalignment quietly undermines performance.

The shift in perspective came gradually but decisively: this wasn't just about customer culture; it was about **human culture**. A human-first approach to everyone connected to the business, employees, partners, customers, and the wider community. This realisation demanded a new perspective, a human lens through which to view our work. Ultimately, growth hinges on people operating with the right mindset, behaviours, and practices—it's about engagement! This pivotal insight ignited a significant leap forward in our methodology, prompting us to revisit our MRI database and our extensive global experience to uncover new, crucial connections.

Looking back through the lens of human centricity, we realise that the seeds of this idea were sown in *The Customer Culture Imperative*. While writing the book, Linden would regularly meet with Dr Donald Williamson, a former clergyman and leadership coach, and Jerry Gleason, a longtime engineer at Hewlett-Packard. Each month, they offered feedback on the latest chapter over coffee.

During one of those meetings, Donald made a profound observation: "I believe the concept of 'customer' has a much broader application.

When a person sees another, whether a colleague, boss, partner, or buyer as a customer, it opens the door to stronger, more respectful relationships." He added, "If you want to be a leader, you first have to be an authentic person. To be customer-centric, you must be person-centric".

Donald was speaking a fundamental human truth: "when people are treated as human beings, seen and heard, both inside and outside an organisation, it builds powerful connections and lasting loyalty".[8]

Another powerful insight came from a conversation with former New Zealand All Blacks rugby coach, Graham Henry. After the team's unexpected exit from the World Cup semi-final against France in 1999, Graham recognised that the problem wasn't just tactical it was cultural. He saw the need to transform the mindset of the entire organisation: players, coaching staff, and administrators alike. The focus shifted to embedding collaboration, resilience, innovation, and sound decision making under pressure both on and off the field. Following a comprehensive review, Graham and his leadership team adopted a powerful belief: "Better people make better All Blacks". He assembled a dedicated support team whose mission extended beyond fitness, diet, and skills. Their true purpose was to help players grow in character and leadership, and to deeply understand their responsibility to each other, the team, and their fans across New Zealand and the world. The result? The All Blacks returned stronger and went on to win the next Rugby World Cup.

The MRI doesn't just measure how customer-centric an organisation is compared to the best in the world. It does so much more. It actively drives engagement within the organisation. It sparks meaningful, customer-focused conversations between leaders, employees, and ultimately, with customers. This point underscores a deeper insight: sustainable growth stems from genuine human engagement at every level of the business.

That is how this book differs from *The Customer Culture Imperative*. That book was grounded in rigorous academic research and offered a structured approach to defining and measuring a customer-centric culture, focusing on the *"why"* and the *"what"*. This book is about the *"how"*. By integrating the human element, it introduces an eighth discipline— **empowerment**— that connects to employee satisfaction and retention. It's this human dimension that powers what we now call the "growth engine", where culture, engagement, and performance align to drive lasting success.

The Human Engagement Solution

In times of volatility, human connection is key. Organisations that build cultures focused on engagement and strong relationships with employees, customers, and partners are best equipped to not just survive, but thrive. However, bringing culture to life requires more than good intentions. It demands a structured, actionable approach. Our research has identified a powerful, three-part system designed to help leaders embed culture into the fabric of their organisations and drive sustainable growth. It consists of a framework, a methodology, and a measurement tool.

1. **The framework**—*The Three Pillars of Human Engagement* provides a clear foundation for building a thriving, human-centric culture.

2. **The methodology**—Grounded in *Eight Behavioural Disciplines* that translate cultural values into daily practices.

3. **The measurement tool**—*The Market Responsiveness Index (MRI)* captures actionable insights to align strategy, behaviour, and performance through measurement.

This integrated approach equips leaders to turn cultural ambition into measurable business impact.

The Framework—The Three Pillars of Human Engagement

In a time of constant disruption, the important work of rebuilding trust and alignment can be achieved by building a foundation of three interconnected pillars: leadership engagement, employee engagement, and customer engagement. While many leaders believe they already have these in place, the real test of effectiveness is whether the pillars are driving meaningful change and growth.

Our research shows that strong listening, communication, and relationships fuel engagement. When leaders, employees, and customers connect positively, trust and personal value grow, driving business success. This must happen consistently across all areas, not just on the frontline, but throughout leadership, operations, and support teams.

True engagement isn't the result of mandates; it's nurtured through active listening, authentic care, empowering individuals, and taking meaningful action to build emotional connections.

At a recent leader's conference hosted by Abundium, Cynthia Scott, MD and Group CEO, Zip Co, shared a powerful employee engagement strategy she uses. This is a simple, yet impactful practice called the "Magic Wand Moment".

A rotating group of employees would be invited to a session where they were asked two key questions.

1. "What's the one thing you never want to see change here?" This opened the door for recognition of what the company was doing well and reinforced positive behaviours and culture.

2. "If you had a magic wand and could change one thing tomorrow, what would it be?" This encouraged honest, constructive feedback and highlighted areas for improvement that might otherwise go unnoticed.

This approach created a consistent rhythm for listening, empowering employees to share their views openly. It gave leaders direct insight into both the strengths and challenges within the organisation. More than just a feedback session, it was a tangible demonstration of human-centered leadership, one that builds trust, fosters engagement, and drives cultural improvement from the ground up.

In the next chapter, we'll take a closer look at each of each of these three pillars and how to uncover their full impact on the organisation.

The Methodology—The Eight Behavioural Disciplines

At the foundation of every customer-centric organisation are eight behavioural disciplines that shape how it listens, understands, and responds to employee and customer needs. These disciplines span every level of the business from leadership alignment and strategic clarity to frontline empowerment and deep customer insight. The eight disciplines have been proven through both rigorous research and real-world client results to directly drive measurable business performance outcomes. Together, they form a practical roadmap for embedding customer focus throughout the organisation transforming insight into action and culture into a lasting competitive advantage. In Chapter 3, we'll take a deeper dive into each of the eight behavioural disciplines.

CUSTOMER INSIGHT	CUSTOMER FORESIGHT	COMPETITOR INSIGHT	COMPETITOR FORESIGHT	PERIPHERAL VISION
This measures the extent to which employees monitor, understand, and act on current customer needs and satisfaction.	This measures the extent to which employees anticipate customer needs, recognise unspoken needs, consider future needs and take action to satisfy them.	This measures the extent to which employees monitor, understand, and act on current competitor activities and take action to incorporate these in their actions to improve customer experience.	This measures the extent to which employees identify and consider possible future competitors and how they might affect the value that will be offered in the future.	The extent to which employees monitor understand and respond to trends in the larger environment (Political, Economic, Social, Technological, Environmental and Legal).

EMPOWERMENT	CROSS-FUNCTIONAL COLLABORATION	STRATEGIC ALIGNMENT
This measures the extent to which employees are able to make decisions that are best for the customer without the explicit approval of senior leaders.	This measures the extent to which employees interact and collaborate cross-functionally. This includes spending time with people from other work groups, taking a cross-functional perspective, sharing information, and inviting contributions.	This measures the extent to which employees understand, attend to, and enact the vision, mission, objectives and strategic direction of the company in their day-to-day activities, specifically focusing on the customer.

The Measurement Tool—The Market Responsiveness Index (MRI)

The MRI is a powerful, data-driven tool that provides a clear and actionable benchmark for building a high-performing, customer-centric organisation. Grounded in eight behavioural disciplines based on our validated research, the MRI helps leaders assess cultural strengths, pinpoints areas for improvement, and focuses on what truly drives business performance.

Beyond measurement, the MRI gives employees a meaningful voice, capturing candid, open-ended feedback that uncovers real insights and opportunities for change. Results are presented in a clear, visual format that makes it easy to see strengths, expose blind spots, and take focused action.

In Chapter 4, we'll explore the power of the MRI and the pivotal role of measurement in driving cultural change, demonstrating its direct link to business performance and the ultimate proof point: "Show me the money".

This circumplex[9] is an example of an organisation that completed the MRI, clearly highlighting areas of strength, weakness, and untapped opportunity. It tells a clear and powerful story, one that everyone in the organisation can see, understand, and act on. Study it just for a minute.

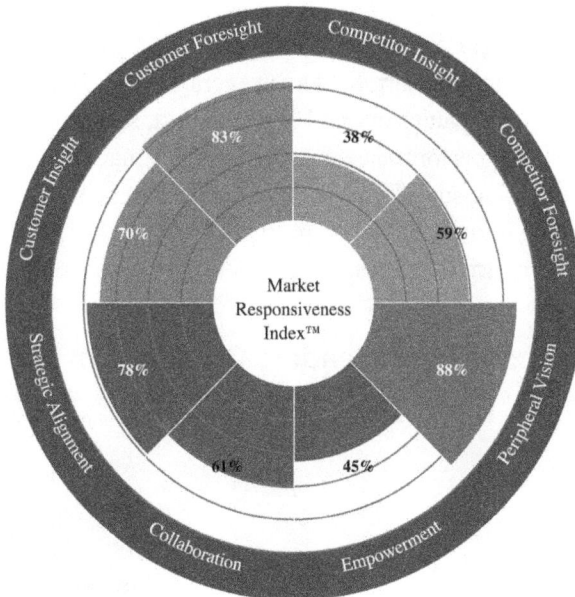

What if this were your company?

- What strengths would you build on?
- What weaknesses need urgent attention?
- Where do the greatest opportunities lie?
- And how would you inspire your leadership team to take action?

Create your own circumplex and see where your organisation stands. Start the exercise at <u>marketculture.com/mri-exercise</u>.

The Growth Multiplier: Show Me the Money

There is compelling evidence that directly links the three pillars of leadership engagement, employee engagement, and customer engagement with increased profitability and growth. This is a critical insight for leaders focused on the bottom line.

Gallup's research[10] shows that companies with high levels of engagement experience 21% higher profitability. Moreover, organisations that cultivate a strong internal culture see a direct positive impact on customer loyalty metrics, such as customer retention. Engaged leaders and employees are not just more committed, they are also more innovative. They actively propose new products and drive valuable process improvements, contributing to organisational growth.

Customer experience research further supports this. Watermark Consulting's analysis,[11] depicted in the chart, tracks the average stock price growth of publicly traded companies over a 16-year period, segmented by their customer experience performance. The data reveals that companies consistently delivering superior customer experiences achieve significantly higher cumulative returns, outperforming the S&P 500 Index and generating 5.4 times greater return than those lagging in customer experience.

Customer Experience Leaders Outperform The Market

16-Year Stock Performance of Customer Experience (CX) Leaders vs. Laggards (2007-2022)

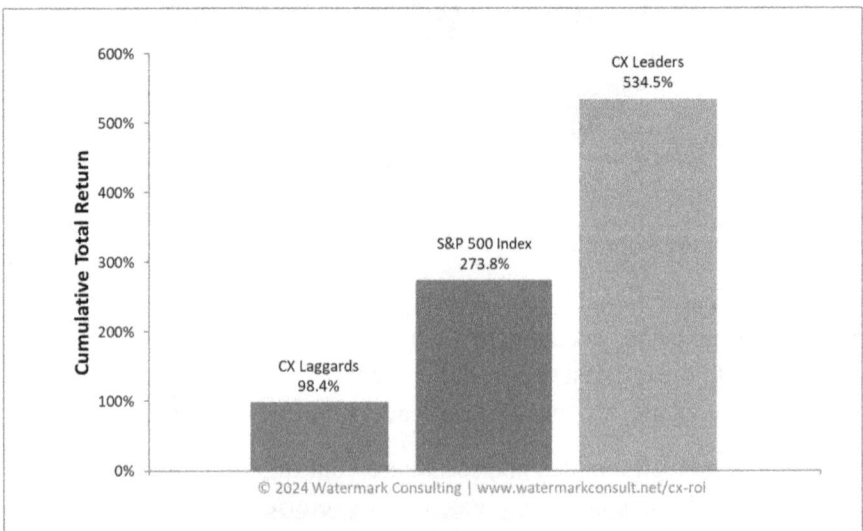

Bar chart — Cumulative Total Return:
- CX Laggards: 98.4%
- S&P 500 Index: 273.8%
- CX Leaders: 534.5%

© 2024 Watermark Consulting | www.watermarkconsult.net/cx-roi

Our MRI research into customer-centric cultures further supports this connection, demonstrating a clear correlation between improvements in the MRI score and a corresponding increase in profitability, as detailed in the figure.

Our cross-sectional analysis of an extensive database reveals a clear trend: organisations that improve their MRI scores consistently show greater profitability and growth over those that don't. This indicates that strategies aimed at improving your organisation's MRI score are likely to drive higher profitability, based on the performance patterns observed within our database. The MRI is a proprietary tool designed to quantify cultural behaviours that are validated as key drivers of both customer and employee satisfaction and retention, which in turn influence profit and revenue growth.

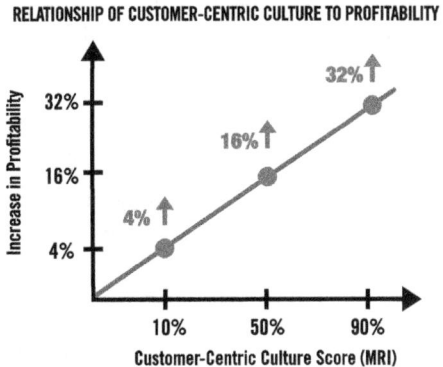

RELATIONSHIP OF CUSTOMER-CENTRIC CULTURE TO PROFITABILITY

Increase in Profitability

32%

16%

4%

32% ↑

16% ↑

4% ↑

10% 50% 90%

Customer-Centric Culture Score (MRI)

The convergence of this research highlights several compelling reasons to cultivate a human engagement culture centred on customers.

The vital role of human judgment and culture: As technology grows more advanced, human insight, oversight, and decision-making become even more important for ethical and successful organisations.

Engagement as a competitive advantage: Organisations that build strong connections with leaders, employees, and customers gain a lasting edge that technology alone can't replicate.

Resilience through engagement: Highly engaged organisations are better at handling disruption and adapting to change.

The chart below, utilising the MRI measurement tool, illustrates the key performance metrics that are positively influenced by a culture of high engagement. Additionally, it showcases various ways the MRI can be applied within an organisation to drive strategic insights and improvements.

The many applications of the MRI provide both quantitative metrics and qualitative insights for leaders, teams, and individuals, pinpointing strengths and areas for improvement in their customer-centric culture compared to top-performing global organisations. At the same time, using the MRI enhances leadership, employee, and customer engagement, which in turn sparks innovation and drives proactive efforts to accelerate growth.

MRI Application	Description
Organisation	Applied to leaders and employees in the entire organisation
Team	Applied to leaders and team members in one or two teams
Partner	Applied to leaders and employees in partner organisations
Customer	Applied to segments of customers of the organisation

The examples below of Saffire, WD-40, and Bank Al Etihad, three distinct businesses from different continents, vividly demonstrate how a culture of human engagement, underpinned by a strong customer focus, fosters long-term, sustainable growth.

The Growth of Saffire—The True Value of Saffire "Their People"

Saffire is one of three luxury hotels within the Federal Group in Tasmania, Australia. Launched during the 2010 global financial crisis, Saffire anticipated a 70% international guest base but instead served 70% domestic travellers. This unexpected shift brought challenges, including occasions when guest numbers were so low that just one couple was staying at the luxury property. Yet, its steadfast commitment to an all-inclusive model led to eventual success.

When the pandemic hit, General Manager Ross Boobyer told the Federal Group CEO, "If we lose our people, we will be starting from scratch again, losing a decade of effort". The CEO agreed, and they prioritised staff support through financial aid, free housing, and regular communication actions that made Saffire a "beacon for the hospitality industry".

Ross noted that guests returned not for new experiences but to reconnect with familiar staff. Guests would ask, "Are Phil and Corinne still here? Is Ian still the head chef?" This highlighted that, in luxury hospitality, authentic human connections matter more than amenities.

Today, Saffire maintains 80% average year-round occupancy, with 20% repeat guests. Staff are loyal and engaged, and guests often rebook before leaving. Leaders enjoy their roles, and the owners take pride in a respected, profitable, and growing brand.

The Growth of WD-40—Sustained Growth in Market Value, Revenue and Regional Expansion

Under Garry Ridge's leadership at WD-40 Company (1997–2022), employee engagement reached 93%, with turnover under 5%. A remarkable 98% of employees felt proud to work there, and 97% trusted and respected their managers.

During his tenure, market cap soared from $250 million to over $2.5 billion, revenues quadrupled, and shareholder returns grew at a 15% CAGR. The company expanded consistently across 176 countries.

Garry credited this success to the company's culture: "Our job is to create an environment where our tribe members are inspired to come to work, feel safe and valued, learn and grow, and leave fulfilled". He believed that a positive employee experience drove engagement, customer satisfaction, and ultimately, financial performance.

The Growth of Bank Al Etihad—A Culture of Growth, Innovation, and Trust Driving Market Leadership

Over its 30-year history, the bank has successfully transformed from a specialised corporate-only institution to a comprehensive, full-service provider, now catering to retail, SME, and corporate clients. This has been led by Isam Salfiti, founder and former chairman, who pioneered adoption of a people-first approach with leaders, employees, and customers, supported by the innovative use of technology.

Originally a small player focused on a corporate niche, the bank has grown to become one of the top three in Jordan, ranking highly across key indicators such as customer market share, profitability, total assets, and liabilities. With a clear focus on regional expansion, the bank is currently prioritising entry into the Iraqi market as a critical component of its growth strategy.

Significant customer base growth has been fuelled primarily by digital acquisition strategies, minimising reliance on physical branch expansion. Today, almost all banking services are accessible digitally, offering customers enhanced convenience and simplifying operational processes.

The bank currently leads the Jordanian banking sector with the highest Net Promoter Score (NPS), demonstrating strong customer satisfaction and loyalty. Its Customer Experience Index has steadily improved, reaching 80% in 2024. Additionally, its employee Net Promoter Score (eNPS) has surged from the mid-40s to the mid-70s by 2024, reflecting improved employee engagement and satisfaction.

The Common Thread: People-Centred Engaging Leadership

Leaders such as Ross Boobyer, Garry Ridge, and Isam Salfiti share a foundational belief: when you create an environment in which individuals feel valued, are free to learn and grow, and are connected to a meaningful purpose, extraordinary outcomes are not only possible, they're inevitable.

Their leadership styles, though varied, were grounded in core human principles.

- They shifted the focus from fear of failure to a culture that celebrates learning and growth.
- They aligned individuals with a purpose that went beyond just profit.
- They genuinely regarded employees as their most valuable asset, investing in their development.
- They consistently delivered exceptional value to customers, building deep loyalty.
- They generated outstanding returns for shareholders, earning admiration and strong support from stakeholders.

The powerful takeaway from these leaders' journeys is both clear and motivating: the most impactful thing a leader can do is cultivate an environment in which people are empowered to reach their full potential. When this happens, success naturally follows, benefiting not only leaders and employees, but also customers and the entire organisation.

The Primacy of Human Engagement: Unlock Your Organisation's Greatest Potential "Your People!"

Does your organisation sound like those in the stories we've shared? Is your growth trajectory sustainable, or are there untapped opportunities for improvement?

As leaders, you possess a strategy, a team, products and services, market channels, and a brand. Your key challenge is to strategically leverage what you've been given. The true key to unlocking growth lies in your ability to listen deeply to your employees, engaging them in the critical actions needed to attract and retain customers. This must then be followed by decisive steps to engage those customers and adapt to their ever-evolving needs.

Looking forward, the organisations that will thrive are those that master what we call the "human engagement growth engine" the intentional design of human interactions, systems, and processes that foster deep commitment among all stakeholders. This approach provides a powerful antidote to the erosion of trust and disconnection that many organisations face today.

When leaders and employees unite with a shared commitment to the customer, exponential growth becomes not just possible, but achievable. But how do you cultivate such a powerful alignment?

In a world of constant disruption, we are firm believers that a strong human-centric culture is the cornerstone of enduring success.

In the next chapter, we will explore the three pillars of human engagement in depth: customer engagement, employee engagement, and leadership engagement. If your aspirations include enhanced engagement, a surge in innovation, and significant organisational growth, then Chapter 2 will help you on your journey toward achieving these goals.

Key Takeaways—Chapter 1

1. Human-Centricity is the New Competitive Advantage

The future belongs to organisations that treat everyone—employees, partners, and customers—as valued humans deserving empathy, care, and respect. This isn't just customer service; it's a fundamental shift in how businesses operate, especially as AI makes human judgment, emotional intelligence, and ethical decision-making increasingly valuable.

2. Culture is Your Growth Engine

A strong, aligned culture creates a powerful chain reaction: engaged leaders empower fulfilled employees, who then deliver exceptional customer experiences, driving loyalty and profitability. The data proves it, demonstrating that highly engaged companies see 21% higher profitability and significantly better market performance. Culture isn't soft; it's your hardest competitive edge.

3. Measurement Drives Transformation

What gets measured gets managed. Tools like the MRI help organisations objectively assess their human engagement across all stakeholders, identify blind spots, and create actionable improvement plans. Without measurement, culture change remains wishful thinking rather than strategic execution.

The Bottom Line

In a world where technology can replicate many business functions, the organisations that win will be those that excel at the fundamentally human elements—connection, trust, and shared purpose. This isn't about being nice; it's about building a sustainable competitive advantage through authentic human engagement.

**Scan or click to listen
to our Podcasts**

CHAPTER 2

EXPONENTIAL GROWTH IN PRACTICE

The Framework—The Three Pillars of Human Engagement

At MarketCulture, we've worked with thousands of leaders around the world. One trait consistently stands out among the most successful: they know how to engage their people, listen to what matters, and take meaningful action to help them deliver great customer experiences.

But over time, we noticed something important was missing. Leaders who didn't directly engage with customers were often blindsided and disconnected from the reality of what was truly happening in their business.

Sean recalls a conversation with David Procter, then Head of Sales at Konica Minolta. He said, "If we gave the sales reps everything, they said the customer wanted, the company would go broke". His point was clear, listening to employees is essential, but it's not enough. Leaders also need to hear directly from the customer.

That's what inspired David to launch an initiative called the *High Activity Day*. On these days, sales reps would bring senior leaders into the field to meet customers face-to-face. The insights they gained firsthand became a powerful guide for decision-making.

Over time, the initiative expanded and employees in non-customer-facing roles also began visiting customers. It brought a new level of alignment across the organisation. At Konica Minolta Australia, this customer-centric approach helped to significantly increase market share, as leaders, employees, and customers all started working from the same playbook.

That's when it became clear: sustainable organisational success isn't the result of isolated efforts. It depends on three key pillars working in unison—customer engagement, employee engagement, and leadership engagement. These pillars are not separate strategies or departments; they're interconnected forces that, when aligned, create momentum that drives real growth.

Too often, organisations focus inward, with leaders investing in employee programs, team-building initiatives, and internal culture. While important, these are only part of the equation. It's not enough for leaders to focus solely on their people. To truly thrive, they must also be outward facing, actively engaging with customers, listening to their needs, and understanding their experiences.

At the same time, employees need more than just direction; they need to clearly understand and connect with their leaders' vision. When that vision also reflects the voice of the customer, something powerful happens. Alignment takes root. Employees see purpose in their work, leaders make better-informed decisions, and customers feel heard and valued.

It's in this alignment between leader, employee, and customer that real, lasting success is born. Companies that understand and implement this triad create cultures of responsiveness, resilience, and relevance. They're not just reacting to change; they're anticipating it and leading through it.

Linden

Have you ever had one of those moments where you think, "Surely something this simple must already be part of every organisation's framework". But it wasn't. And then it became clear, what's the real risk of *not* doing this?

Over the years we've spoken with countless customers, across the many organisations we've worked with, and often ask them the same question: When was the last time you had a conversation with a senior leader or even a back-office employee from the company you buy from?" The responses are consistently eye-opening, often not what we expect to hear. It's such a simple thing, yet it's frequently overlooked.

We've seen countless companies shrink in size, lose market share, or disappear entirely. How many were blindsided by disruption when the warning signs were already right there on their doorstep overlooked simply because they were too inwardly focused to notice?

In Chapter 1, we introduced the three pillars of human engagement. Sustainable growth is achieved when leaders, employees, and customers are all engaged through a continuous cycle of listening and empowering. Each pillar supports and reinforces the others, creating a unified, high-performing culture.

In this chapter, we'll examine three real-world case studies that show how applying this methodology with the right support can lead to higher employee engagement, stronger customer satisfaction, and ultimately, sustainable growth and profitability.

Leadership Engagement: The Catalyst for Organisational Vitality

Recent studies by Harvard Business Publishing[12] underscore the importance of leader engagement as a pivotal driver of organisational transformation. Engaged leaders are characterised by three essential attributes.

1. Acting out the vision

Engaged leaders embody the vision through their actions, not just their words. They consistently demonstrate the organisational vision in their daily decisions and behaviours. Isam Salfiti, founder and former chairman of Bank Al Etihad in Amman, Jordan, offers a powerful example.

"I take a gentle but firm approach, especially on values and competence. I have high expectations, but I care deeply for my team. They are like family." He prioritised visiting branches to connect with managers, who appreciated his personal engagement. His vision for Bank Al Etihad focused on empowering customers, especially women. "Our commitment to making things easy and meeting customer needs was key to our success", he said, proving that customer experience can outweigh technical expertise.

Isam's human-centered leadership inspired employees to perform their best, blending care with accountability. He's widely described as a leader who values "humanity".

Daniel Sharaiha, Director of Human resources and Customer Experience, at Bank Al Etihad explained: "We have extended our human approach to providing new skills for women who have become disconnected from the workforce, initially to train them for jobs in the bank but also to enable them to start their own businesses. This initiative has led to other large organisations in Jordan joining this program."

Dalia Ajlouni, Director of Learning and Development, noted, "Our founder leads by example. He always says, 'My people are the ones who made me'." She highlights that this mindset lives on in today's leadership, strengthening trust seen in gestures like executives serving food at company events themed around servant leadership.

2. Shaping and role modelling culture

Engaged leaders shape culture through intentional actions, consistent behaviour, and measurable outcomes.

David Thodey, former CEO of Telstra, exemplified this with a story about a time early in his tenure that reinforced customer-centric values. He introduced the Net Promoter Score (NPS) and required executives to call both high- and low-rating customers, sharing insights monthly.

One planning director spoke with a man who had rated Telstra 10 out of 10 but shared that his wife had died a week after they signed a two-year mobile contract. When he tried to cancel, he was told it would cost over $2,000. The director wasn't sure what to do.

David asked, "How would you want this handled if it were you?" The director replied, "Waive the fee". David then said, "Then why wouldn't we do that? Don't our values of fairness override policy?"

This moment became legendary at Telstra, powerfully illustrating how values-driven decisions should guide action and how leaders must model the culture they want to create.

3. Enabling high performance

Engaged leaders drive high performance by creating environments where success naturally emerges from the efforts of their engaged teams.

A man once asked his gardener why his plants grew so strong and vibrant. The gardener replied, "I don't force them to grow. I simply remove what stops them".

Engaged leaders recognise that fostering high performance isn't about pushing growth, it's about cultivating the right conditions for it to thrive. Much like the gardener, these leaders don't compel their teams to grow, they remove the barriers that hinder progress. By clearing the path for their teams, engaged leaders eliminate obstacles, ensure clarity around how individual roles contribute to broader organisational goals, and empower their teams to make decisions that best serve customers and colleagues. They nurture an environment that supports individual growth, which, in turn, propels organisational growth.

This approach requires leaders to actively identify and tackle hidden barriers that may be slowing their teams' progress. David Tudehope, CEO of Macquarie Technology, articulated this mindset: "I establish the framework, including the goals, strategy, and measurement systems, to give my teams a clear sense of purpose. Then, I step back, trusting them to do the right thing."

The science of leadership, as emphasised by the *Harvard Business Review*,[13] shows that engaged leaders are catalysts for positive change. Their engagement sparks positive emotional responses that lead to trust-building behaviours, creating a ripple effect that extends throughout the organisation.

Employee Engagement: The Engine of Innovation and Customer Satisfaction

In recent decades, the "employee engagement" industry has grown substantially. However, for many organisations, this has become a superficial "check-the-box" exercise. Despite the wealth of data collected through surveys and analyses, much of it ends up gathering dust, with no meaningful action taken. Employees rarely hear about the results ... until the next survey rolls around, and the cycle repeats itself, often yielding the same lack of impact.

This repetitive cycle not only frustrates and disengages employees but also undermines genuine engagement efforts, wasting both time and resources. Have you observed this dynamic within your own organisation?

Linden

I remember an early experience in my career when senior leadership tasked me with creating a corporate plan for a subsidiary of a multinational corporation. After three months of hard work, the plan was approved and submitted to headquarters, but then it disappeared without a trace. The following year, I was asked to do it all over again. This time, I handed the task to my assistant with the cynical advice: "Do your best, but make sure it's a bulky plan, it doesn't really matter because we'll never hear about it again". She took me at my word and padded the report with some of her favourite recipes to make it seem more substantial. True to my prediction, the plan was never heard of again. Later, my wife, Marie-Noelle, used some of the recipes and asked, "Where did you find these?" I replied, "They're from our corporate plan". I added, "The best part of it!"

In stark contrast to this ineffective approach, genuine employee engagement represents what we can think of as the "beating heart" of organisational success. It's more than just satisfaction, rather it's an emotional commitment that transforms everyday tasks into meaningful contributions. From our experience we have seen firsthand that truly engaged employees exhibit:

- improved problem-solving abilities
- a stronger focus on customer needs
- higher levels of innovation and creative thinking
- greater resilience when facing challenges

The following three examples highlight how authentic employee engagement can be deeply embedded within an organisation.

Saffire Boutique Hotel, Tasmania, Australia

Saffire
FREYCINET

Ross Boobyer, General Manager of three luxury hotels within Tasmania's Federal Group, builds employee engagement from day one. "We can teach skills, but not character", he says, so he screens for values before resumes, seeking culture-enhancers over experience.

At induction, Ross tells new hires, "You're the newest member ... even those here 15 years ago went through this. It's now your job to motivate and re-energise them". This flips hierarchy, empowering new staff as culture carriers.

He grants frontline autonomy, saying, "If it aligns with your values, make the call, you won't be penalised". Ross fosters a positive culture: "I want this to be a fun place. If you dread work, customers will feel it". His leadership rests on "care, consideration, and connection ... if you don't genuinely care, this isn't the right fit".

Staff meet three times daily to discuss guests' motivations, preferences, and how to deliver a "plus one" moment a memorable, personal experience that deepens the guest connection and defines the Saffire brand.

WD-40, San Diego, USA

Garry Ridge, former CEO of WD-40 Company, transformed the culture by introducing a "tribal leadership" model to drive engagement, innovation, and growth. "When I became CEO in 1997, many saw their jobs as just a pay cheque", he said. "I wanted to build a tribe united by values and purpose".

Central to this was the mindset, "Don't mark my paper, help me get an A", encouraging learning over blame. Garry banned the word "failure", calling mistakes "learning moments" and asking, "What did you learn? What will you do differently?"

One employee made a $600,000 mistake during a product launch. Instead of punishment, Garry focused on lessons learned. That same employee later led innovations worth millions.

He also introduced the "Maniac Pledge", promoting ownership, respect, and creating positive memories. Those who lived these values became known as "WD-40 Maniacs", passionate, values-driven brand ambassadors.

Bank Al Etihad, Amman, Jordan

At Bank Al Etihad, employee engagement soared through a cultural transformation rooted in co-creation and inclusivity. Employees weren't passive recipients of change—they helped shape the bank's future.

Daniel Sharaiha, Director of Human Resources and Customer Experience, has been instrumental in shaping the culture of the bank. Since joining in 2010, he has personally interviewed and appointed nearly every new hire, embedding the values of the organisation from day one.

Under the guidance of Chairman Isam Salfiti, Daniel has helped the bank achieve a remarkably balanced workforce, looking for an even distribution of gender and age across the organisation. Women represent about 48% of the total workforce at the bank, up from around 20% when he joined. His hiring philosophy is grounded in a deep respect for character and growth. As Daniel puts it, "We have employed people with genuine humility with an ambition to learn and improve. And we have created a culture where employees can advance based on their increased learning, skills and demonstration of the company's values."

This ethos has led to a unique organisational approach where senior leaders embrace a servant leadership model. Daniel explains, "It's almost as if the organisation is turned around, where the senior leaders adopt a servant leadership approach to role model the humility of leadership that has been the hallmark of the founder".

Ledi Lapaj, Director of Customer Experience, explains, "Our culture was built on humility and youthful energy, but we needed to formalise it.

We involved people from all levels, which created a sense of ownership, where employees felt like co-founders." She adds, "We stay focused by using employee feedback to set our priorities. Then we measure our culture and its impact because we don't want to walk in the dark."

Dalia Ajlouni, Director of Learning and Development, emphasises, "Culture can't be dictated, it must feel authentic". She notes that promotions are no longer solely manager driven. Now, two-thirds of promotion criteria are based on personal growth, learning, and living core values. This shift has empowered staff to own their career paths.

With strong training and cultural education, Bank Al Etihad has built a highly engaged workforce driven by purpose and personal ownership.

Customer Engagement: The Ultimate Measure of Success

The third essential pillar of our framework is customer engagement. According to research by Jamali and Caldwell,[14] customer engagement naturally emerges from effective engagement of both leaders and employees. Driven by meaningful engagement with customers, it goes beyond traditional satisfaction measures, encompassing:

- an emotional connection to the organisation and its brand
- deep and consistent interactions with customers across all relevant touchpoints
- active involvement of customers in the company's ongoing development and improvement
- strong customer advocacy and the creation of a sense of community around the brand

The stories of Saffire, WD-40, and Bank Al Etihad serve as compelling examples of customer engagement, demonstrating how leadership engagement and employee engagement can profoundly impact and strengthen customer engagement.

Saffire

At Saffire, GM Ross Boobyer champions the "plus one" philosophy, personalised moments that leave lasting impressions. During a daily briefing, Ross noticed guests Mark and Sarah hadn't had a "plus one" yet. Josie, a team member, stepped up.

Knowing the couple's love for Tasmanian Pinot Noir, especially Gala Estate, Josie discovered their hometown in Sydney and found a local Dan Murphy's that stocked the wine.

Saffire—continued

She added a note to their departure bag: "Mark and Sarah, it was a pleasure hosting you. I found the Gala Pinot at Dan Murphy's near you. We hope every glass reminds you of us."

This simple, thoughtful gesture turned a wine into *their* wine, sparking memories, future enjoyment, and word-of-mouth advocacy. It perfectly illustrates the cornerstones of customer engagement: meaningful interaction, emotional connection, advocacy, and community.

WD-40

Former WD-40 CEO Garry Ridge defines the company's purpose simply: "We exist to create positive, lasting memories by solving problems in factories, homes, and workshops worldwide." He adds, "We're not just in the lubricant business, we're in the memories business".

Customer engagement, he explains, comes from consistently meeting needs and delivering exceptional service. "It's about reliably fulfilling our brand promise, not just satisfaction, but delight".

He illustrates this with the product's iconic status: "Show someone a blue and yellow can with a red top, and they'll say, 'I used this with my dad', or 'My parents always had one'". For Garry, those memories are proof that true customer engagement goes far beyond the product, it's about emotional connection and trust built over time.

Bank Al Etihad

Ledi says, "Customer success is our primary value.
We lead with empathy; understanding customers is just as vital as
understanding employees. Our humility shapes how we engage."
(The picture is the team at Bank Al Etihad)

Dalia adds, "We focus on building personalised, long-
term relationships. One family has banked with us for four
generations." She shares, "A corporate client in crisis once relied
on our trust, no collateral, just his word. He's now one of Jordan's
largest corporate owners."

Ledi sums it up: "We don't treat customers as numbers, we see them
as people". This human-centered, trust-based culture fuels lasting
engagement, loyalty, and growth.

Bank al Etihad Case Study: https://www.marketculture.com/product-page/
bank-al-etihad-case-study

The stories of Saffire, WD-40, and Bank Al Etihad show that organisations
of any size, industry, or region can successfully implement an engagement
strategy that connects leaders with employees, and together with their
customers. These are not extraordinary industries—but they are led by
extraordinary people who embrace human engagement as a catalyst for
innovation and sustained growth. This approach forms the foundation of

a proven framework and measurement system that drives both human and organisational success.

In Chapter 3, we'll take a closer look at the eight-disciplines methodology and how it can be actively managed and embedded across any organisation to bring this engagement model to life, making it tangible and actionable within the organisation, and, ultimately, making it easy to implement in your organisation. We'll show practical examples, share proven strategies, and warn against the risks of complacency. Through real-world examples from our partner organisations, we reveal how this approach has fuelled sustainable growth and profitability.

Key Takeaways—Chapter 2

1. True Growth Comes from Alignment

Sustainable success requires all three forces—leaders, employees, and customers—to be engaged and aligned. When leaders listen, empower, and model values, employees connect more deeply with the vision, and customers feel genuinely valued.

2. Leadership Engagement is the Catalyst

Engaged leaders drive transformation by acting out the vision, shaping culture, and removing barriers to performance. Their behaviour sets the tone for organisational vitality and trust.

3. Employee and Customer Engagement Go Hand-in-Hand.

When employees are empowered and emotionally committed, they deliver better customer experiences. Organisations like WD-40, Saffire, and Bank Al Etihad show how this creates a ripple effect that boosts loyalty, innovation, and advocacy.

The Bottom Line

Organisational growth isn't just about internal culture or customer-facing strategies, it's about integrating leaders, employees, and customer engagement into one unified system. When these three pillars work together through listening and empowering, businesses become more resilient, responsive, and relevant.

**Scan or click to listen
to our Podcasts**

CHAPTER 3

THE GROWTH ACCELERATOR

The Methodology - The Blood in the System

At MarketCulture we speak with leaders across a wide range of industries and organisations. Over time we have seen a clear pattern—despite genuine efforts to engage employees and improve performance, many organisations struggle to link their cultural initiatives to measurable business outcomes. Without that connection, cultural efforts often lose momentum and, in many cases, are deprioritised altogether.

Despite strong intent and investment, many organisations lack something tangible, something practical they can see, measure, and act on to shape culture meaningfully. These organisations have no clear metrics, no consistent behavioural patterns, and no direct link between engagement efforts and business performance. Many leaders in organisations like these have confided that culture feels too abstract or fluffy, that it's impossible to work on because there is no structured way to bring it to life or link it to financial performance. Our foundational research set out to change that.

The MarketCulture approach outlined in our original work, *The Customer Culture Imperative*, identified seven disciplines—clear, observable behavioural practices deeply embedded in the DNA of high-performing, customer-focused companies such as Apple, LEGO, Amazon, Canva, and Salesforce. These disciplines weren't isolated programs or initiatives; they formed a cohesive cultural system that extended across teams, departments, and geographies, all united by a relentless focus on the customer.

Originally developed as a leadership framework, we soon discovered something even more powerful: the greatest impact came when these practices were adopted and lived by employees at every level of the organisation. This insight led to the emergence of a vital eighth discipline, empowerment.

Have you ever encountered an organisation where decisions seem to get stuck in a loop, constantly delayed because everyone is waiting for someone else to make the call? That's the absence of empowerment in action.

Sean

I recall a conversation, in the early days of Amazon, with a senior executive who told me that their call centre employees have the authority to refund a customer's purchase, no questions asked. At the time, I was sceptical. It sounded too good to be true.

But just weeks later, I experienced it firsthand. I had ordered several books from Amazon, and after five days without delivery, I contacted their customer service. Without hesitation, they apologised and immediately processed a full refund. No approval chain. No delays. Just empowered action focused entirely on customer satisfaction.

The kind of responsiveness Sean highlights at Amazon doesn't happen by accident. It's the result of an intentional culture where empowerment is built into the system. And it's one of the most critical disciplines for creating speed, trust, and loyalty both internally and externally.

The eight disciplines offer a blueprint for embedding engagement into the fabric of an organisation and driving measurable business outcomes. Our research and consulting experience have shown they directly contribute to long-term performance, fuelling sustainable growth, profitability, customer loyalty, and employee retention. The eight disciplines offer leaders a clear, actionable framework for turning culture into a lived experience, not just a concept. With the support of measurement tools, organisations can pinpoint where they stand, identify gaps, and take targeted steps toward meaningful cultural improvement. The eight disciplines activate the three pillars of human engagement—customer, employee, and leadership engagement. They form the foundation for a high-performing culture, one that unlocks the organisation's full potential by embedding a customer-first mindset and fostering an environment where employees feel empowered, valued, and inspired to contribute.

In this chapter, we bring these disciplines to life. We'll break down each one, show how it works in practice, and highlight best-in-class examples from organisations that have used them to achieve sustainable, customer-led growth. But before we do this, let's look at a company example that shows how all eight disciplines have been applied at different times to make important decisions that shaped its competitive advantage and growth.

The Overseas Shipping Services (OSS) story powerfully illustrates how a human-centric approach, even from an inexperienced start, can lead to remarkable success.

Linden

Looking back on the history of OSS, I now realise we instinctively embedded all eight disciplines into our culture without even knowing it. From the very beginning, when Richard Overton and I co-founded OSS, *customer insight and foresight* were at the core of our approach. A key influence was Stan Glaser, who made a pivotal early contribution. Not only did Stan design our first logo capturing the essence of "substance and security" he also gave us foundational advice: "Build your business around customers and always seek feedback and observe their behaviour". That simple but powerful insight became the cornerstone of everything that followed.

Our journey started with *customer insight*. At Sydney's wharves, we didn't just see trucks we saw stories unfolding. Greek families were returning home with a lifetime of memories and belongings.

This wasn't simply about transporting boxes; it was about trust, emotion, and cultural connection.

By immersing ourselves in the Greek community and spending time at the Greek Club, we uncovered a real need: a dependable, trustworthy mover. Greek travel agents who were already held in high regard became frustrated by ongoing complaints about existing providers. They quickly became our most valuable partners.

This deep understanding led naturally to *customer foresight*. We anticipated the impact of cheaper air travel on migrant communities and responded with a breakthrough: the UPAK service. It was a DIY moving solution that gave customers full control. They packed their own goods, knew the cost upfront, and delivered everything to the OSS depot. It offered transparency, security, and exceptional value. Launched through trusted Greek travel agents who earned commissions, UPAK took off rapidly capturing the entire Greek market for overseas moves within just three months and paving the way into other migrant communities.

The foundation of OSS was its strong, deliberately cultivated culture driven by *empowerment, cross-functional collaboration, and strategic alignment*. It wasn't just about leadership; everyone, from drivers and packers to accounts and frontline sales, saw themselves as part of the customer service team. United by a shared vision, they met weekly, felt empowered to act in the customer's best interest, and made OSS remarkably easy to deal with. Streamlined processes ensured smooth documentation and tracking, while a motivated team focused on delivering outstanding service reducing complaints and strengthening collaboration across the business.

As we pursued growth in new markets and faced off against a dominant industry leader, we leaned heavily on both *customer and competitor insight*. When our largest competitor launched a major advertising campaign, we sidestepped an expensive ad war with a simple, strategic message: "Get your second quote from OSS".

Knowing most customers sought at least two quotes, this positioning kept enquiries strong and ultimately won us the majority of the business. Our *competitor foresight* was just as important. We spotted the rise of corporate relocation service companies early and responded by entering the market with a tailored, premium solution designed specifically for corporate clients.

At weekly warehouse townhalls, everyone from the floor to the front office was encouraged to share ideas for improving service. One such conversation sparked a bold, forward-thinking concept: using the internet to help clients buy and sell goods, optimise their shipments, and even purchase replacements at their destination. This outward-looking, collaborative culture exemplified true innovation and what we now recognise as *Peripheral Vision* in action.

The OSS story is more than just a success, it's a blueprint for sustainable, thriving growth. By deeply understanding customers, anticipating their needs, staying ahead of competitors, and empowering every team member within a unified culture, any organisation can achieve lasting impact and resilience.

In what follows—in what is for good reason the longest chapter in this book—we take a deep dive into each of the eight disciplines. Think of it as a practical reference guide, your playbook, structured so you can easily navigate to the specific discipline you're looking to develop or improve.

The Eight Disciplines that Drive Engagement

Walking through the offices of companies we've worked with, we often see powerful words proudly displayed on the walls: "Customer", "Collaboration", "Empowerment", "Strategy", "Teamwork", "Empathy", and more. These words are meant to define culture, signal intent, and shape behaviour. But are these words just décor? Or are they the foundation of the organisation? When we ask people we meet in these companies, "how do you bring these words to life?" the answers are often unclear, inconsistent, or even missing entirely.

The eight disciplines discussed below have become the cornerstone for organisations around the world, providing a practical framework that transforms these values from words on a wall into daily actions and measurable impact. Let's begin with an overview of the eight disciplines shown in the figure, which clarifies their purpose and key functions.

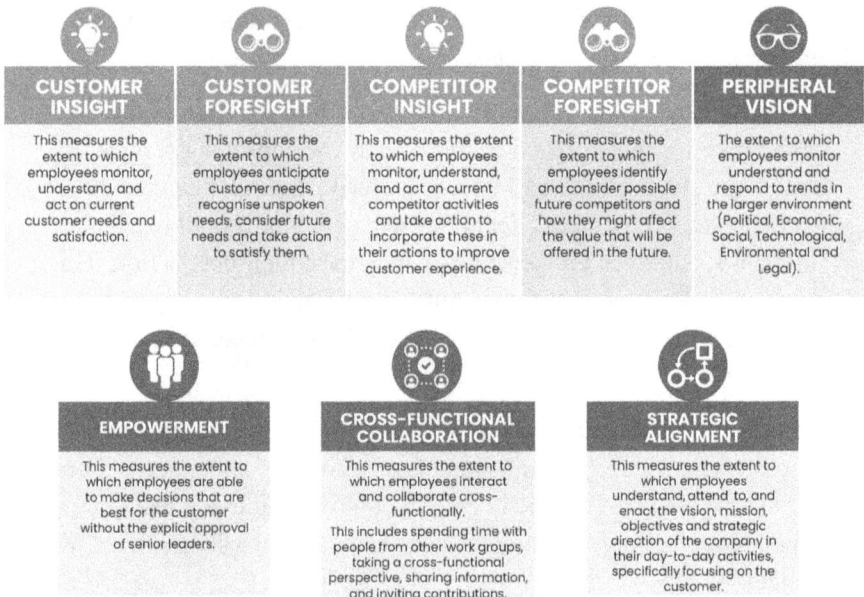

CUSTOMER INSIGHT	CUSTOMER FORESIGHT	COMPETITOR INSIGHT	COMPETITOR FORESIGHT	PERIPHERAL VISION
This measures the extent to which employees monitor, understand, and act on current customer needs and satisfaction.	This measures the extent to which employees anticipate customer needs, recognise unspoken needs, consider future needs and take action to satisfy them.	This measures the extent to which employees monitor, understand, and act on current competitor activities and take action to incorporate these in their actions to improve customer experience.	This measures the extent to which employees identify and consider possible future competitors and how they might affect the value that will be offered in the future.	The extent to which employees monitor understand and respond to trends in the larger environment (Political, Economic, Social, Technological, Environmental and Legal).

EMPOWERMENT	CROSS-FUNCTIONAL COLLABORATION	STRATEGIC ALIGNMENT
This measures the extent to which employees are able to make decisions that are best for the customer without the explicit approval of senior leaders.	This measures the extent to which employees interact and collaborate cross-functionally. This includes spending time with people from other work groups, taking a cross-functional perspective, sharing information, and inviting contributions.	This measures the extent to which employees understand, attend to, and enact the vision, mission, objectives and strategic direction of the company in their day-to-day activities, specifically focusing on the customer.

Discipline 1. Customer Insight

CUSTOMER INSIGHT

'The most important single thing is to focus obsessively on the customer. Our goal is to be earth's most customer-centric company.' –Jeff Bezos, Amazon

Customer insight begins with a simple but often overlooked question: Who is the customer? You'd be surprised how often organisations can't agree on the answer.

Yet, that clarity shapes every function in the business from product development to marketing communication. Everyone should know exactly who is the customer. But ask the same question across departments in most companies, from warehouse, to IT, finance, and marketing, and you're likely to get different answers.

Without consensus on who is the customer, even the most sophisticated insights risk being misdirected. Yet, this kind of misalignment isn't unusual. In fact, it's alarmingly common. Many employees who aren't on the front lines believe their customer is internal—this creates an entirely different mindset.

🠖🠖

Sean

Facilitating a two-day workshop for a car insurance company I presented a detailed MRI report to the senior leadership team. What followed caught everyone off guard. A heated debate erupted over the fundamental question: "Who is our customer?" Half the team insisted it was the car dealership, their car insurance partner. The other half argued it was the end user, the car owner. I wondered what the rest of the company believed. I had a completely different experience at Dulux, the paint company. Presenting the MRI results to over 100 executives across Australia, there was no confusion. Why? Because they had made a deliberate, strategic shift from prioritizing retail partners to focusing on the end consumer.

Once You Know Who the Customer Is, You Can Begin to Understand Them

🠖🠖

Chris

I asked one of the early leaders at Stayz.com, Australia's original answer to Airbnb, how they'd transformed a modest holiday rental directory into a household name. His answer was simple: *"We let our customers drive the roadmap".*

By listening closely to feedback and analysing booking data, the team uncovered a powerful insight hidden in plain sight: most travellers start dreaming about their next getaway while still enjoying their current one. People were browsing villas from the pool lounge and eyeing ski chalets before their sunscreen had dried.

That single realisation reshaped their strategy. Stayz redesigned its confirmation emails and mobile app to offer "next-trip inspiration" as soon as guests settled into their stay. These included surfside cottages, alpine retreats, and city lofts tailored to the kind of trip they were already enjoying. It felt like a friendly suggestion, and it worked. Follow-on bookings surged by nearly 30%.

True customer insight goes beyond demographics or surface behaviours. It's about uncovering what your customers genuinely value. At Amazon, for example, consumers consistently rank convenience as a top priority. That insight doesn't sit in a PowerPoint deck it drives everything Amazon does.

Think of customer insight as your organisation's collective empathy. It's not just a set of data points; it's a living, breathing understanding of customer experience. Companies like online retailer Zappos embody this. Every employee, from warehouse staff to executives, spends time in customer service. Why? Because customer understanding isn't something you outsource or delegate, it's something you live.

Some of the Most Impactful Decisions Are Made by People Who Never Speak to a Customer

It's a surprising fact that in many organisations, major decisions, especially those that affect the customer experience, are made by teams who never interact with customers at all. Finance, legal, IT, and operations often make choices they believe are "in the customer's best interest", yet their understanding is based on assumptions, not actual insight.

Sean

I remember an example from my time at Konica Minolta back in 2010. The finance department developed a new rental agreement for clients. It was 16 pages long, dense, complex, and full of legal jargon. One client joked it was like reading the Bible. Another told me that having it reviewed by their lawyer would cost nearly as much as the first six months rental. Meanwhile, our competitor had a simple, two-page agreement that was clear and easy to understand.

The root issue? The agreement was created with little to no input from actual customers or even sales. No one from finance sat down with a client. No one asked, "How easy is this to use?" or "Does this build trust or erode it?"

The result? It took six months to fix. And during that time, we lost countless deals, not because of price or product, but because of paperwork.

Customer Insight Must Transcend the Entire Organisation

Customer understanding isn't the responsibility of just one department, it must be embedded across every function and every level of the business. Making decisions without the customer in mind isn't just risky, it can be costly, time-consuming, and damaging to your brand.

Our research consistently shows that when a deep, organisation-wide understanding of the customer is present, the impact is significant: higher customer satisfaction, stronger loyalty, and measurable sales revenue growth.

What is the impact on customers when businesses lack customer insight?

Insight	Description	Impact
Irrelevant products and services:	Customers receive what they don't need	Frustration, wasted time, unmet needs.
Generic experiences	Interactions feel impersonal and disconnected	Customers feel undervalued
Confusing journeys	Processes don't make sense to customers	Effort, confusion, dissatisfaction

Insight	Description	Impact
Ignored feedback	Feedback leads to no action	Customers feel unheard and disengage
Weak emotional connection	Brands miss chances to build real relationships	Customers go to brands that "get" them
Missed value opportunities	Helpful solutions are overlooked	Lost loyalty and missed growth
High effort, low satisfaction	Customers must work harder to get what they need.	Frustration › Churn › Negative word of mouth.

Businesses that fail to improve customer insight risk falling behind in today's customer-driven marketplace. Without a deep understanding of customer needs and behaviours, they face wasted investments, poor experiences, lost sales, ineffective marketing, and increased customer churn. Competitors with better insights will innovate faster and capture more market share. Internally, misaligned teams lead to inefficiencies, while brands that don't evolve lose relevance and trust. Improving customer insight is not optional, it's essential for growth, innovation, and staying competitive in the long term.

Customers expect businesses to know them, not just sell to them. In today's competitive landscape, customer insight isn't optional, it's a core driver of business success.

Discipline 2. Customer Foresight

CUSTOMER
FORESIGHT

"What I had to do was take stock of the company and look forward 10 to 15 years at the big megatrends that were going to impact the consumer products industry, food and beverage in particular, and PepsiCo even more specifically." —Indra Nooyi, PepsiCo

When Apple released the first iPad, many industry observers and bloggers were quick to criticise it, some calling it an "utter disappointment" and even "an abysmal failure". But Apple wasn't reacting to customer requests. They were responding to something deeper: an emerging lifestyle shift, a latent need for intuitive, mobile computing. And now, of course, we know how that story turned out. The iPad has become one of the most successful and widely adopted tech products in history.

Customer foresight is one of the most powerful yet underutilised capabilities within organisations. It's the ability of employees, not just those in marketing or innovation, but across the business, to anticipate emerging customer needs, uncover unspoken expectations, and take proactive steps to address them. Foresight isn't just about today's customer. It's about uncovering the hidden and future needs of both existing and prospective customers. They might not be your customers today, but they could be tomorrow.

To do this well, you need to blend a deep understanding of your customers' world with a clear grasp of your own organisation's technical strengths and capabilities. It's not enough to simply ask customers what they want. Many companies rely on that approach and end up with incremental improvements at best. True innovation requires more. Why? Because customers often can't articulate what they don't yet know they need. They can't envision the future; we have to show it to them.

Sean

In the early years of production print at Konica Minolta, just before we introduced a digital printing press to the traditional offset printing market, my role was to speak with commercial printers and gather their feedback on whether this new technology was something they'd consider implementing into their business. Let's just say, it wasn't an easy sell or even discussion. These were businesses that had invested millions in offset printing equipment, and the idea of adopting a product that could potentially devalue that investment was not well received. They firmly believed that a digital press had no place in their business. They saw it as a toy. Based on the resistance I encountered, I could have easily reported back to management that the product was destined to fail.

If I asked them what they wanted, their answer was always the same: a faster, cheaper, better quality, more cost-effective offset press. They couldn't imagine a world where digital printing would play a central role in their operations. And yet, fast-forward to today, and all of them are using digital presses.

It taught me a powerful lesson; customers often can't see the future until you show it to them. True innovation isn't about responding to what people say they want; it's about anticipating what they'll need next.

Many organisations look beyond their traditional markets to uncover new opportunities for growth. By building flexible structures and adaptive capabilities, they position themselves to introduce new products and services that deliver greater value to both existing and future customers.

Take Amazon as a prime example. What began as an online bookstore has evolved into one of the world's most diversified companies. Through a relentless focus on innovation and customer value, Amazon has expanded into new markets, from cloud computing and logistics to streaming and grocery retail. The acquisition of Whole Foods in the US marked a bold move into physical retail, demonstrating how the company continually redefines its market boundaries to stay ahead of customer needs. In each of these markets it continually innovates to meet future customer needs.

Our research shows that when organisations cultivate a deep understanding of customer foresight, the results are powerful, driving breakthrough innovation, and retaining and attracting new customers.

What is the impact on customers when businesses lack customer foresight?

Insight	Description	Impact
Outdated offerings	Products no longer meet evolving needs	Frustration and unmet goals
Disconnected experiences	Services feel irrelevant to customers' future direction	Customers feel misunderstood
Loss of trust	Brands seem out of touch	Loyalty erodes, customers consider switching
Missed solutions	Innovations that could help are never delivered	Customers settle for less
More effort for customers	Customers have to piece together solutions themselves	Frustration and wasted time
Forced to switch	Brands that don't evolve lose relevance	Loyalty lost, customers disconnect emotionally
Lower confidence in the brand's future	Customers question if the brand will keep up	Hesitation to continue the relationship

Failing to improve customer foresight leaves businesses vulnerable to disruption, irrelevance, and missed growth opportunities. Customer foresight is about anticipating future needs and market trends, helping organisations stay ahead of competitors and create lasting value. Without it, businesses fall into short-term thinking, miss critical innovations, and lose customers to brands that predict and meet emerging demands. The result is wasted investment, declining relevance, and erosion of trust. In contrast, organisations that embrace foresight drive innovation, build stronger relationships, and maintain a clear competitive advantage in an ever-evolving market.

Customers want brands that grow with them, not ones that leave them behind. Customer foresight isn't just a skill, it's a mindset. And in a world, that's changing faster than ever, it may be one of the most important competitive advantages you can build.

Discipline 3. Competitor Insight

COMPETITOR
INSIGHT

"We compete with FX, with AMC, with HBO, with so many networks... Amazon is one of those bidders, they're not even the biggest of those bidders. So, it's one more bidder and they're doing some great work." —Reed Hastings, Netflix

We first saw how critical competitor insight is as a cultural capability while advising the senior leadership team of a market-leading company in a mature, highly competitive paper products industry. Their biggest competitor had just slashed prices for high-volume customers. In response, the leadership team debated whether to follow suit or go even lower. Emotions ran high. Conflicting opinions filled the room, yet none were backed by solid market intelligence. It was a classic case of a knee-jerk reaction driven more by instinct than informed strategy. Does this sound familiar? There was:

* no shared understanding of the competitor's pricing strategy or intent
* no insight into the actual profit implications of a price cut
* no discussion of what customers truly valued
* no alignment around the organisation's own value proposition

Sales, marketing, finance, operations, and customer service all gave conflicting advice. With no unified framework or insight guiding the decision, the business was on the brink of initiating a self-destructive price war, one that would harm not only its own profitability, but the value it could deliver to customers and the entire industry.

Under pressure to respond quickly, we worked with the company to gather fresh intelligence. We analysed the competitive landscape and, more importantly, spoke directly with its customers. What we found was eye-opening: many of the assumptions held by leaders were inaccurate and out of sync with what customers valued.

Rather than matching the competitor's price drop, we recommended maintaining current prices while introducing a new service enhancement that customers had specifically asked for. This feedback came from speaking with their customers. The result? The competitor reversed course and raised its prices back to its original levels. A destructive price war was avoided, and the company preserved both its profitability and customer trust.

This experience reinforced a key fact: competitor insight helps remove emotion from decision-making and replaces it with clarity and confidence. Emotional reactions to aggressive competitor actions can often result in decisions that destroy long-term customer value. While price cuts may bring short-term wins, they often erode the margins necessary to invest in quality, innovation, and service, ultimately hurting customers in the long run. This is what's known as a race to the bottom—no one wins not even the customer.

Competitor insight is the ability to deeply understand your current competitors, their strategies, intentions, and how they compete, so you can determine the unique, differential value you need to deliver to maintain a sustainable competitive advantage. It's not just about tracking market movements; it's about interpreting competitor behaviours through the lens of your customers and aligning your response accordingly.

An organisation with a strong competitor insight capability doesn't simply react to competitors, it anticipates, evaluates, and acts decisively in ways that reinforce its strategic position. Businesses that underperform in this area often struggle to compete effectively, falling victim to short-sighted decisions and eroding value for both the customer and the organisation.

When an organisation shares competitor insight broadly, every team member can see the bigger picture:

- they understand how their role contributes to the company's value proposition
- they can align their actions with what differentiates the business in t he market
- they become more agile and responsive to change, with a clear understanding of "why"

Facilitating workshops with a wide variety of organisations has offered invaluable insight into how different teams perceive competitor insight. These sessions often include both frontline and back-of-house employees, and one of the most common challenges comes from those in support roles. They question the relevance of concepts like competitor insight to their day-to-day work. This is where it's important to listen respectfully and find ways to challenge that perspective.

Sean

During a client workshop, I spoke with a member of the accounts team who was openly dismissive, saying they had no idea who the company's competitors were and considered any discussion about them a waste of time. Rather than debate, I simply asked: "How do your competitors handle accounting for their customers? What could we learn from them? What are they doing that could take your customers away?" These questions shifted the discussion. It reminded everyone that no matter the role, we all have a part to play in delivering superior value and knowing how others do it can be a game-changer.

With competitor insight as a core discipline, companies can:

- make better strategic decisions with confidence
- align cross-functional teams around customer value
- innovate in ways that truly differentiate
- respond to competitor moves in ways that build, not destroy value

Our research shows that when organisations develop strong competitor insight, the impact is significant, driving increased profitability, sustained revenue growth, and long-term profit performance.

What is the impact on customers when businesses lack competitor insight?

Insight	Description	Impact
Fewer choices, less value	Businesses offer outdated or overpriced products	Customers miss out on the best solution
Inferior products	Competitors deliver better, more innovative offerings	Customers feel they're settling for second-best
Higher prices without value	Pricing doesn't match market expectations	Customers feel overcharged and undervalued
Poorer experiences	Competitors provide smoother, faster service	Frustration rises, customers compare and switch
Loss of trust in the brand	Seeing competitors lead shakes confidence	Loyalty erodes, customers try other brands
Customers forced to research	Customers must search for better alternatives	More effort › frustration › switching
Brand seen as outdated	Competitors feel fresher and more relevant	Customers associate the brand with stagnation.

Failing to improve competitor insight risks businesses losing their competitive edge, relevance, and long-term growth. Competitor insight equips organisations with the knowledge needed to anticipate market shifts, position offerings effectively, and respond to emerging threats. Without it, businesses fall behind in innovation, miss key trends, and waste resources duplicating what competitors already do better. This leads to declining market share, damaged brand reputation, and vulnerability to disruption by more agile competitors. Investing in competitor insight is essential for staying ahead, making smarter decisions, and consistently delivering value that keeps customers loyal.

By embedding competitor insight into your culture, you empower your organisation to compete from a position of strength, not fear.

Discipline 4. Competitor Foresight

COMPETITOR FORESIGHT

"Disruptive technology where you really have a big technology discontinuity... tends to come from new companies." —Elon Musk, Tesla

Google exemplifies competitor foresight in action. As a company built on innovation, Google is constantly looking around the corner to anticipate future challenges and opportunities. Whether through bold internal R&D or strategic acquisitions, Google has consistently stayed ahead of both current and future competitors.

- Google Glass represented an early bet on wearable technology and new ways to access information.
- Project Loon, using weather balloons to deliver internet access to remote areas, showcased Google's long-term vision for connectivity.
- When mobile advertising began to gain traction, Google identified Jumptap as a rising competitor and acquired AdMob to strengthen its position in the mobile space.
- As search behaviour moved from desktop to mobile, Google doubled down on mobile innovation by developing Android and acquiring Motorola Mobility, securing a dominant role in the mobile ecosystem.

Google's acquisition of YouTube, outbidding both Microsoft and Yahoo!, was another move grounded in competitor foresight. Google correctly anticipated that video would become central to how users engage with content online.

Beyond individual moves, what truly sets Google apart is its culture of curiosity. Teams are encouraged to think about what's next, to scan both internally and externally for ideas and innovations that align with the company's mission. This mindset is embedded across the organisation, empowering employees to look beyond today's landscape and actively shape tomorrows.

Chris

There is one question I always love to ask senior leaders at a strategy workshop: *"What would Amazon do if they entered your industry?"*

At first the room would erupt in laughter. Executives would joke, *"Lose money!"* and to be fair, they weren't wrong. In its early years, Jeff Bezos' long-term strategy was often dismissed by Wall Street as reckless or unsustainable.

Chris—continued

But fast forward to today, and that laughter has turned to silence. Now, when I ask the same question, the mood shifts. People sit up. They know Amazon has proved time and again that it can disrupt virtually any industry it targets.

They've taken on Netflix in streaming, challenged Google and Apple with Alexa, pioneered checkout-free retail, launched grocery subscriptions, and even stepped into healthcare with online medical appointments.

That's the essence of competitor foresight: imagining bold moves like these before they happen and ensuring you're already delivering the kind of value a company like Amazon might bring, before they ever get the chance.

A standout example is iFood in Brazil, which holds more than 80% of the home food delivery market. Its early entry and strategy of securing exclusivity agreements with restaurants effectively blocked Uber Eats from gaining traction prompting Uber Eats to exit the market in 2022 and later re-enter via a partnership with iFood. This collaboration now allows iFood users to access Uber's ride-hailing platform, while Uber users can tap into iFood's delivery services. Still, iFood must stay alert: recent regulatory changes have curtailed its ability to enforce exclusivity, lowering barriers for new competitors to enter the market.

Like iFood, if you can see them coming, you can start moving now and stay a step ahead.

Competitor foresight is the proactive discipline of identifying and preparing for future competitors before they disrupt your market. It's about acting today to mitigate tomorrow's threats and capitalising on the opportunities they create. Businesses with strong competitor foresight can pre-empt market shifts, sustain competitive advantage, and drive innovation that fuels new revenue streams, customer growth, and product success.

This is not a reactive capability, it's a forward-looking mindset embedded across the organisation. It means continuously scanning the horizon for emerging players, technologies, and models that could challenge your position and being ready to act decisively.

A deep understanding of emerging competitors, what they're doing, where they're headed, and how they could impact your business equips companies to innovate with purpose and shape the future rather than chase it.

Disruption is relentless and most never see it coming. Take the printing industry as a prime example of how disruption can blindside even the most established players. For years, the dominant belief was that digital presses wouldn't have a significant impact on the market. Companies like Heidelberg and Komori once held a firm grip on the commercial print sector, but not anymore. That stronghold has crumbled as digital technology reshaped production, customer expectations, and market dynamics.

Look at the newspaper and magazine industry. It didn't adapt quickly enough to the rise of online media, and we've seen the consequences. The collapse of traditional newsprint giants happened faster than anyone predicted. And it's not just print. The hotel industry was blindsided by Airbnb, a company that saw what customers truly wanted: more personalised, authentic, and flexible travel experiences. Traditional hotels didn't see it coming or refused to take it seriously, until it was too late. Uber did the same to the taxi industry, transforming customer expectations around convenience, transparency, and pricing. And now, that disruption continues with autonomous vehicle technology threatening to replace drivers altogether.

The list of disrupted industries grows by the day and it's not slowing down. Disruption isn't a possibility. It's a certainty. Organisations must accept a critical truth: you will be disrupted. The only question is when, how, and whether you'll be ready.

Linden

Sean and I had the privilege of interviewing Luke Jecks, the founder and CEO of Naked Wines, an innovative company that connects independent winemakers directly with customers. In their model, customers are referred to as "angel investors" because they fund winemakers up front in exchange for exclusive access to high-quality wines at better prices.

During our conversation, Luke shared something deeply profound, something that has stuck with me ever since. He asked me: "What's kryptonite to a disruptor?" Caught off guard, I admitted I didn't know. His response was simple but powerful: "The kryptonite to a disruptor is to love your customer so much that no competitor, present or future, can ever get a foothold".

That insight hit hard. In a world where new competitors can emerge overnight, and disruption can come from anywhere, the most effective defence isn't technology, pricing, or scale, it's an unwavering commitment to customer love. If your customers feel deeply understood, valued, and supported, they won't be looking elsewhere. And no disruptor will be able to steal them away.

New entrants, often smaller, nimbler, and digitally native aren't burdened by legacy systems or thinking. They can move faster, adapt to shifts in customer behaviour, and deliver value in ways established companies never considered. That's why competitor foresight is no longer optional, it's a strategic necessity. You must continuously scan for emerging threats and anticipate changes in technology, customer expectations, and market structures. The ability to adapt isn't just about survival. It's how market leaders are created.

Organisations that embed competitor foresight into their culture don't just survive, they thrive. They anticipate disruption rather than react to it. They innovate intentionally rather than defensively. And most importantly, they ensure long-term relevance by continually evolving with, and ahead of, the market. By empowering your teams to ask, "Who could disrupt us next?" and "What can we learn or adopt before they do?", you lay the foundation for sustainable competitive advantage.

Our research proves that competitor foresight directly impacts the success of innovation, new products and services.

What is the impact on customers when businesses lack competitor foresight?

Insight	Description	Impact
Limited innovation	Without anticipating competitors, businesses fail to innovate	Customers miss out on better, smarter solutions
Outdated products	Competitors introduce new features or services first	Customers feel stuck with second-best
Higher effort	Customers expect easier, faster, more tailored experiences	More frustration, more work for customers
Lower perceived value	Competitors offer more for the same or lower price	Customers feel overcharged or undervalued
Loss of confidence in the brand	Customers notice when competitors lead	Trust erodes; future relevance is questioned
Forced to switch	Customers migrate to brands that meet evolving needs	Loyalty weakens, switching becomes inevitable
Negative word of mouth	Disappointed customers share frustrations	Brand reputation suffers

Failing to improve competitor foresight leaves businesses exposed to sudden disruption, missed opportunities, and long-term decline. While competitor analysis focuses on current actions, foresight prepares organisations for what's coming next. Without it, companies' risk being blindsided by innovation, overlooking emerging trends, and investing in outdated strategies. As a result, they lose market share, weaken their brand relevance, erode profits, and shift from leaders to followers in their industries. Competitor foresight is essential for staying ahead, protecting profitability, and building sustainable growth in an increasingly competitive world.

Customers expect brands to grow with them if you don't, they'll find someone who will.

PERIPHERAL
VISION

Discipline 5. Peripheral Vision

"The pandemic has accelerated our digital lives. During the first quarter of last year, we saw a 25 percent increase in watchtime around the world". —Susan Wojcicki, YouTube

The day the world changed was 9 March 2020, when the COVID-19 pandemic triggered a lockdown in Europe that soon went global, redefining how we live, work, and connect. Virtually overnight, entire industries were brought to a standstill, and life as we knew it was upended. COVID had a significant impact on us all and brought many industries to their knees, including, but by no means limited to, travel and hospitality, retail, food, health, and fitness. Few organisations were truly prepared for such a massive external shock, one that would not only disrupt business operations but reshape societal norms and customer expectations. The initial response wasn't driven by strategy or foresight, it was driven by human instinct, a collective scramble to adapt, survive, and find new ways to function in a world turned upside down. What if we had been prepared? More importantly are we prepared now, or are we still leaving it to chance?

A strong customer culture demands that organisations consistently consider the full spectrum of external forces and market trends shaping customer value. What is relevant, valuable, and expected by customers is constantly evolving, driven by political, economic, social, technological, environmental, and legal (PESTEL) shifts. To stay ahead, leaders and their teams must actively track and respond to these forces, not only to understand their markets today, but to anticipate where they are heading tomorrow.

A striking example of external influences of which organisations have no control is unfolding as we write—that is, the imposition of new tariffs on countries exporting goods to the US. This geopolitical manoeuvre is dramatically reshaping global trade flows and compelling companies to rapidly reassess their supply chains, pricing structures, and go-to-market strategies. For businesses like Apple that are heavily reliant on US imports, the stakes are high. If Apple does not localise manufacturing within the US, escalating tariffs could drive production costs exponentially, potentially tripling the price of an iPhone. Such a shift would send shockwaves through consumer demand, global competitiveness, and Apple's long-term strategic outlook. But the broader and more urgent question is this: what will it truly cost to manufacture at scale within the US? The most recent indication in August 2025 is that Apple has announced it will invest $600 billion into the American Manufacturing Program (AMP). These are the kinds of external forces companies cannot ignore because when they hit, they do not ask for permission.

The rapid decline of industry giants like Kodak, Borders, and Nokia wasn't due to a lack of awareness. These were iconic brands with vast resources and customer reach. They saw the changes coming but they failed to build peripheral vision into their cultural DNA. They lacked the shared early-warning system and organisational agility needed to translate market insight into decisive action. As a result, they couldn't realign their business models fast enough to match evolving customer behaviour.

Technology has become both a powerful disruptor and a transformative enabler for every industry. Artificial intelligence is revolutionising how businesses and employees operate and it's not a passing trend. It's here to stay, and it's accelerating. The key question is not whether technology will change your business, but whether you'll be ready when it does. The era of reactive leadership is over. To truly benefit from future technological shifts, organisations must become proactive anticipating change, embedding agility into their culture, and investing now in the capabilities that will define tomorrow's success.

Chris

Recently, I sat down with Jim Penman, the founder of Jim's Mowing, one of Australia's most iconic and successful businesses, with over 5,500 franchisees internationally. While it may seem like a simple lawn care service on the surface, Jim has leveraged technology to transform what began as a one-man operation into a large-scale enterprise. These franchises have grown from mowing and gardening to cleaning, trades like plumbing to home improvements, automotive and pet care. By embracing digital systems, streamlining operations, and enhancing customer responsiveness, Jim's Group has become a powerful example of how even the most traditional industries can scale dramatically through smart use of technology.

Peripheral vision must be a collective competency, shared across leadership, teams, and functions. It is not the job of a few strategists or market researchers; it must become part of how the entire business thinks and operates. Key components of this discipline include:

- workforce behaviours that monitor and assess external trends
- leadership commitment to acting on early signals, not waiting for certainty

- dynamic strategy and innovation that respond to future-focused market realities
- cross-functional alignment around what customers will value next

With strong peripheral vision, businesses can see around corners, spotting opportunities and threats early, adjusting priorities quickly, and shaping the future rather than reacting to it. Given that today, disruption is constant—from digital transformation, including AI, to shifting customer expectations, to the convergence of entire industries—companies that thrive in this environment will be those that:

- consistently scan the horizon for change
- embed agility and foresight into every level of the organisation
- mobilise swiftly to deliver new products, services, and business models that reflect future customer value

Our research proves that peripheral vision directly impacts the success of innovation and employee retention.

What is the impact on customers when businesses lack peripheral vision?

Insight	Description	Impact
Outdated products and services	Companies miss changing behaviours or trends	Customers feel stuck with irrelevant solutions
Limited innovation	Emerging trends go unnoticed and competitors provide options	Customers feel like they're missing out
Higher customer effort	Customers must piece together solutions elsewhere	More work, more frustration
Loss of trust and confidence	Brands slow to adapt lose relevance	Customers hesitate to stay loyal
Forced to switch	Customers move to brands that stay ahead	Increased churn, lost loyalty
Poor alignment with customer values	Social or cultural shifts catch brands off guard	Customers see the brand as out of touch
Lower satisfaction	Missed chances to add value or differentiate	Frustration › disengagement › exit

Businesses without strong peripheral vision and the ability to detect emerging trends, threats, and opportunities beyond their immediate focus face significant risks. Without it, they can be blindsided by disruption, miss new growth markets, develop strategic blind spots, and react too slowly to change. Innovation suffers when trends in adjacent industries go unnoticed, and resilience weakens when external shocks occur.

Peripheral vision is not optional, it's a strategic necessity for long-term relevance, innovation, and resilience. Companies that fail to develop it risk stagnation, irrelevance, and, ultimately, disappear from the market.

Customers expect organisations to evolve alongside them and the world around them. When they don't, they leave. Peripheral vision is not just a competitive advantage, it's a necessity for long-term relevance, growth, and leadership in an unpredictable world.

Discipline 6. Empowerment

"The key to the culture change was individual empowerment".
—Satya Nadella, Microsoft

EMPOWERMENT

Empowerment is the degree to which employees are trusted and enabled to make decisions in the best interest of the customer without needing constant approval from senior leadership. Ask yourself a question now: "Are your employees truly empowered?" It means giving your employees the authority, confidence, and capability to act, innovate, and take the initiative in how they serve customers and execute their work.

True empowerment is not simply about delegation; it's about creating a culture where everyone feels responsible for delivering exceptional customer value. It fuels innovation, accelerates decision-making, increases engagement, and reduces inefficiencies. When organisations lack empowerment, decisions are delayed, bureaucracy grows, and customer experience suffers.

Linden

Sean and I were sitting in a meeting with Luke Jecks, the founder of Naked Wines, when suddenly a loud cheer erupted from the office floor behind us. Curious, we looked out of the meeting room and saw a group of employees jumping up and down, high-fiving, and celebrating what they called a "Giraffe Moment". Intrigued, Sean turned to Luke and asked, "What's a Giraffe Moment?" He smiled and explained, "It's when an employee sticks their neck out, just like a giraffe, to go above and beyond for a customer without asking for approval".

This simple, joyful celebration wasn't about hitting a sales target or closing a deal, it was about empowerment in action. Employees were encouraged, even celebrated, for taking initiative, making bold decisions, and solving problems in real time for the customer. That kind of empowerment wasn't just permitted, it was part of the culture.

The Giraffe Moment was a powerful symbol of trust, ownership, and customer obsession. And more importantly, it fostered a workplace where people felt valued, supported, and proud of the impact they made.

Empowerment becomes a powerful engine of performance when it's deeply embedded in a company's culture and everyday behaviours. Yet, in many organisations, this potential is stifled, not by lack of talent, but by a lack of trust. When employees are restricted by rigid hierarchies, approval bottlenecks, or fear of making mistakes, innovation stalls and customer experience suffers.

By contrast, companies that lead with empowerment unlock extraordinary value. Consider these standout examples. Apple transformed the retail experience by empowering its staff to not just sell products but to educate, support, and resolve customer issues on the spot. Employees at Apple Stores are trained to take ownership of the customer's experience and make independent decisions to ensure satisfaction. UK retailer Waitrose launched a bold initiative called "Licence to Thrill", which empowered frontline employees to break the rules if it meant delivering an exceptional customer moment. This trust-driven approach fostered loyalty and elevated everyday service into memorable experiences

Sean

In a recent conversation, Peter MacMillan, Director of 3E Advantage, spoke about the transformative power of empowerment within his organisation.

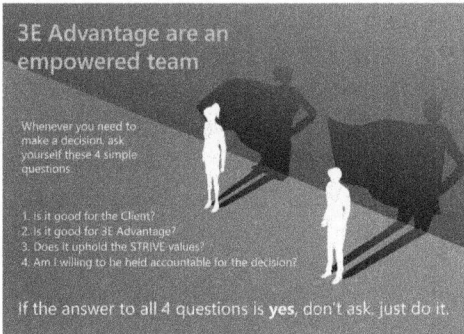

"Empowerment is central to 3E's culture. Every team member is trusted to act without permission if it's good for the client, good for the company, aligns with their STRIVE values, and they're willing to be accountable. Don't ask—just do it," Peter says. This trust has driven consistent double-digit growth, with a 31% increase in the past year alone.

Peter believes the real asset is people, both customers and employees. Every interaction can be a "plus one" moment, making 3E the highlight of someone's day. Trust is non-negotiable, and cutting corners for short-term gain is never an option.

For Peter, profit is the outcome, not the goal. By protecting relationships, empowering his team, and simplifying the customer experience, he's built more than a finance company, he's built a culture where growth is a natural result of doing the right thing.

Uber replaced traditional taxi regulations with a simple, empowering principle: delight the customer. Drivers have the autonomy to deliver service in flexible, customer-centric ways, supported by a platform that listens, learns, and evolves based on user feedback. Luxury automaker Lexus places trust in its customer-facing staff to make high-stakes decisions. In one legendary case, a Lexus executive replaced a customer's car with a Mercedes at a discount because the Lexus model couldn't sync with the customer's garage door. That customer's next car? A new Lexus. Empowerment isn't just a policy; it's a relationship strategy.

Chris

Several years ago, I attended a Zappos vendor party in Las Vegas. It was vibrant, full of energy, and offered a rare chance to connect with Zappos team members, Zappos customers, and even Tony Hsieh, the legendary founder and CEO.

Tony shared a story from the company's early days. When he launched Zappos, many said it would never work: *"No one will buy shoes online, shoes are too personal. People need to try them on."* But Tony saw things differently. He didn't view Zappos as just an online shoe store, he saw it as a customer service company that happened to sell shoes.

His mission was to create a workplace where people could be themselves, have fun, and build authentic connections with customers. In that kind of culture, exceptional service wasn't forced it happened naturally.

As I mingled with staff, it was clear his vision had become reality. Everyone I spoke with was upbeat, enthusiastic, and proud to work there. More than a few said it was *"the job they'd been waiting for their whole lives"*.

Tony also told me he used to call the Zappos call centre pretending to be a regular customer not to order shoes, but to ask, *"Where's the best pizza place in town?"* The answers were never scripted or rushed. He'd get thoughtful, passionate recommendations often with personal stories.

That's true empowerment: when people are trusted to be themselves, they go beyond the transaction. They don't just resolve a need. They create a moment of connection. And that's when customer service becomes a memorable customer experience.

The common thread across these examples is clear: empowerment drives performance by unlocking people's potential. When employees are trusted to make decisions, solve problems, and innovate, they don't just follow processes, they own the outcomes.

Our research proves that empowerment directly fuels customer satisfaction, innovation, successful product launches, revenue growth, and profitability.

In a truly customer-centric culture, empowerment isn't a luxury, it's a necessity. It serves as the engine behind customer loyalty, business growth, and long-term success. Empowered teams drive higher customer satisfaction and are essential to delivering meaningful innovation.

What is the impact on customers when businesses lack empowerment?

Insight	Description	Impact
Slow, frustrating service	Employees can't solve issues on the spot	Customers wait longer, escalate issues, and lose patience
Poor resolutions	Staff lack authority to fix problems properly	Customers feel their issues are unresolved and are dissatisfied
Increased customer effort	Customers must repeat themselves or chase answers	More frustration, less trust
Generic experiences	Employees can't personalise help	Customers feel like "just another number"
Loss of confidence in the brand	Poor frontline support damages credibility	Loyalty drops, competitors look better
Forced escalation	Basic issues get unnecessarily pushed upward	More wasted time, more friction
Negative word of mouth	Frustrated customers share bad stories	Brand reputation suffers, fewer referrals
Switching to competitors	Customers leave for brands that value them	Higher churn, loyalty disappears

Empowerment is the foundation of high-performing teams and exceptional customer experiences, giving employees the authority, tools, and confidence to act in the best interests of customers and the business. Without it, organisations face slow decisions, poor customer service, disengaged teams, operational bottlenecks, missed innovation, higher customer effort, leadership overload, and an inability to adapt to change.

Improving empowerment isn't just about employee morale, it's about speed, innovation, growth, and building a resilient organisation where empowered employees deliver better outcomes for customers and long-term success for the business.

Empowered employees create empowered, loyal customers. Without empowerment everyone loses.

Discipline 7. Cross-Functional Collaboration

CROSS-
FUNCTIONAL
COLLABORATION

"Coming together is a beginning. Keeping together is progress. Working together is success". —Henry Ford, Ford Motor Company

In a recent engagement with a major energy company, we partnered with senior leadership and frontline teams to build and embed a truly customer-centric culture. Both the company and our team firmly believed that long-term business success is directly linked to a strong customer focus. However, one of the most significant barriers we encountered was not a lack of will or vision, but a lack of internal collaboration. Senior leaders and middle managers were overwhelmed by a sea of emails and non-strategic meetings that left little room for genuine cross-functional dialogue. Departments operated in silos, rarely interacting, or aligning around the question: "How do we increase value for our customers?"

Unfortunately, this is not unique. Across organisations of all sizes and industries, we consistently see silos, misalignment, and even internal competition often at the expense of customer satisfaction and business performance.

Sean

Like many large organisations, Konica Minolta began as a deeply siloed company. Different departments operated independently, with little cross-functional communication, particularly when it came to solving customer issues.

One day, I returned from a difficult meeting with one of our largest clients. The customer was understandably frustrated because, despite our strong relationship, we consistently failed to get his billing right.

I left the meeting determined to fix it. I gathered all his invoices, identified the errors, and highlighted the necessary corrections. Back at the office, I brought the issue to my sales manager. I suggested visiting the accounts team in person to walk them through the problem and collaborate on a fix. I was told not to do that; I should send an email instead. "That's not how we do things", was the implied message. Sound familiar?

Three days passed. Multiple emails were exchanged. Still, no resolution. Eventually, the issue had escalated into an email chain that copied-in half the company, yet the client's problem remained unresolved. Frustrated and committed to doing the right thing for the customer, I made the decision to walk down to the accounts department myself. But moments after I arrived, I was quickly intercepted by a group of managers and asked, rather forcefully, to leave. Apparently, I had crossed an invisible line.

As I was being ushered out, the Managing Director happened to witness the scene and asked what was going on. I explained the situation to him. Without hesitation, he looked at me and said, "Go back into accounts and fix it". That moment changed everything.

What began as a painful customer issue became the trigger for something far more powerful. It sparked a cultural shift within the business. Silos began to break down. Cross-functional relationships started to form. People from different departments began working together, really working together, to solve customer issues and improve outcomes. From that day forward, a stronger sense of unity and shared purpose took root in our organisation. We stopped viewing problems as someone else's responsibility and started approaching them collectively, with the customer at the centre.

That experience remains etched in my memory, not because of the conflict, but because it marked the beginning of a more collaborative, customer-focused culture. It was a powerful lesson: when we break down internal barriers, we unlock the full potential of our people and deliver the service our customers truly deserve.

Cross-functional collaboration is the degree to which employees actively engage, share knowledge, and support colleagues across different teams or departments, with the shared goal of creating superior customer value.

This discipline is vital to delivering exceptional customer experiences. When customer insights, requests, and feedback are trapped within departments, opportunities for innovation and value creation are missed. Cross-functional collaboration enables teams to align, adapt, and act quickly in service of the customer.

Don Tapscott, renowned author on digital transformation, explores the next wave of workplace collaboration in his book Radical Openness.[15] In an interview with McKinsey Quarterly,[16] Tapscott highlights how the limitations of traditional tools like email are stifling productivity and innovation. He likens email to what Mark Twain once said about the weather: "Everyone talks about it, but nobody does anything about it".

Instead of receiving dozens of emails about a single project, teams should have centralised hubs where updates, discussions, documents, and decisions are all transparently shared. Real-time input, digital brainstorming, and peer-to-peer problem solving are no longer optional—they are essential.

To truly embed a customer-centric culture, businesses must go beyond structure, they must cultivate a culture where cross-functional collaboration is instinctive. This means:

- breaking down silos and creating shared accountability for customer outcomes
- redesigning workflows to prioritise cross-functional touchpoints
- equipping teams with digital tools that enable fast, visible collaboration
- encouraging shared language around customer value across departments

Our research proves that a strong collaboration directly influences customer satisfaction, accelerates innovation, drives new product and service success, boosts sales and profit growth, and improves overall business performance.

What is the impact on customers when businesses lack cross-functional collaboration?

Insight	Description	Impact
Inconsistent experiences	Different teams give conflicting messages	Customers feel confused or frustrated
Slow problem resolution	Poor information sharing delays fixes	Customers repeat themselves or wait too long
Broken journeys	Team handoffs fail, breaking customer processes	Errors, frustration, incomplete service
Higher customer effort	Customers must navigate silos themselves	More work › frustration › churn risk
Weak personalisation	Disconnected data makes personalisation ineffective	Customers feel like "just another number"
Missed added value	Upsells or cross-sells that help are missed	Customers lose out on useful solutions
Loss of trust and loyalty	Disorganised brands lose credibility	Loyalty weakens, fewer repeat purchases
Switching to competitors	Competitors offer smoother, easier experiences	Customers leave for better alternatives

Cross-functional collaboration is critical for delivering seamless customer experiences, driving innovation, and achieving sustainable growth. When teams and departments operate in silos, businesses face misaligned priorities, inconsistent customer journeys, slow execution, poor communication, duplicated efforts, and missed revenue opportunities. These breakdowns not only increase costs but also erode employee engagement and reduce agility. Improving collaboration isn't optional it's essential for delivering value to customers, executing strategy effectively, and building a resilient, competitive organisation. Companies that foster teamwork and align around shared goals win, inside and out.

Customers expect seamless experiences when teams don't collaborate, the customer pays the price.

Discipline 8. Strategic Alignment

"You build your own strategy. You don't define it by what another competitor is doing" —Ginni Rometty, IBM

STRATEGIC ALIGNMENT

Is your strategy truly centred around the customer? Strategic alignment is a vital organisational discipline that ensures every employee understands and lives the company's vision, mission, objectives, and strategic direction. It is the backbone of a strong customer-centric culture, enabling the company to consistently create and deliver superior value to both customers and shareholders.

Sean

Shortly after I joined MarketCulture, we were engaged by Peter Cooke, the International President of Wright Medical Group. A US-based company, Wright Medical, had recently acquired Tornier, a French organisation. The merger aimed to establish a global medical devices leader in the extremities (shoulder, elbow, hand, ankle and foot) and biologics market by broadening the product portfolio and accelerating growth in the rapidly expanding orthopaedics sector.

However, we quickly discovered that despite the strategic intent, the two companies continued to operate largely as separate entities, with significant cultural differences shaped by their distinct national backgrounds. Our mission was clear: to bridge these cultural divides and forge a unified, high-performing organisation.

We focused on building a shared strategy that placed the customer at the heart of both businesses, a vision that transcended simply offering outstanding products and services. Over the following years, through deliberate alignment and integration efforts, the combined company developed a cohesive identity and collaborative culture.

The results spoke volumes. When the organisation was eventually acquired by Stryker, the integration had driven an increase in share value of more than 40% underscoring the power of strategic alignment and a customer-centric focus in unlocking innovation and sustainable business growth.

Without strategic alignment, businesses suffer from inefficiencies that frustrate customers and disengage employees, ultimately harming performance and satisfaction. But when alignment is strong, teams don't just know the strategy, they actively embody it. They:

- engage in ongoing discussions about company goals
- align their daily work and projects with strategic priorities
- eliminate activities that do not contribute to value creation
- adapt swiftly when strategy evolves

Bryan Jago, Executive Manager—Service at Canon Medical Systems ANZ Pty Ltd described his experience leveraging the eight disciplines to improve their strategy and performance: "At Canon Medical Systems, we operate in a highly regulated, fast-evolving, and technologically advanced market where competition is fierce and global. To stay ahead, we are always on the lookout for fresh ideas and innovative concepts that can become real differentiators and growth drivers for our business." Bryan describes attending a conference where Philip Kotler spoke about the *Customer Culture Imperative* book (MarketCulture's original book). It had just been named the 2015 Marketing Book of the Year. What really stood out to Bryan was the book's accessibility; no need for a PhD to grasp or implement its concepts.

He explains, "We saw a natural connection between the book's principles, the eight disciplines, and our own Made for Life philosophy, where customer intimacy was already a cornerstone of our strategy and a key competitive advantage. We seamlessly integrated these ideas alongside frameworks from other influential business thinkers to create a robust approach."

Since then, Canon Medical Systems has adopted a practice of focusing on two key disciplines each year. Every team member sets personal development goals aligned with these priorities, enabling the company to track individual contributions toward its broader objectives. This is called the customer success index. Today it's a critical driver of Canon's employee engagement, customer connection, and sustainable business growth. It creates a foundation for its strategy. Bryan says, "We've consistently delivered solid results across all our key performance indicators. Beyond that, it has given us peace of mind by uncovering blind spots through employee feedback, flagging customer risks early, and highlighting continuous improvement opportunities."

This example describes how strategic alignment is a foundational pillar for any organisation seeking to deliver exceptional customer value. It's not enough for strategy to be written in a document or discussed in leadership meetings—it must be clearly understood, embraced, and acted upon by every team and individual across the business. True alignment occurs when day-to-day decisions, behaviours, and priorities at every level consistently reflect and reinforce the organisation's overarching strategic direction.

When teams are strategically aligned, their efforts become focused, coordinated, and customer driven. This alignment transforms disconnected initiatives into cohesive value-creation engines that serve both customer needs and business goals.

Our research proves that high levels of strategic alignment lead to stronger innovation, higher customer satisfaction, accelerated sales growth, and increased profitability. In essence, strategic alignment ensures that the entire organisation is travelling in the same direction with the customer as the compass.

What is the impact on customers when businesses lack strategic alignment?

Insight	Description	Impact
Inconsistent experiences	Teams operate with different priorities	Customers feel confused or frustrated
Slow responses	Misalignment causes hesitation and duplication	Customers face delays and poor service
Products that miss the mark	Teams build features that don't solve real problems	Customers feel misunderstood
Higher customer effort	Customers must navigate disconnected departments	More frustration, lower satisfaction, higher churn
Broken journeys	Lack of teamwork breaks the customer journey	Customers abandon purchases or switch brands
Missed value opportunities	Poor coordination means missed upsells and solutions	Customers miss out on real benefits
Loss of confidence	Disorganised brands lose trust	Loyalty weakens, customers look elsewhere

Strategic alignment is critical for ensuring that everyone in an organisation is working toward the same goals with clarity and purpose. Without it, businesses risk conflicting priorities, wasted resources, slow decision-making, frustrated employees, and fragmented customer experiences. Even the best strategies will fail without coordinated execution across teams. Misaligned organisations not only struggle to deliver value to customers but also fall behind competitors who move faster with clearer focus.

Strategic alignment transforms strategy into measurable results, creating stronger, more resilient businesses. Without it, organisations risk confusion, inefficiency, and long-term decline.

Customers want one seamless experience not a collection of disconnected departments.

Each of the eight disciplines is interconnected with the others. Focusing on one inevitably influences the rest. In practice, organisations typically concentrate on one or two disciplines that best support their strategy and business priorities.

Later, in Chapter 7, we'll take a deeper dive into each of the eight disciplines, exploring both strategic and tactical initiatives that can be applied across any organisation. But first, in Chapter 4, we address a critical challenge facing today's leaders: how to gain clear, actionable insight into their organisation's culture and performance. We introduce the MRI, a proven tool that empowers leaders to diagnose cultural strengths and weaknesses. It uncovers hidden barriers so that leaders can take positive action.

Key Takeaways—Chapter 3

1. Culture Must Be Measurable to Be Effective

Many organisations struggle to connect culture with business performance because it feels abstract. This chapter has introduced eight behavioural disciplines as a practical, measurable system for embedding culture into day-to-day operations and aligning it with financial outcomes.

2. Customer Insight Is Everyone's Job, Not Just Marketing's

One of the most damaging blind spots in business is when teams, especially in finance, legal, or IT make decisions that have an impact on customers without ever interacting with customers. This chapter emphasises that deep, organisation-wide customer understanding must be embedded across every department and level. Companies that align around a shared view of "who the customer is" make better decisions, reduce friction, and build stronger relationships.

3. Engagement Must Span Customers, Employees, and Leaders

The eight disciplines activate the three pillars of human engagement: customer, employee, and leadership. When fully embraced, they create a customer and human-first culture where every person and every function contributes to value creation.

The Bottom Line

Chapter 3 delivers a clear, actionable blueprint for transforming culture from a vague concept into a performance-driving system. Organisations that implement the eight disciplines consistently outperform competitors, achieving innovation and sustainable growth, higher profitability, stronger customer loyalty, and deeper employee engagement.

Scan or click to learn more about the 8 Disciplines

Scan or click to listen to our Podcasts

CHAPTER 4

MEASUREMENT DRIVES BUSINESS PERFORMANCE AND GROWTH

The Measurement—Show Me the Money

Culture Eats Strategy and the MRI Measures the Appetite.

Without clear, measurable insights, even the most well-intentioned strategies risk falling flat. In other words, how can we accurately measure our current state and track progress with confidence over time? Without that visibility, improvement is just guesswork.

That was the challenge the MarketCulture research team set out to solve: how do we take the eight disciplines and turn them into a practical, actionable tool that clearly pictures where an organisation is today, and tracks its progress over time? The feedback was clear: leaders want to know if their organisations are actually improving.

We set out to develop a measurement tool that could provide a clear, accurate picture of an organisation's strengths and weaknesses, specifically through the lens of the eight disciplines. The goal was to give leaders the insight needed to make informed decisions and take purposeful, strategic action. But as the idea evolved, so did the vision. We began to ask a bigger question: Could we create a benchmark for organisations to compare themselves against the best in the world? What if we could build a global database that not only assesses an individual company's performance, but also compares it to others? That became the foundation for a broader ambition: to give organisations both self-awareness and context.

We soon realised that measurement alone isn't enough. Knowing an organisation's strengths and weaknesses is just one piece of the puzzle. It's like stepping on a scale, you might see the number, but it doesn't tell you what it means or what to do next. We needed more than data; we needed insight. A way for the business to speak for itself. A method to uncover hidden risks, highlight roadblocks, and bring to the surface the often-invisible barriers that silently limit performance. Because real progress doesn't just come from knowing where you are. It comes from understanding "why" and knowing exactly how to move forward.

And the rest is history. The MRI was developed and has now been used by over 1,000 organisations worldwide to assess what they have done and where they are going. It's helped countless leaders tackle meaningful action to increase innovation and achieve sustainable growth.

Does this phrase sound familiar? "What gets measured gets managed".

Measurement has become deeply woven into the fabric of our everyday lives. From an early age, we're surrounded by metrics that shape how we understand progress and performance. Today, we wear smartwatches that track our steps, weigh ourselves to monitor our health, and check our bank accounts to measure financial goals. And one thing we all keep tabs on? Our age, perhaps the most universal metric of all.

In business, measurement is even more pervasive. Sales teams chase revenue targets, accounts receivable teams focus on reducing outstanding debts, and executives monitor dashboards to steer strategy and performance. Regardless of your role, metrics influence behaviour and, ultimately, drive results.

As outlined in the previous chapters, the three pillars of human engagement offer a powerful framework to align customers, employees, and leaders in building a sustainable, customer-centric culture. We also identified eight essential disciplines. Yet even with this structure in place, a critical gap remained: how do we know where we are today? Are we improving? What are our strengths and weaknesses and how do we find the blind spots that might be getting in the way of success?

The MRI is a tool for answering these questions, bringing the three pillars and the eight disciplines to life in a practical, actionable way. In this chapter, we take a closer look at the MRI: how it works, how it's applied in organisations, and its real-world impact. You'll see how leaders have used the MRI not only to drive meaningful change but also to actively engage employees and accelerate business success. We'll explore the science behind it and how it's been proven to link directly to measurable business performance outcomes. Because the MRI and the success it achieves is grounded in data and results.

More importantly, we'll share case studies and examples of organisations that have leveraged the MRI to outperform their competitors. In short, we demonstrate what's possible when insight meets action.

What is the Market Responsiveness Index (MRI)?

Bryan Jago, Executive Manager Service at Canon Medical Systems ANZ, shared a compelling analogy when describing the Market Responsiveness Index. He likened it to a medical MRI scan: "When you're experiencing persistent headaches, you visit a doctor. The doctor can assess the symptoms, but to truly understand what's happening beneath the surface, they'll refer you for an MRI. The scan provides a deeper, more detailed diagnosis revealing underlying issues that may not be immediately visible."

The MarketCulture MRI works in much the same way for a business. Leaders can observe what's happening on the surface, in terms of customer feedback, team performance, operational challenges, but those surface indicators probably don't tell the whole story.

Bryan explained, "The MRI gave us the ability to look deeper into the organisation to diagnose issues that weren't visible from the outside. It helped us uncover root causes and areas of misalignment that we would've otherwise missed."

Bryan considers the MRI an essential tool for strategic clarity and cultural transformation, offering insights that go far beyond those provided by traditional performance metrics. This is because the MRI is a statistically validated diagnostic tool designed to help uncover, benchmark, and strengthen the cultural drivers that shape a company's financial future. It focuses on what truly matters, the culture that fuels customer value, innovation, and sustainable growth.

The MRI serves as the vital bridge between leader and employee engagement, and customer satisfaction. By offering an inside-out view of organisational culture, it equips leaders with the insights they need to take targeted action that empowers teams to deliver exceptional customer experiences that drive loyalty, retention, and advocacy. It empowers leaders and employees to share open, honest, and constructive feedback, fuelling meaningful cultural change and improved business outcomes.

The MRI is completed anonymously by leaders and employees, encouraging candid responses without fear of repercussion. The assessment asks questions based around the best practices of high-performing, customer-centric organisations known for their sustained growth and competitive agility. It features 40 targeted questions, each aligned with the eight disciplines that underpin market responsiveness. Additionally, and most importantly, employees can provide open-ended comments, giving leaders deeper insight into the *why* behind the scores, offering context, clarity, and direction for action.

What Does the Market Responsiveness Index (MRI) Measure?

While corporate culture is broad and multifaceted, the MRI focuses with precision on the cultural behaviours that most directly drive and sustain long-term competitive advantage. It provides a clear, actionable benchmark for assessing and improving based on the eight disciplines that define high-performing organisations.

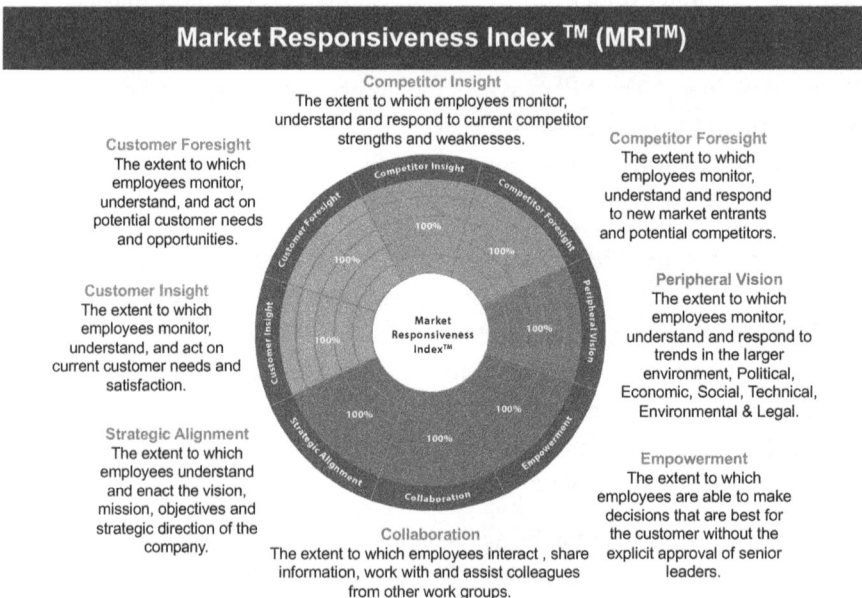

Market Responsiveness Index ™ (MRI™)

Competitor Insight
The extent to which employees monitor, understand and respond to current competitor strengths and weaknesses.

Customer Foresight
The extent to which employees monitor, understand, and act on potential customer needs and opportunities.

Competitor Foresight
The extent to which employees monitor, understand and respond to new market entrants and potential competitors.

Customer Insight
The extent to which employees monitor, understand, and act on current customer needs and satisfaction.

Peripheral Vision
The extent to which employees monitor, understand and respond to trends in the larger environment, Political, Economic, Social, Technical, Environmental & Legal.

Strategic Alignment
The extent to which employees understand and enact the vision, mission, objectives and strategic direction of the company.

Empowerment
The extent to which employees are able to make decisions that are best for the customer without the explicit approval of senior leaders.

Collaboration
The extent to which employees interact, share information, work with and assist colleagues from other work groups.

The MRI does more than show where your organisation stands. It delivers a clear, actionable roadmap for cultivating a culture that consistently creates and delivers superior customer value. With the ability to conduct ongoing measurements, leaders can track progress over time, monitor cultural shifts, and ensure continuous alignment with strategic goals.

How is the MRI Implemented?

The MRI is a web-based employee assessment designed to capture feedback at the organisational, departmental, or team level. It is easy to administer, intuitive to complete, and highly effective in delivering clear, detailed, and actionable insights for leaders aiming to strengthen customer culture and accelerate business performance.

During a conversation with Beatrix Kapitány, Head of Customer Experience, Transformation, and Business Steering at Deutsche Telekom, she shared an insight that fundamentally shifted the direction of our business. At the time, Deutsche Telekom was actively using the MRI, with the implementation and management handled entirely by our team at MarketCulture. While discussing their experience, Beatrix offered a simple yet powerful suggestion: "If we could run the MRI ourselves, it would make the tool so much more versatile." That moment was a turning point. Her comment highlighted a crucial opportunity to transform the MRI from a consultant-led assessment into a self-service platform that could scale across small medium and large organisations with ease.

Over the past two years, we've taken the MRI to the next level by developing the MRI Platform: a fully online, intuitive tool that any organisation can access, from anywhere, at any time. It's built for ease of use, scalability, and measurable impact. The MRI is fully automated and requires no specialised facilitation, anyone in an organisation can deploy it. Once completed, the assessment generates a comprehensive report that is available instantly online, enabling rapid decision-making and immediate action. Included is an online training course to help leaders interpret the results.

And the best part? You don't have to wait. You can try it now and experience the value firsthand. We often say to leaders who are hesitant to try something new, "What's the real risk of not doing anything?" Because in today's fast-moving world, standing still is often the biggest risk of all.

Understanding the MRI Benchmark Results

In a recent executive presentation, a senior leader questioned the value of benchmarked scores, asking instead for the raw data. Our answer was straightforward: a raw score reflects how your employees perceive your organisation's market responsiveness on its own without comparing it to any other organisation. To create a benchmark, your score is measured against those of other organisations. Benchmarking reveals how you stack up, including against the best. Your people provide their perspective; the benchmark shows where that perspective sits in the wider market. It reveals whether you are ahead, behind, or on par. Without that context, you can't know if 'good' is actually good enough.

One of the most widely understood and relatable examples for raw score vs benchmark score is the school test:

- **Raw score** = Your individual test mark. For example, you scored 78/100. This tells you how you did in isolation from others in the class.

- **Benchmark score** = Your test mark compared to all others in the class. For example, your raw score of 78/100 may translate to a benchmark score of 70%. This means your score was higher than 70% of the people in your class. This tells you where you stand in relation to others.

Raw scores offer internal insight, but benchmark scores provide essential context, allowing you to understand your position relative to others and identify where real competitive advantage lies. The MRI benchmark results are expressed as percentiles, with a ranking scale ranging from 1 (lowest) to 99 (highest), with 50 representing the median. A percentile rank:

- reflects the percentage of organisations in the norm group that scored equal to or lower than the reported score
- does not represent the percentage of correct or ideal responses; rather it shows how a group's cultural behaviours compare to those of other organisations

The norm group includes data from over 1,000 organisations worldwide, making the percentile scores both meaningful and reliable. Percentiles are used because raw scores can be misleading, often lacking context or comparative value. In contrast, normed percentiles offer a clear benchmark, revealing how your organisation stacks up against others across the world.

Extensive empirical research, including our own, confirms that MRI percentile scores are valid and comparable across industries, regions, and organisational demographics, making them a trusted metric for cultural performance evaluation. You aren't just being compared with your direct competitors; you are being compared with the best organisations globally.

Interpreting the MRI Circumplex Graphics

When developing the MRI we faced a challenge: how could we present the results in a way that resonated not just with leadership, but with the entire organisation? Creating engagement was essential. After all, how many surveys or assessments have been conducted in organisations only for the results to fall flat, lost in reports that fail to inspire action?

That's why the circumplex visuals included in every MRI report are so powerful. They deliver a clear, intuitive, and immediately meaningful snapshot of your organisation's performance across the eight disciplines. These graphics make it easy for everyone from the executive team to frontline and back-of-house employees to understand where the organisation excels and where there's room to improve. Most importantly, they spark dialogue, foster ownership, and drive momentum for meaningful cultural change. Even more powerful is the ability to compare results over time; when the MRI is conducted a second time, it provides a clear, data-driven view of progress, trends, and impact. Below is an example of 2 very different organisations.

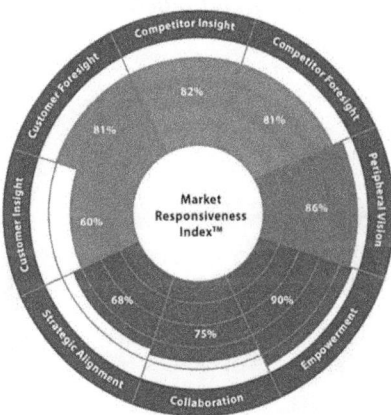

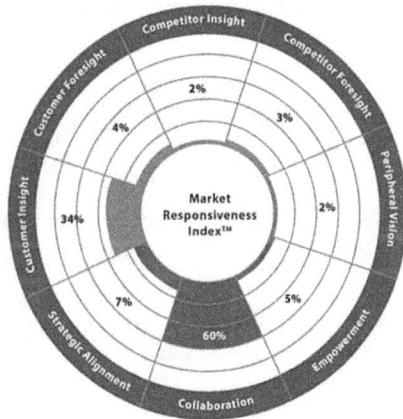

HIGH PERFORMER   LOW PERFORMER

- The graphic on the left represents a high-performing organisation
- The graphic on the right shows a lower-performing organisation
- Each of the eight segments corresponds to one of the MRI disciplines
- The colour intensity within each segment reflects the percentile performance, the more colour, the stronger the performance
- Each discipline also displays a numerical percentile score for precision

These visuals are powerful diagnostic tools, as higher circumplex scores have been shown to strongly correlate with superior business outcomes, including growth, innovation, and customer advocacy.

What Does a Circumplex Chart Tell Us? Diagnosing Your MRI

When we look at the MRI circumplex chart, we get an instant snapshot of what an organisation is experiencing—its relative strengths, weaknesses, blind spots, and the key areas that may need attention.

Adding the verbatim comments from respondents brings this picture to life, explaining *why* the chart looks the way it does. Even deeper context emerges when we factor in external conditions, such as market growth rates and competitive pressures.

Yet even on its own, the MRI chart offers powerful insights into what's really happening inside the organisation. The examples below illustrate diagnoses made using just the MRI chart, before adding any additional data.

Example 1: Externally Focused vs Internally Focused Organisation

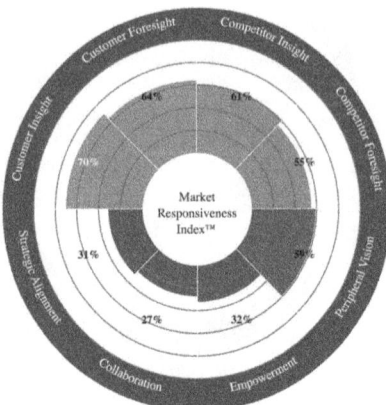

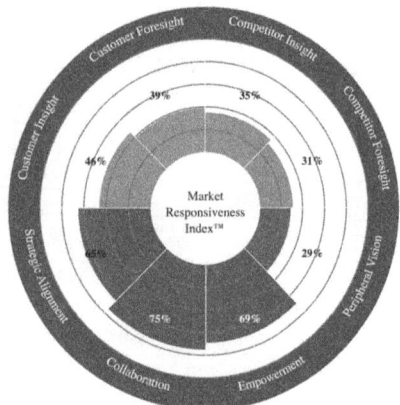

Externally Focused Organisation   Internally Focused Organisation

Example 1 shows organisations analysed using the MRI framework. The results highlight two contrasting profiles: one organisation excels at internal alignment and operational execution but struggles to connect with its external market. The other shows strong external awareness and market focus but is held back by critical internal weaknesses.

Example 2: A Perception Gap between Leaders and Employees in One Organisation

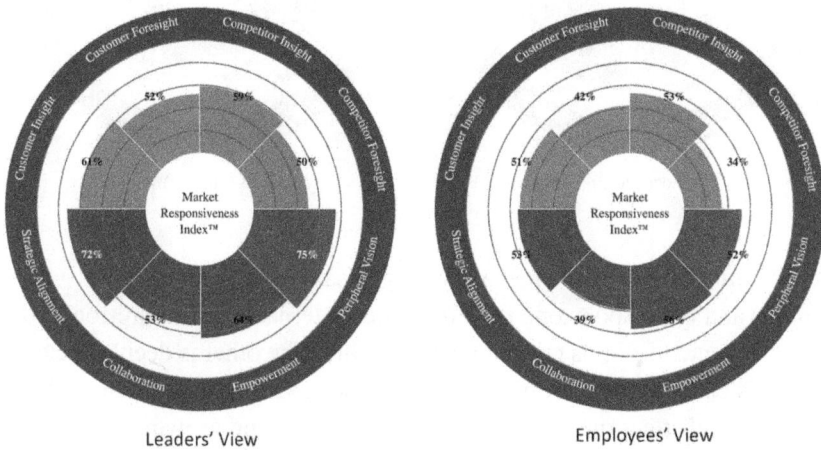

Leaders' View   Employees' View

The two circumplexes in Example 2, while showing a similar pattern, reveal a critical disconnect: leaders see the organisation as strong and responsive with an overall score of 61%, while employees experience it as somewhat weaker, with internal friction, and a lack of future vision at 48%. This gap is the greatest risk the company faces, as leadership may be making strategic decisions based on flawed assumptions, fostering disengagement, and leaving the organisation vulnerable to market shifts and competitive threats.

Example 3: Present Focused vs Future Focused Organisations

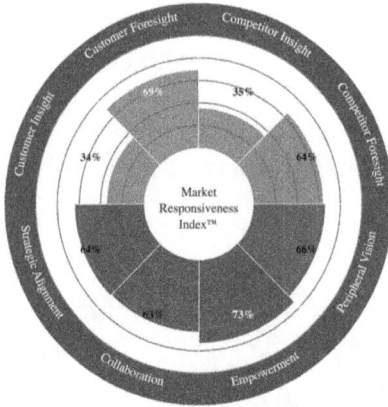

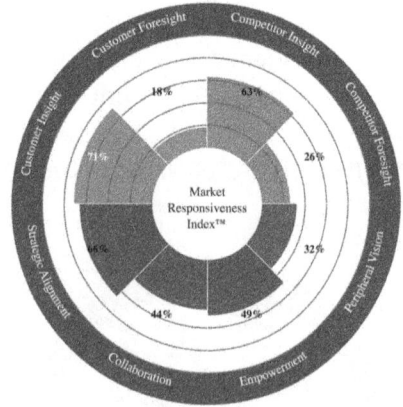

Future Focused Organisation · Current Focused Organisation

The Example 3 MRI charts reveal two organisations with contrasting strengths and blind spots: one is well-aligned internally and future-focused but disconnected from its current market reality. The other is deeply focused on today's customers and competitors but lacks a vision for the future. Both profiles pose distinct risks to sustained performance and growth.

Example 4: Competitor Focused vs Customer Focused Organisations

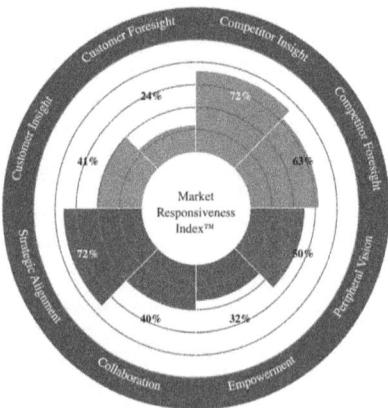

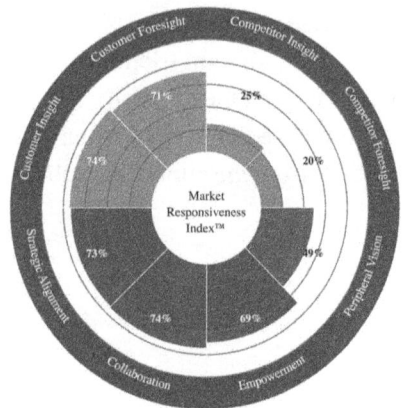

Competitor Focused Organisation · Customer Focused Organisation

The competitor focused organisation in Example 4 is so fixated on its rivals that it's dangerously blind to its own customers. The customer focused organisation excels at serving customers and nurturing a strong culture but ignores the competitive landscape. Both are strategically vulnerable: one risks fighting hard for a market that has moved on, and the other, by relying on its strong customer base, risks being blindsided by an unseen competitor.

Show Me The Money!

During our research, we encountered many challenges, but one stood out: could we directly link the MRI methodology to business performance? This was the critical question. It wasn't enough simply to build a methodology— we had to prove that strengthening the eight disciplines and performing better on the MRI benchmark over time would lead to measurable improvements in the bottom line. In other words, could we demonstrate that developing the eight disciplines drives real, tangible financial results?

Having attended conferences around the world and engaged with countless customer experience professionals and consultants, one question is asked more than any other: "How do we prove to leadership that what we do drives financial return?"

The biggest challenge is not about intent or effort—it's about quantifying impact. Leaders want to see clear evidence that customer experience initiatives translate into measurable progress and tangible business outcomes. They demand tools and methods that don't just tell a story but demonstrate value in financial terms. That's because too many projects and initiatives begin without clearly defined performance metrics. Without a structured way to measure impact, how can we credibly return to the executive team and ask for additional funding or support? If we can't demonstrate that our initiatives are contributing to the bottom line, we risk losing momentum, buy-in, and future investment. To drive meaningful change and secure sustained executive backing we must connect our work to tangible business outcomes and show precisely how it adds value.

During the height of COVID-19, Beatrix Kapitany engaged MarketCulture to help drive a customer-focused cultural shift in Deutsche Telekom. A clear goal was set to identify strengths and weaknesses across two departments to improve customer satisfaction and demonstrate measurable change to leadership. A virtual kick-off session brought together 140 employees, with the aim of completing the MRI assessment live, and 90% of participants completed the survey in-session, enabling the overall results to be developed quickly. Two clear priorities became clear.

- Customer Insight—Deepening understanding of customer needs
- Cross-Functional Collaboration—Breaking down silos and improving teamwork

These became the focus of an eight-month improvement plan. When the team was reassessed, the impact was undeniable.

- Marked improvement in both target areas
- Stronger collaboration and alignment
- Higher customer satisfaction
- Noticeable growth in business performance

Most importantly, the initiative sparked a profound shift in the relationship between the two departments building mutual respect, stronger collaboration, and a unified sense of purpose.

The MRI did more than measure—it validated that meaningful change was taking place and that it was translating into real business results. It proved the change occurred. With measurable improvements in the MRI Benchmark score, Beatrix was able to confidently demonstrate to senior leadership that a transformation had occurred that directly contributed to enhanced business performance and customer outcomes.

The good news is this: the MRI has not only been scientifically validated to drive business performance it has now been proven in practice. With over 1,000 organisations having implemented the methodology, we're seeing clear, consistent evidence that strengthening the eight disciplines using the MRI directly contributes to bottom-line results.

When we first launched the MRI, we relied solely on rigorous academic research. Today, it's backed by a growing body of real-world success stories from companies that have embraced the MRI methodology. Chapter 5 offers an in-depth look at organisations that have achieved meaningful, measurable, and financial improvements through the implementation of the MRI.

The Vital Link to Business Performance

To innovate successfully, organisations must deeply understand their customers, not just as they are today, but as they will be tomorrow. This requires more than market research; it requires active listening, empowerment, and cross-functional collaboration.

When employees feel valued and are encouraged to share insights from the field, the business is better positioned to align its strategy, innovation, and execution, ultimately delivering products that succeed not by chance, but by design.

Sean

Over my career in sales, I often found myself frustrated by the lack of success in new product launches. Time and again, I watched products hit the market that simply didn't fit, like trying to force a square peg into a round hole. No one wanted them, and frankly, they were a waste of time and resources.

That all changed in 2007, when I received an unexpected invitation to attend a product development meeting in Japan for Konica Minolta. For the first time sales, not management, had been invited to contribute to product strategy. Three months before the meeting, I was asked to visit customers and gather insights to present.

At first, the questions I was given to ask customers were focused on improving product features. But I realised that wouldn't get us where we needed to go. Instead of asking what customers thought of our products, I asked them where they saw their business would be in five to ten years. Their answers changed everything.

Sean—continued

They painted a picture of the future with new challenges, evolving needs, and emerging opportunities. They did not give me specific features, instead thinking big about what their business required. Armed with this perspective, I headed to Japan and sat through two full days of PowerPoint presentations before sharing my findings. There was one catch: I didn't speak Japanese.

As I presented, I received no reaction. Maybe it was the language barrier. It was hard not to feel deflated. But deep down, I knew it wasn't that I was speaking English to a Japanese audience—it was that I was the voice of the customer speaking to an audience of people who were used to telling the customer what they wanted. My message was not about what we wanted to sell, but what the customer needed to succeed. Three years later, that insight became reality. A new digital printing press was launched, one that aligned perfectly with the vision our customers had shared. The result? We dominated the market, with huge demand. Konica Minolta emerged as a major force in the production print space, and I experienced some of the most rewarding years of my career.

The eight MRI disciplines have been proven to exert a decisive influence on a wide range of critical business outcomes, including sales growth, profit growth, overall profitability, customer satisfaction, innovation, new-product success, employee engagement, and retention.

The image below illustrates how each discipline directly drives key performance outcomes, reinforcing the powerful connection between customer-centric culture and sustainable business success. The tick marks represent a strong correlation between each cultural discipline and a key driver of business performance. We're often asked, *"How can I make my organisation more innovative and more successful at launching new products?"* The answer lies in this table: focus deliberately on the disciplines that fuel innovation and product success. For example, seven of the eight disciplines directly drive innovation, while four are critical for new product success. So, what are the most important business outcomes you want to achieve? Look at the table. Your roadmap is there.

When you evaluate your MRI chart alongside the performance drivers in this chart and your business objectives, your action priorities for sustainable growth will become clear.

Disciplines	Customer Satisfaction	Innovation	New Product Success	Profit Growth	Profitability	Sales Revenue Growth	Employee Satisfaction (Engagement)	Employee Retention (Cost)
Customer Insight	✓	✓	✓			✓	✓	✓
Customer Foresight		✓						
Competitor Insight				✓	✓	✓		
Competitor Foresight		✓	✓					
Peripheral Vision		✓						✓
Empowerment	✓	✓						
Cross-Functional Collaboration	✓	✓	✓	✓	✓	✓	✓	
Strategic Alignment	✓	✓	✓	✓	✓	✓	✓	✓

Let break this down. Take Customer Insight, for example. Ask yourself: "If your entire organisation had a deeper understanding of your customers, would you deliver a higher level of customer satisfaction?" Of 100 business leaders, 99 would answer with a resounding "yes". And the one who wouldn't? Chances are, they're no longer in business. This simple fact underscores the power of these cultural drivers. They're not just nice to have; they're essential to staying competitive and relevant.

Let's look at one more, arguably the most critical: Strategic Alignment. This factor shows a strong correlation with every key business performance outcome. Why? Because when a company builds a clear, customer strategy and aligns the entire organisation behind it everything improves. Ask yourself: "If we crafted a sustainable strategy anchored in customer value, would it drive business performance across the board?" The answer is simply yes. We've consistently seen that when strategic alignment starts at the top and cascades throughout the organisation, it boosts employee engagement, retention, satisfaction, and, ultimately, customer outcomes and profitability. It's not just theory; it's proven in practice.

Every discipline marked with a tick has been scientifically shown to strongly correlate with business performance, reflected in an overall correlation of 0.57, a significant result. Some areas, while intuitively important, don't have a tick because they didn't meet the minimum threshold of 0.25 to qualify as validated drivers in this analysis. That said, we recognise many of these disciplines still contribute meaningfully to organisational success—they just didn't meet the statistical bar here.

To appreciate the strength of a 0.57 correlation, consider this: aspirin and reduced heart attack risk correlate at just 0.02, ibuprofen and pain relief at 0.20, and SAT scores with college GPA at 0.35. Even adult height and weight only show a 0.44 correlation. So, a 0.57 link between customer culture and business performance is remarkably strong, stronger than many trusted medical outcomes or educational predictors.

In business, correlations above 0.25 are considered meaningful. At 0.57, this is a standout result, one of the strongest real-world relationships we're likely to encounter. This comes from the original correlation comparison chart, which remains highly compelling for anyone familiar with statistics.

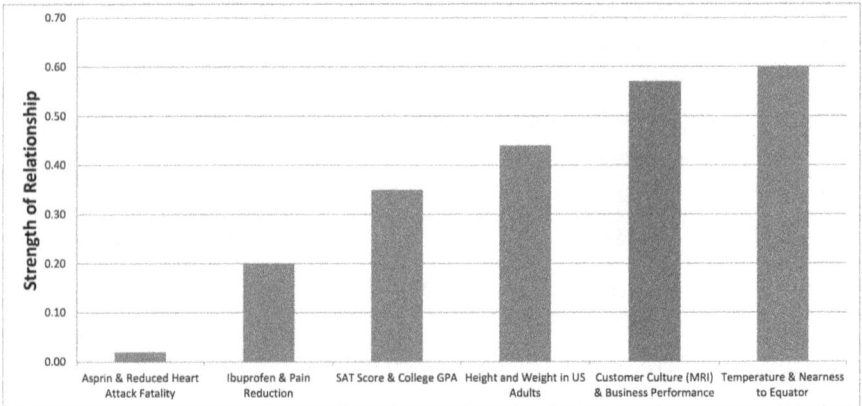

Correlation vs Causation Made Simple

Correlation means two things move together, like ice cream sales and drownings in summer, without one necessarily causing the other. Causation means one thing directly drives the other, like turning a steering wheel causes a car to turn.

Why the MRI Shows Causation, Not Just Correlation

The MRI doesn't just measure a vague idea like "customer culture", it breaks it down into eight specific, actionable disciplines. When companies improve in these areas, performance reliably follows. That's not coincidence; it's causation. It also means that the MRI is a lead indicator to where a business is heading in relation to future performance.

More than a measurement tool, the MRI is a practical diagnostic. Companies use it to identify gaps, make targeted improvements, and see real business gains. That proven cause-and-effect makes it far more powerful and more compelling than any other culture diagnostics available.

For those who enjoy diving deeper into the data and methodology behind the study, we invite you to explore the Market Responsiveness Index Foundation Study. Visit www.marketculture.com/resources to download the full report and gain detailed insights into how the research was conducted.

Using the Market Responsiveness Index to Spark Alignment

Over the past 15 years, organisations across all industries have leveraged the MRI in a variety of ways across the entire organisation, within leadership teams, inside departments, or even with select groups of employees. Its flexibility is one of its greatest strengths.

Sean

One of the most impactful experiences I've had was working with a financial services organisation during an offsite executive retreat. I had been invited to deliver a keynote on building a sustainable, customer-centric culture. But in my experience, a keynote alone often isn't enough to create lasting change, so I suggested a more hands-on, workshop-style session.

Instead of just listening, the executive team would experience the MRI in real time. As they arrived, each leader completed the MRI assessment, a process that takes about 25 minutes. Thanks to our digital platform, the results were instantly available and projected in the room. What followed was far more than a standard workshop.

Sean—continued

The session quickly turned into a dynamic and candid conversation. Executives debated the results, some surprised by lower-than-expected scores, others nodding in agreement. What emerged wasn't just data it was clarity, alignment, and a shared realisation: there was significant room for improvement, and now they had the insight to act on it. By the end of the day, the entire leadership team was fully engaged and aligned around key initiatives that could drive real, measurable change.

The MRI doesn't just inform, it ignites. It creates a common language for culture, surfaces blind spots, and turns abstract goals into focused action. When used in the right setting, it can transform any team from a group of individuals into a unified force committed to building a culture that truly puts the customer at the centre.

Benefits of the MRI for Different Roles in the Organisation

In our initial studies and work, we focused on leadership as the primary drivers of change. However, we have since discovered that meaningful transformation can begin at any level especially when departmental leaders are empowered with the right tools and understanding. Equally important is full organisational buy-in, particularly from senior leadership. Changing an organisation's culture starts at the top, but real, lasting impact only happens when everyone is aligned and engaged.

Let's consider eight key roles within organisations, including one external role, and explore how the MRI methodology delivers unique benefits to each. Feel free to skip ahead to the role most relevant to you.

The Chief Executive Officer: *"The MRI opened a whole new dimension in understanding the customer. It showed me where my perspective had been quite blinkered and revealed blind spots I hadn't considered before."*
—Peter Cooke, International President Wright Medical Group

The MRI empowers CEOs to cultivate market-aware, customer-driven cultures that fuel strategic alignment, accelerate performance, and secure long-term competitive advantage. It enables CEOs to measure, benchmark, and transform organisational culture, turning insight into action and strategy into measurable results. CEOs that embed this capability enterprise-wide are:

- more innovative
- faster to market
- more aligned around customer needs
- and, ultimately, more profitable

The Board of Directors: *"I found that the MRI converts the intangible—culture, agility, customer-centricity into a quantified, benchmarked, and financially validated early-warning system. It lets directors and the board steer growth and risk with the same precision it brings to the balance sheet. It is most valuable when used as a measurement tool that is integrated with the strategic plan. It creates alignment between the board, senior leadership and employees to drive sustainable growth and profitability."*
—Norman Newbon FAICD, Director, StateCover Mutual

The MRI helps boards uncover critical organisational and leadership blind spots that can hinder performance and erode shareholder value. It enables more informed governance and helps ensure the company is well-positioned to deliver sustained growth and superior financial returns. By evaluating the customer-obsessed culture of a company, the board can:

- support new CEOs in driving transformational change
- reinvigorate existing leadership teams
- ensure alignment between culture, strategy, and performance

The Chief Human Resources Officer: *"The MRI provided alignment that galvanised employee engagement and built trust in how they interacted with customers".*
—Sonja Sandral, Moneytech

Today's CHRO is a strategic architect of culture, capability, and competitive advantage. To meet this mandate, HR must move beyond traditional talent practices and adopt smarter, data-driven tools to identify, attract, develop, and align the right people those who can drive growth in a rapidly evolving market landscape. The MRI equips HR leaders with a powerful platform to:

- assess organisational mindset and readiness
- identify critical talent and capability gaps
- drive re-skilling, development, and cultural alignment
- and, ultimately, build a more agile, innovative, and high-performing workforce

The Chief Financial Officer: *"The MRI provides clarity of purpose and focus that added $15 million to the bottom line by reducing fraud and bad debt".*
—John Stanhope, CFO Telstra

People are both the greatest asset and the most significant investment in any organisation. Maximising their effectiveness in delivering customer value, driving market responsiveness, and enabling competitive agility is critical to achieving higher returns and operational efficiency. In an environment where every dollar must deliver measurable value, the CFO plays a key role in ensuring that human capital is aligned with business outcomes. The MRI offers CFOs a powerful, data-driven tool to:

- quantify cultural effectiveness in driving performance
- identify areas of underperformance and risk
- support strategic decisions around resource allocation, transformation, and ROI
- and partner with the CEO to drive sustainable business performance and cultural accountability

The Chief Marketing Officer: *"The MRI was a key tool in the impetus and planning around the global restructuring of the kitchen systems division. It became a tool to communicate at a strategic level for the entire organisation. The MRI was a game changer for Franke and me personally."*
—Charlie Lawrence, Former CMO, Franke Group, North America

The role of today's CMO is evolving rapidly, expanding from brand and communications to owning business growth, customer experience, and enterprise-wide alignment. With rising expectations for measurability, impact, and innovation, CMOs are now at the forefront of driving transformation that connects the voice of the customer to the heart of the business strategy. The MRI empowers CMOs to:

- embed a customer-obsessed mindset across global marketing teams and the broader organisation
- foster a collaborative, agile culture that adapts quickly to market shifts
- equip teams with the skills, behaviours, and insights needed to engage customers more effectively
- elevate marketing's strategic role as a growth engine and catalyst for enterprise transformation

The Customer Experience Officer: *"The MRI provided concrete measurement for concrete actions and that gained the attention and buy-in of senior leadership".*
—Raja Al-Khatib, Global CXO, Vodafone

The Chief Experience Officer (CXO) is the leader responsible for ensuring the entire organisation consistently delivers experiences that meet and ideally exceed customer (and often employee) expectations in ways that create measurable business value. The MRI provides the framework to make this possible and underpins all effective CX initiatives. The MRI:

- makes CX a board-level priority that is strategic, measurable, and fully integrated into how the business competes and grows
- measures real customer-centricity not just in statements, but in daily behaviours, systems, and culture
- builds a compelling internal case for change with credible data that earns senior leadership support
- highlights strengths and blind spots, pinpointing exactly where to focus for the greatest impact
- tracks progress over time, proving whether culture shifts are taking hold and delivering results
- sparks wider alignment, opening conversations across leadership, HR, sales, operations, and product

The Head of Strategy and Planning: *"The MRI results were built into Gippsland Water's strategy, making customer focus a core part of its long-term plan, not just a one-off project".*
—Paul Clark, General Manager Customer & Community, Gippsland Water

In today's dynamic market environment, it's not enough to build smart strategies they must be executed effectively across the organisation. That requires alignment, capability, and a deep understanding of where the business stands today. The MRI provides:

- data-driven insight into organisational strengths and weaknesses that directly impact strategic execution
- a platform to engage leaders and employees, ensuring strategy is shaped by those closest to customers and operations
- clear, actionable priorities to support short- and mid-term strategy implementation
- enterprise-wide alignment and buy-in, helping to ensure that everyone is working toward the same strategic goals

The Head of Learning and Development: *"We've integrated the MRI into several of our leadership development programs with clients, and it has consistently delivered deep insight and impact. The tool helps leaders understand how well their organisations are aligned to market needs and where they can become more responsive. It creates a strong foundation for strategic dialogue and practical change."*
—Jill Blick, Principal Learning Partner, Harvard Business Impact

The MRI helps L&D leaders to cultivate the next generation of customer-centric leadership, equipping both current and emerging leaders with the mindset, skills, and experiences needed to thrive in a customer-driven world. We provide L&D executives with the tools, expertise, and structured programs needed to:

- develop leaders with a customer-obsessed mindset
- drive behaviour change through immersive learning experiences
- align leadership development with strategic business outcomes
- create long-term value through more connected, adaptive, and effective leaders

Entrepreneurs and High-Growth Company Leaders: *"If you want to understand CX, start with EX; the MRI is a practical way to get the employee's view of customer experience. That's rare."*—Vivek Bhaskaran, QuestionPro

We help founders and growth-stage leaders embed customer-centric thinking deep into the fabric of their organisations, ensuring that rapid expansion doesn't dilute what made them successful in the first place. The MRI serves as a powerful diagnostic and alignment tool that:

- assesses the current cultural strengths and gaps that influence customer experience and execution
- identifies the capabilities needed to scale a customer-obsessed mindset across new hires and evolving teams
- acts as a strategic checkpoint along the growth journey to ensure the customer remains at the centre of decisions
- fosters ongoing alignment and buy-in across the business, helping teams rally around a shared purpose and scalable strategy

Consultants: *"The MRI has become one of the most powerful tools in helping organisations transform their cultures. It is the missing link between vague conversations about 'culture' and concrete, measurable actions. It makes culture understandable and tangible. Are you doing this or not?"*—Olga Guseva, Integria CX Consulting

The MRI provides a clear, repeatable method to assess client organisations' cultural strengths, gaps, and customer-centric capabilities, helping consultants deliver consistent, data-backed insights. It:

- boosts credibility and trust, signalling a disciplined, data-driven approach, instantly elevating professionalism and earning client confidence
- streamlines onboarding and discovery by quickly uncovering where attention is needed most, allowing consultants to focus time and energy where it will make the biggest impact
- tracks progress with hard evidence by providing clear benchmarks and measurable progress over time, helping to demonstrate value and celebrate client wins
- aligns leadership and teams by surfacing blind spots and building shared understanding; when everyone sees the same data, it's easier to get buy-in and drive meaningful change
- delivers tailored, high-impact strategies by allowing tailored solutions that are sharply focused on each client's unique challenges and opportunities
- scales with growth so that whether a consultant is working with one client or 20, the MRI adapts, giving a repeatable, professional framework to grow the consulting business efficiently
- opens the door to strategic dialogue, naturally leading to high-value conversations about strategy, culture, and customer experience, positioning the consultant as a trusted advisor.

No matter your role within the organisation, the MRI serves as a foundational tool for success. Start-ups use it to shape customer-driven strategies from day one, while established teams apply it to deepen alignment and execution. We've seen individuals at all levels embrace the methodology not only to contribute more effectively today but also to prepare themselves for future leadership roles.

In the next chapter, we bring the MRI framework, methodology, and measurement to life, showcasing how organisations have successfully implemented it to drive alignment, customer-centricity, and scalable growth.

Key Takeaways—Chapter 4

1. What Gets Measured Gets Managed and Improved

Without measurement, culture change is just wishful thinking. Chapter 4 introduces the MRI as a practical, validated tool that translates the eight disciplines into measurable, trackable data. It turns abstract cultural goals into clear benchmarks and actionable insights that show exactly where an organisation stands and how to move forward.

2. The MRI Links Culture Directly to Financial Performance

The MRI isn't just a survey—it's been statistically validated and proven in the real world to drive measurable results. Organisations that use the MRI see clear improvements in customer satisfaction, innovation, new product success, employee engagement, and profitability. This gives leaders the evidence they need to secure buy-in and funding for cultural initiatives.

3. Insight Sparks Alignment, Ownership, and Action

The MRI provides a common language for leaders, employees, and teams. By revealing hidden strengths, gaps, and blind spots, it aligns everyone around where to act and why it matters, fostering shared ownership and accountability. The circumplex visuals make it easy for everyone from frontline teams to boards to understand and engage.

The Bottom Line

Chapter 4 proves that measurement is the bridge between cultural intent and business results. The MRI makes culture tangible, actionable, and financially credible. When organisations measure what matters, they manage what matters and they see the money follow.

**Scan or click to listen
to our Podcasts**

CHAPTER 5

HOW HUMAN-CENTRIC ORGANISATIONS DRIVE EXPONENTIAL GROWTH

I'll Believe It When I See It

Throughout our journey, we've engaged with countless leaders to answer a central question: Can culture truly be changed? Their responses almost always fall into two distinct camps.

The first and most common view is, "I'll believe it when I see it". These leaders prioritise evidence. For them, belief follows proof. They need to witness culture change working, ideally in an organisation much like their own, before they're willing to embrace the possibility.

The second perspective turns that mindset on its head: *"I believe it, so I can see it"*. These leaders operate from a deep conviction in the transformative power of culture. Their belief becomes a lens, one that sharpens perception, tunes them into subtle shifts, and reveals opportunities others might overlook. This mindset allows them to recognise and nurture emerging cultural signals before they're broadly visible.

Both perspectives carry a risk: confirmation bias. Leaders often discount data or experiences that don't align with their expectations. We've seen this sometimes when teams first receive their MRI results. When scores come in lower than expected, the reflex is often defensive. But with thoughtful reflection and open dialogue, that initial resistance often shifts to recognition.

One leader who exemplified cultural responsiveness in action was Russell Stanners, former CEO of Vodafone, New Zealand. Russell rejected the idea of a fixed office. Instead, he worked from various standing desks across the company, staying mobile and immersed in the daily rhythm of both employees and customers. We met him during our MRI rollout, when he spoke passionately about the "buzz" he felt throughout the organisation, an engagement and energy that he described as "electric". For Russell, culture wasn't an abstract concept, it was a tangible force, one he could see, hear, and feel. And it reinforced what he already believed: culture drives performance.

Mary Barra, CEO of General Motors, captured it succinctly: "The most important thing I've learned in my career is that culture is everything". She's a vocal champion of the belief that culture is mission critical for business performance. She also says: "They say culture can't be changed, or it takes 10 years. To me, it's behaviours and that can be changed right away."

Leaders like Russell Stanners and Mary Barra believe that culture must be shaped, actively and intentionally, to support sustained innovation and performance. They both believe it, so they see it.

We recognise that it can be difficult to picture how new cultural frameworks or tools will take root in your own organisation. That's why this chapter shares real stories from leaders navigating challenges not unlike your own. You'll hear from global enterprises and agile SMEs alike. The MRI has been adopted by organisations across a diverse spectrum of industries including banking and finance, telecommunications, insurance, construction, hospitality, healthcare, government, non-profits, and manufacturing.

Each case study demonstrates a simple fact: when customer-centric behaviours are measured, they can be managed, and when they are managed, meaningful change occurs.

Our goal is to illustrate how the MRI enables leaders to align culture with strategy, drive performance, and build organisations that are truly responsive to their customers and markets.

We've featured 14 case studies of organisations that have generously allowed us to share their stories, providing clear, real-world evidence of impact and transformation.

Case Study	Company	Industry
1	Vodafone	Telco
2	Deutsche Telekom	Telco
3	Telstra	Telco
4	Wright Medical Group	Medical
5	Canon Medical ANZ	Medical
6	Allen Medical	Medical
7	Konica Minolta	Technology
8	Blackrock	Banking
9	Westpac	Banking
10	StateCover	Insurance
11	Gippsland Water	Government Utility
12	Sydney Water	Government Utility
13	Speedo	Manufacturing
14	Franke Group	Manufacturing

In Chapter 6, we shift focus to explore a less tangible but equally powerful dimension of the framework and methodology: the human element. We examine how leaders can create lasting impact not just through strategy, but by fostering empathy, building genuine rapport with employees, and shaping a culture that endures. This is where leadership becomes legacy.

1. Vodafone

vodafone **From Stalled Loyalty to Net Promoter Score Leadership**

The Challenge

Vodafone's Net Promoter Score (NPS) had flatlined. Years of investment in systems and initiatives weren't moving the dial. In telecom, even a 1% NPS shift can mean millions, so this wasn't just a stagnation; it was a strategic threat. And the root issue wasn't operational it was cultural.

The Spark

It began unexpectedly. A voicemail at 3am: "This is the Chief of Staff to the CEO of Vodafone. We need to speak urgently about your book." A follow-up email from Raja, Global Head of Customer Experience, confirmed it: "We want to talk about culture".

Within 24 hours, a meeting was arranged with Hatem Dowidar, then Group Chief of Staff. His words were blunt: "We've been stuck for years. Nothing we've tried has worked."

The Turning Point

Leadership agreed: a cultural transformation was essential. Over 3,500 leaders participated in the MRI, with an 80%+ response rate, personally driven by Group CEO, Vittorio Colao. The data was eye-opening and confronting.

A two-day workshop series followed. Some leaders welcomed the findings. Others resisted. One CEO pushed back publicly: "These results are wrong. My team doesn't think this way." Then, something shifted.

A Moment of Truth

Vittorio Colao, a former McKinsey partner, shared a revealing story: "At a business summit, CEOs were scrambling for the Wi-Fi password embarrassed to submit roaming fees. I realised: we ask customers to trust us, yet we nickel and dime them."

That insight led to a bold decision: Vodafone eliminated roaming fees across 40 territories including the EU. Finance resisted. But the customer response validated the move. It became a powerful symbol of change.

From Insight to Impact

Resistance turned to advocacy. Leaders began aligning strategy and behaviour with customer priorities. The MRI became the compass clarifying focus, breaking silos, and embedding new habits.

The Results

- Highest NPS Score in 19 of 22 markets
- EBITDA turnaround: from −8.3% to +5.8%
- Trust rebuilt through roaming reform
- Cultural shift, with leadership aligned and customer-first thinking embedded

Leadership Legacy

- Vittorio Colao later served in the Italian government, taking with him the lesson that small moments can spark massive change.
- Hatem Dowidar is now Group CEO of e& (formerly known as Etisalat), leading customer-centric reform across the Middle East and transforming from a telecommunications provider to a global technology and investment group.
- Raja reflected, "The MRI gave us laser focus helping shift mindsets and align teams around what really matters to customers."

··· **T·· Deutsche** Telekom   2. Deutsche Telekom
A Cultural Shift with Customer Impact

The Challenge

Inside Deutsche Telekom's ATS Division (wholesale infrastructure), rising customer complaints signalled deeper problems. The root cause? A cultural breakdown between ATS and its internal partner, NWI.

Beatrix Kapitány, Head of Customer Experience, recognised the real issue: not just broken processes but broken trust. Yet convincing others was tough. Her view was simple and urgent: if the culture didn't change, the customers would.

The Turning Point

Beatrix partnered with MarketCulture to launch the Customer Experience Initiative, uniting ATS and NWI around a single focus—the customer.

A Moment of Truth

An MRI assessment of 145 leaders and employees revealed the truth: both divisions scored below global benchmarks on customer-centric behaviour. Suddenly, the conversation changed. Data had sparked dialogue. Now there was evidence and urgency.

From Insight to Action

Next came a four-hour online workshop. Voices from both divisions aligned around three priorities:

- Customer insight—get closer to customer needs
- Collaboration—break down silos, rebuild trust
- Strategic alignment—connect daily work with customer goals

Cross-functional teams were formed to drive each priority. Then came the full Customer Experience Masterclass with practical training designed to embed customer focus into everyday work.

The Results

In just eight months:

- MRI scores rose 9 percentile points, a clear culture gain
- Customer conversations increased; teams addressed issues proactively
- Collaboration improved, operational efficiency and service quality rose
- Employee engagement soared, staff felt purpose and pride

Beatrix's leadership was recognised with a promotion to Head of International Sales Network Infrastructure Solutions at Deutsche Telekom Global Carrier.

Leadership Legacy

What started as internal friction became a customer-first transformation. This story proves that customer-centric culture isn't optional, it's essential. With leadership, evidence, and commitment, even entrenched silos can become powerful bridges.

⬤Telstra 3. Telstra's Cultural Reset
Rewiring a Telecom Giant Around the Customer

The Challenge

When David Thodey became CEO of Telstra, he inherited more than 30,000 employees and a $20 billion enterprise. He also inherited a major trust issue.

Telstra's reputation was in decline. Customers saw Telstra as slow, bureaucratic, and indifferent to their needs. Internally, teams were disconnected, process-heavy, and far removed from customers. For David, this wasn't just a perception problem, it was an existential threat in an era of digital disruption and rising competition. He said, "If we don't put the customer at the centre of everything we do, we won't have a future".

The Spark

To shift the culture, Telstra needed a clear framework. It partnered with MarketCulture to introduce the MRI to measure and embed customer-centric behaviours. The first group involved was an important one of 2,500 people, the Finance and Administration Department. The CFO, John Stanhope, was already a believer in customer culture. The MRI revealed deep gaps:

- Customer insight—employees didn't truly understand evolving needs
- Empowerment—teams lacked autonomy to act
- Collaboration—silos blocked innovation and speed

These weren't isolated problems, they were signs of a risk-averse, internally focused culture. John embarked on leading a journey to embed the concept of "value added service". The cultural focus was on engaging all leaders and employees to understand how they were using customer insight to create value for both internal and external customers. The mindset centered on the end customer—considering what impact actions would have on them, how internal customers could be supported, and what was needed internally to ultimately deliver value to the end customer.

It also included how functional teams would collaborate and what was needed to embed empowerment of leaders and employees to lift service and add value. John's relentless focused leadership was essential for a customer-first mindset to take hold.

John believes innovation is sparked by curiosity. "With regard to curiosity I apply a simple approach: What, So What, Now What. For example: What has the customer told us, so what does it mean, now what action do we take."

The Turning Point

After just 10 months, John's department reported an AUD $15 million boost to the bottom line, driven by customer-focused initiatives and a significant improvement in MRI scores. He continued to embed this improvement in the years that followed. The pilot's success led by John was extended company-wide by David.

Telstra Case Study: https://www.marketculture.com/product-page/telstra-case-study-john-stanhope

A Moment of Truth

A critical test came with customers relocating homes or businesses. The experience was painful, confusing handoffs, delays, and frustration. NPS for this service sat at a very low −60.

Over three years, Telstra redesigned the experience from the ground up. The results:

- NPS improved from −60 to 0
- Customer churn dropped; loyalty rose
- Efficiency gains saved hundreds of millions
- Teams rediscovered purpose and pride

From Insight to Impact

Armed with data, Telstra developed a long-term roadmap, based on a multi-year transformation plan:

- Embedding customer thinking in all departments even those not customer-facing
- Breaking down silos through cross-functional collaboration
- Leadership development tied to daily behaviours
- Data-driven marketing and sharper customer segmentation

This wasn't a quick fix—it was a disciplined, enterprise-wide reset.

The Results

New data showed:

- Stronger leadership behaviours
- Greater team engagement
- A cultural shift toward customer focus

Marketing and service strategies became more data-driven, agile, and aligned to market realities, helping reverse customer attrition and reigniting profit growth.

Leadership Legacy

What began as reputation repair became a cultural reinvention. Under the leadership of David Thodey and John Stanhope, Telstra didn't just update processes, it changed how people thought, collaborated, and served.

The Telstra story proves that culture isn't soft, it's a performance multiplier. When customer experience becomes how a company thinks, not just what it does, real transformation follows.

WRIGHT FOCUSED EXCELLENCE

4. Wright Medical
A Journey to Customer-Centric Excellence

The Challenge

Wright Medical's acquisition of a French company, Tornier, promised growth but instead exposed a deep cultural rift. The fast-paced, results-driven US culture clashed with the French team's collaborative style. Silos deepened, decisions slowed, and customer satisfaction dropped.

Peter Cooke, President of International said: *"We needed to shift. Not just structurally, but culturally. If we didn't rally around the customer, we'd continue to lose ground."*

The Spark

Peter turned to the MRI from MarketCulture to uncover cultural drivers behind customer-centricity and enable the organisation to measure what matters.

The Turning Point

The results of the MRI formed the basis of a new approach.

- **Leadership Alignment Workshops** created a shared vision around customer value
- **A tailored roadmap** focused on communication, decision-making, and customer focus
- **Ongoing measurement** ensured progress and accountability

A Moment of Truth

The MRI revealed that:

- Leadership misalignment stalled decisions
- Teams worked in silos, hindering collaboration
- A gap between strategy and delivery was clear to customers

More than diagnosis, the MRI provided a roadmap.

From Insight to Impact

- Internal alignment improved, bridging the cultural divide.
- Customer satisfaction rebounded, clients felt heard and valued.
- Revenue growth returned.
- A sustainable customer culture took hold.

The Results

The MRI didn't just fix problems it fuelled transformation that created the foundation for a model for sustainable grown.

Leadership Legacy

Says Peter Cooke, *"The MRI gave us more than insight, it gave us clarity, alignment, and a path to growth".*

Canon
CANON MEDICAL SYSTEMS
ANZ PTY LIMITED

5. Canon Medical:
From Strategy to Culture in a Customer-Centric Transformation

The Challenge

Canon Medical Systems ANZ had a clear customer experience strategy under Managing Director Monica King. But something was missing. Monica told us "Customer intimacy wasn't yet woven into the fabric of everyday behaviour". Strong processes and a committed team weren't enough, culture needed to catch up with strategy.

The Spark

Originally Canon Medical had a manual measurement system, based on *The Customer Culture Imperative*, which offered insights but wasn't scalable. It needed a more powerful, measurable approach. Enter the MRI.

The Turning Point

Two key elements turned things around at Canon. The first was making culture measurable. While Canon Medical excelled in customer and competitor insight, the MRI uncovered gaps in collaboration and empowerment, which are key to agility and alignment.

The second was unifying the team.

- A leadership workshop, which included 16 ambassadors across the company, set priorities: customer insight, cross-functional collaboration, and strategic alignment
- Later all 200 employees participated in a company-wide conference. They reviewed the MRI data, shared feedback, and embedded activities into individual Success Indexes

This wasn't top-down. It was all-in.

A Moment of Truth

The MRI provided the data that meant the company could turn its vision into everyday behaviour at scale.

From Insight to Impact

One year later, a second MRI showed real change:

- Strategic alignment surged
- Customer foresight improved
- Monthly "Monomania" town hall meetings on meaningful team and customer stories

The Results

- Market share gains in key product lines
- Higher customer satisfaction, especially in service
- Employee retention improved, even amid industry-wide churn

Leadership Legacy

Says Monica King, "A focus on customer centricity is our guide and truly complements who we are…we're still all about 'Made for Life'."

With the MRI, Canon Medical didn't just talk customer-centricity, it built it into the DNA of the business. It brought its customer intimacy strategy to life.

Allen 6. Allen Medical
Growth Found Hiding in Plain Sight

The Challenge:

Allen Medical Systems, a division of Hill-Rom, had a strong innovation culture and a solid track record of launching breakthrough surgical positioning systems. But growth was stalling, and leadership couldn't pinpoint why. "We're constantly having to innovate and find new customers", said CEO Jason Krieser. "That left little energy for existing relationships".

The Spark:

Though strategic alignment was strong, a blind spot had formed: existing customers were being neglected. The MRI assessment confirmed this. "Our Customer Insight score … was very, very low", Jason admitted.

This oversight risked losing Allen's most loyal, profitable clients, especially dangerous in a competitive market.

The Turning Point

Allen had dismissed post-sale engagement because hospitals rarely reordered for years. But private label customers, who bought frequently and in volume, were underserved.

The fix? A dedicated business unit focused solely on this forgotten segment via:

- Direct engagement and feedback
- Training and marketing support
- Custom products and services

A Moment of Truth

Jason explains, "Previously, this group got swept into other projects. Now, it has a dedicated team. We even began selling smaller items we'd once ignored ... unlocking hundreds of thousands in extra revenue." Most notably, Allen avoided layoffs while competitors downsized. "Because of the MRI and the money, we made, we didn't have any layoffs. That's rare in this industry".

From Insight to Impact

- Customer Insight scores doubled
- Private label sales rose 20%, then 30% the following year, despite an industry downturn
- Customers who had to buy now wanted to buy from Allen

The Results

Innovation isn't enough—growth requires nurturing existing customers.

- Segment strategies matter—treat high-frequency buyers differently
- Small wins add up—fulfilling minor requests can lead to major revenue
- Data reveals blind spots—the MRI uncovered what assumptions had hidden

- Structure drives focus—a dedicated unit ensured customer care wasn't sacrificed
- Customer focus builds resilience—Allen grew and protected jobs in a downturn

Leadership Legacy

Says Jason, "Sometimes, the most innovative strategy is simply listening to the customers you already have".

7. Konica Minolta

A Cultural Breakthrough or How One Leader Transformed a Tech Giant by Putting People First

KONICA MINOLTA

The Challenge

When Dr David Cooke became the first non-Japanese MD of Konica Minolta Australia, he saw more than a symbolic role, he saw a chance to redefine success.

In a commoditised market, he believed culture, not product, would be the differentiator. At the time, Konica Minolta Australia was a $250M business. But internally, the mindset hadn't evolved. There was a legacy mindset: "We just sell printers" and "This soft stuff won't help us win".

The Spark

David challenged this thinking. He envisioned a purpose-led company that cared about people, staff, customers, and the community. To understand internal sentiment, David partnered with MarketCulture to run the MRI.

- 90% staff participation showed a deep desire to be heard.
- Key gaps emerged in customer insight and strategic alignment.

The data gave David the confidence to act and bring others with him.

The Turning Point

The results of the MRI inspired cultural transformation based on:

- Purpose-driven vision—in his first public address, David declared a new direction in which values would matter as much as results.
- Cross-functional workshops—departments that never spoke began collaborating.
- Community engagement—partnerships with not-for-profits, including anti-trafficking groups, inspired pride and connection among staff.
- Ethical innovation—David launched a bold ethical sourcing program, auditing supply chains for modern slavery, well before industry giants did.
- Continuous listening—beyond the MRI, regular feedback channels were embedded.

A Moment of Truth

A 25-year-old employee said, "Now I proudly tell people where I work". Staff embraced the shift and quiet voices found platforms. As a result of the MRI silos broke down and transformation became part of the culture.

From Insight to Impact

Employee engagement soared, with staff shaping the vision and approaching their work with a new sense of purpose.

- Top talent joined and stayed, drawn by values
- Customer loyalty grew, relationships replaced product focus
- Industry influence expanded; ethical sourcing set a benchmark
- Even sceptics shifted, they saw cultural change drive business results

The Results

Culture gave Konica Minolta a competitive advantage. It's no longer just a tech provider, it's a purpose-led brand.

Leadership Legacy

"The more profitable we are, the more we can support our not-for-profit partners", says David. "And the more we do for the community, the more customers want to work with us". Empathy and execution worked hand in hand.

BlackRock

8. From Friction to Focus
How BlackRock Reclaimed Customer Confidence Through Culture

The Challenge

Even financial giants can lose their footing. For BlackRock's enterprise clients, cracks were forming, late reports, poor quality, and inconsistent service were eroding trust. Some clients reduced their investments; others walked away entirely. The risk wasn't performance, it was experience.

The Spark

Internally, the signs were misunderstood. Account managers heard the frustrations but couldn't fix the problems. Back-office teams weren't aware of the impact, and even when they heard, there was no urgency. What should have been service recovery became a cultural standoff. The leadership realised: "It wasn't denial, it was disconnection".

The Turning Point

Implementing the MRI revealed the root cause—internal misalignments. The results confirmed what account managers already knew were the problem:

- Cross-functional breakdowns
- A culture where the customer's voice wasn't being heard by back-office teams

Verbatim feedback across the company revealed a consistent view: internal silos were undermining client trust.

A Moment of Truth

BlackRock launched a Customer Immersion Program designed by MarketCulture. Internal teams experienced the real-world effects of their work or lack of it:

- Delayed reports
- Client frustration
- Missed deliverables

From Insight to Impact

Teams put themselves in the client's shoes. Empathy replaced apathy. Urgency replaced resistance.

This wasn't training. It was an awakening.

The Results

Within months, BlackRock had made measurable gains and a cultural shift, achieving:

- 10% improvement in client retention
- Increased investment allocations from existing customers
- Millions in recovered fees
- Stronger internal collaboration and cross-team ownership

Leadership Legacy

"Trust was rebuilt, not with new tools, but with cultural alignment". The leadership at BlackRock realised that customer experience isn't a department, it's everyone's job. By exposing blind spots through the MRI and humanising the data with real stories, BlackRock reconnected people to purpose.

"Great service isn't about process. It's about empathy, urgency, and alignment."

Westpac
9. From Collections to Retention
How Westpac Humanised Debt Recovery and Boosted Performance

The Challenge

In banking, "collections" typically means tough conversations and consequences. At Westpac, it was business as usual until it stopped working. Collection rates had stalled. Customer relationships were strained. Morale was low. "We were effective in process but disconnected in purpose."

The Spark

The mission was clear: recover the money. But over time, this narrow mindset damaged customer loyalty and trust. Recovery became harder. Leadership began asking: "What if we changed how we think not just what we do?"

The Turning Point

Westpac used the MRI methodology to assess culture, not just outcomes. The results were stark:

- A transactional mindset dominated
- Low collaboration, little empowerment
- No clear link to customer wellbeing

A Moment of Truth

A leadership workshop sparked a new identity: "We collect money" became "We help customers stay in their homes and businesses."

There was a mental shift from collectors to enablers. The Collections Department became Customer Retention.

From Insight to Impact

The new mindset led to action, based on the idea that empathy drives efficiency:

- Financial advice and budgeting support
- Personalised repayment plans
- Services tailored to customer needs

The Results

In six months:

- Collections improved
- Revenue recovered increased
- Customer trust and advocacy rose

Leadership Legacy

"What was once the bank's most contentious touchpoint became one of its most admired". Morale lifted. Employees felt proud of their impact.

The transformation reached beyond the department. Westpac's leadership saw that culture is a financial lever.

The Westpac story proves that you don't need to change people, just how they see their purpose. By shifting from enforcement to empowerment, Westpac didn't just recover money. It recovered trust.

10. StateCover's Quiet Revolution
How a Regional Insurance Mutual Turned Culture into a Competitive Edge

The Challenge

Though once dominant, StateCover Mutual, serving local Australian councils as members, was facing increased competition from players like iCare. Its members were leaving and insurance board director Norman Newbon acknowledged: "Losing just one or two major councils could unravel everything".

The Spark

CEO Linda Bostock, is a leader focused on culture, not marketing gimmicks. She had seen what happens when leadership falters: *"Empty promises, collapsing morale, and lost customers"*. She wasn't going to let that happen at StateCover.

The Turning Point

The MRI was used to assess customer-centric behaviours across the organisation. The first score just above the median was where Linda thought it would be. Gaps in collaboration and internal alignment became clear.

A Moment of Truth

Rather than impose change, Linda engaged the entire company.

- Over 90% of employees participated
- Findings were shared at a company-wide Town Hall, sparking cross-team engagement

From Insight to Impact

New initiatives were introduced. They weren't big restructures, just focused, meaningful actions.

- "We Go Beyond" celebrated real customer service moments
- "In the Know" kept staff updated on member needs
- Groups like the Vault Team empowered employee-driven innovation

The Results

One year later, the MRI results told a powerful story:

- The workforce increased by 19%, yet scores rose to 65%, placing StateCover in the top 35% globally
- Member foresight jumped 8 points

Though collaboration dipped during growth, leadership acted quickly

By department:

- Shared Services: 65% → 72%
- Member Services & Workplace Risk: 57% → 68%
- Leadership: consistent 71–73%

Leadership Legacy

StateCover didn't chase disruption; instead, it strengthened from within. It used the MRI as a blueprint for resilience. The MRI became a long-term metric for risk reduction and customer growth. Linda said: "Cultural transformation wasn't a campaign. It became the way we did business." Linda's approach, using the MRI, harnessed the quiet power of looking inward. One employee said: "Our reputation has strengthened with the specialised service our members now experience."

In a world chasing fast change, StateCover chose focus, authenticity, and consistency. What was once its biggest risk, a fixed customer base, became its foundation for growth.

Says Linda Bostock, "Constraints don't limit innovation, they focus it".

Gippsland Water

11. Restoring Trust, Transforming Culture
Gippsland Water's Journey to Customer-Centric Leadership

The Challenge

In regional Victoria, Gippsland Water, a water utility monopoly faced growing community dissatisfaction, particularly when price rises were discussed with their community. Customers didn't see transparency and trust was eroding. Despite service improvements, the disconnect remained.

The Spark

"It had to pass the auntie test", said MD Sarah Cumming, meaning decisions had to genuinely serve the community. When she started, she found Paul Clark, General Manager of Customer and Community, struggling to influence the organisation in the direction needed. Paul understood this wasn't a communication issue, it was a cultural one and Sarah gave his thinking momentum and traction.

The Turning Point

MarketCulture was engaged to deploy the MRI with 20 senior leaders. The aim was to uncover not just performance, but behaviours behind customer alignment like collaboration, empowerment, and strategic focus.

A Moment of Truth

The MRI data exposed what Paul and Sarah suspected: leadership misalignment was a core issue. Through transparent, small-group conversations and a powerful leadership workshop where verbatim MRI feedback was shared, sceptics became advocates. "Trust wouldn't be earned through slogans … it had to be modelled from the top".

From Insight to Impact

Leaders committed to specific, visible customer-focused initiatives, tracked publicly for accountability. Crucially, the customer culture approach was embedded into the strategic plan, tying leadership performance directly to culture outcomes.

The Results

- Net Trust Scores (NTS) turned positive and today are very good
- Stronger leadership alignment
- Clear cultural shift, staff began centring decisions around the customer
- MRI embedded into strategy to sustain change

Leadership Legacy

Sarah and Paul's leadership surfaced three key takeaways that are particularly relevant for the public sector:

- Leadership commitment is non-negotiable
- Trust is a core metric, not a soft one
- Embed the mindset or lose it, this wasn't a campaign, it was cultural transformation

Says Sarah, "Even monopolies must earn trust. And trust comes from the top."

Sydney WATER — 12. From Pipes to People
The Sydney Water Transformation Story

The Challenge

For decades, Sydney Water delivered reliable service, but internally it operated like many monopolies: siloed, process-driven, and disconnected from the people it served.

The customer was an abstraction. Until one leader changed the story.

The Spark

Dr Bhakti Devi, a Liveability Strategist, blended engineering expertise with human empathy. She asked a radical question: "What if we put the customer at the centre of everything we do?" To drive this, she introduced the MRI to measure Sydney Water's cultural alignment with customer needs.

The Turning Point

The MRI acted as a cultural X-ray. The results were clear:

- Customer data existed but rarely influenced decisions
- Departments operated in silos
- Projects lacked alignment with community needs

Engineers weren't ignoring customers - they had simply never been asked to listen. Workshops turned data into dialogue. Scepticism gave way to curiosity. Mindsets began to shift.

A Moment of Truth

Change at Sydney Water began to flow through its culture.

Small changes created real momentum:

- Customer feedback started to inform design
- Teams shared insights across silos
- Engineers began asking, "What would the community think of this?"

The Results

Innovation became grounded in relevance, not just technology. Solutions reflected community values, not just compliance checklists. What began in the Strategy and Planning Group spread. Inspired by the shift, senior leaders adopted customer-centricity as a company-wide priority, practising, not just preaching, it. "We make a positive impact, achieving together. We are customer-centric and innovative."

Leadership Legacy

Sydney Water's transformation showed that cultural change isn't quick, but it is possible with the right leadership and tools:

- Leadership is the lever: Bhakti's blend of empathy and strategy sparked the shift
- Alignment is essential, customer thinking must guide both vision and execution
- Culture takes time but with focus and persistence, even large utilities can learn to listen

speedo 13. Speedo's Cultural Reboot
From Manufacturing Mindset to Market Momentum

The Challenge

Speedo, the iconic swimwear brand, had global recognition but behind the scenes, performance was slipping. Margins were down, profits declining, and market share shrinking. Internally, the company remained manufacturing-led, but externally, it was losing customer relevance.

The Spark

Leadership acknowledged, "Speedo didn't just need new tactics; it needed a mindset shift."

The Turning Point

Speedo used the MRI tools to guide its strategic planning process. The diagnosis was revealing:

- Customer Insight: teams lacked a deep understanding of customer behaviour
- Competitor Insight: Speedo had underestimated new market entrants
- Strategic Alignment: daily operations weren't supporting broader market goals

A Moment of Truth

Utilising the MRI tools executives began the shift to a market-driven mindset. It realised it didn't need a new product, it needed to realign around the customer. A company-wide cultural transformation began.

From Insight to Impact

- Customer value programs extended beyond marketing
- Teams engaged in customer observation exercises and cross-functional initiatives
- Every function, not just marketing, was reoriented around the customer

Marketing itself was rebuilt:

- New strategic capabilities introduced
- Deeper customer research conducted
- Channel strategies refined

One breakthrough: identifying swim centres as a new retail channel, increasing Speedo's footprint by 30%.

The Results

In just 18 months:

- Customer satisfaction and retention surged
- Revenue grew 20%
- Speedo regained momentum in a mature and competitive market

Leadership Legacy

Speedo's leadership realised that even market leaders can fall behind when customer understanding fades. But when the culture shifts, performance follows. "Customer insight isn't a function. It's a foundation."

FRANKE 14. Franke Group
Rediscovering Customer Culture

The Challenge

In the luxury kitchen systems market, Franke North America had ridden the housing boom comfortably. But when the market shrank, complacency was exposed. "We made really good stuff and for years, that was enough", said Charles "Charlie" Lawrence, who joined as CMO just as the downturn hit.

The company had lost sight of its customers. Service cuts, especially in a luxury business, backfired. Charlie said: "We're a luxury products business, but the first thing we cut were customer service people ... stepping over dollar bills to pick up pennies". Customer frustration mounted: long wait times, shipping delays, and order errors became the norm. Yet leadership lacked consensus on the root issues.

The Spark

To get clarity, Charlie turned to the MRI. The results revealed broad weaknesses in customer focus, competitor insight, collaboration, and strategic alignment. "The MRI simplified the issues … feedback came from every single employee, not just another management idea."

The Turning Point

Charlie shared the MRI results transparently, creating a sense of ownership across the company. His bold, data-driven leadership earned him a promotion to General Manager of the Luxury Products Group.

A Moment of Truth

With such low scores, ignoring the results would've meant growing customer churn, falling revenues, and an eventual need for costly reinvestment just to recover lost ground.

Charlie tackled the turnaround in two phases:

1. **Internal Alignment:** getting teams working across boundaries with a cohesive strategy
1. **External Focus:** ensuring everyone understood customer expectations, competitor moves, and how to respond

"I started immediately trying to change our culture and get the organisation focused on the customer", Says Charlie Lawrence

From Insight to Impact

Key lessons from the MRI included:

- Growth can hide weakness
- Cutting service in luxury markets is costly
- Objective data builds alignment
- Transformation begins inside
- Market-focused culture wins, even in tough conditions
- Customer champions often become company leaders

The Results

- Revenue grew by 16%
- EBITDA doubled within a year
- The organisation unified around a shared, customer-centric vision

"Showing employees what customers said about our business made them part of the solution, not bystanders". Charlie emphasised the MRI's role in enabling alignment across a complex organisation, fragmented by past acquisitions.

Leadership Legacy

There were significant lessons learned at Franke, where Charlie had to rebuild the business from the customer up. Says Charlie, "Sometimes the most valuable business tool is a clear mirror and the leaders who hold it up often rise with it."

These company stories reveal how the MRI ignited change by fostering leadership and employee engagement with customers driving measurable performance improvements and sustainable growth. In the next chapter, we explore how leaders have built enduring legacies, guided by a higher purpose that transcends profit.

Key Takeaways—Chapter 5

1. Culture Change is Possible and Proven

Many leaders doubt that culture can truly shift. Chapter 5 dismantles that doubt with real-world proof: case studies from Vodafone, Telstra, Deutsche Telekom, Canon Medical, and more show how organisations across industries used the MRI to measure behaviours, realign mindsets, and turn customer-centricity from theory into everyday practice.

2. Human-Centric Leadership Unlocks Growth

Behind every transformation is a leader (or leadership team) who believes it so they can see it. CEOs like Russell Stanners (Vodafone) and David Thodey (Telstra) modelled visible, human-first leadership, staying close to employees and customers, challenging fixed mindsets, and turning culture into a daily habit that directly drives performance.

3. Measurement + Stories = Culture in Action

The MRI provides the measurement, but stories bring it to life. Organisations that combine clear data with human stories create understanding, alignment, and ownership at every level. They don't just fix problems; they build resilient, responsive cultures that adapt and grow stronger in competitive markets.

The Bottom Line

Chapter 5 shows that human-centric culture is a proven driver of exponential growth, not an abstract ideal. It brings a competitive advantage that any organisation can build. When leaders measure what matters, model what they believe, and connect data to real human impact, culture shifts and the bottom line follows.

Scan or click to watch the Case Study videos

Scan or click to listen to our Podcasts

CHAPTER 6

THE HIGHER PURPOSE BEYOND PROFIT

The Human Legacy of Leaders

When people thrive, businesses don't just succeed, they shape the future.

In today's world, many leaders are driven by a purpose that transcends profit. They seek more than financial performance; they aspire to leave something meaningful behind. Some are, as we say, *pining for a legacy,* not in a nostalgic sense, but as an intentional act of building something enduring. They understand that some of the most vital aspects of business, like community impact, the personal growth of people, emotional connection with customers, integrity in relationships, can't be neatly quantified on a balance sheet. These things are real. They matter. And they multiply.

A legacy isn't just what you leave behind; it's what continues to grow in your absence. It's about the ripple effects of your values, behaviours, and decisions echoing through employees, customers, partners, and communities, sometimes in ways you may never see.

Take the stories shared in Chapter 2 about Saffire, WD-40, and Bank Al Etihad. Each represents a profound example of leaders shaping human legacies that extend far beyond their own tenure.

Ross Boobyer viewed his leadership at Saffire not simply as managing a luxury destination, but as stewarding a long-term legacy, protecting and nurturing something of significance for the region, the people, and future generations. His team of just 40 people shaped unforgettable experiences that reverberate through guests, their families, and the broader Tasmanian community.

At WD-40, Garry Ridge famously prepared for succession—not as a transition, but as a continuation of purpose. Over two years, he worked closely with his successor to ensure the company's unique culture, its *tribal wisdom* and shared values, would endure. He strongly believes that culture is the real asset and that its preservation is the true test of leadership.

At Bank Al Etihad, Isam Salfiti took the long view. He collaborated closely with his senior team to ensure the organisation remained grounded in its values while evolving for the future. This wasn't just about protecting the institution; it was about empowering people to carry that legacy forward with integrity and conviction.

Now consider the human impact behind the numbers. If each employee influences, on average, four people in their family or close circle, then:

- Saffire's 40 employees touch 160 lives
- WD-40's 650 employees influence around 2,600 people
- Bank Al Etihad's 1,000 employees affect roughly 4,000 individuals

And that's just the beginning. Add customer relationships, partner networks, community volunteering, and philanthropic outreach, and the ripple effect grows exponentially. The result? A powerful *human multiplier effect* that can touch tens of thousands, perhaps millions, of lives over time. This is legacy in motion. It's not bound to a timeline, a job title, or even a single business. It's about the dissemination of values.

What's most remarkable is that you may never fully grasp the scale of your impact. But occasionally, the legacy makes itself known.

Linden

I recall meeting a former student from India, years after he had taken his university course. "I don't remember much from your lectures," the student told me, "Except one story about your early days with the Blue Banner pickled onion business." That story, simple and practical, stayed with him. When he returned to India, he used the principles he learned to start his own food business. Today, that business supports families, nourishes communities, and sustains a growing local economy all sparked by a story shared in a classroom half a world away.

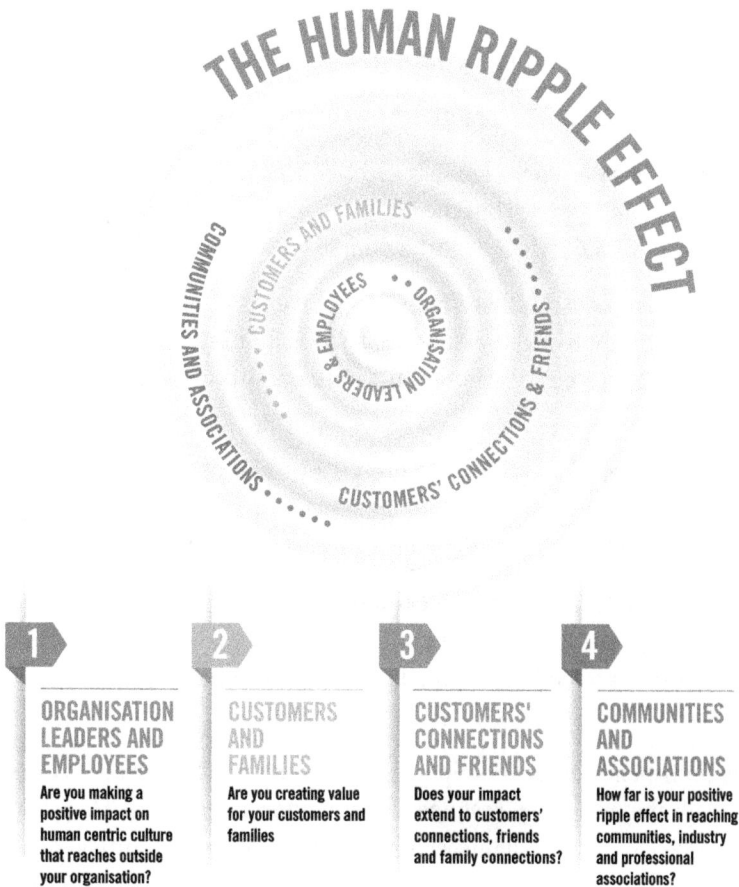

THE HUMAN RIPPLE EFFECT

1	**2**	**3**	**4**
ORGANISATION LEADERS AND EMPLOYEES	**CUSTOMERS AND FAMILIES**	**CUSTOMERS' CONNECTIONS AND FRIENDS**	**COMMUNITIES AND ASSOCIATIONS**
Are you making a positive impact on human centric culture that reaches outside your organisation?	Are you creating value for your customers and families	Does your impact extend to customers' connections, friends and family connections?	How far is your positive ripple effect in reaching communities, industry and professional associations?

Leadership legacy often emerges not from grand gestures, but from everyday actions, consistent values, and the courage to do what's right, even when no one's watching. When you lead with purpose and invest in people, your influence becomes limitless.

Path-Benders: Leaders Who Shape the Journey, Not Just the Destination

In a world craving authenticity and purpose, a new archetype of leader is emerging, one grounded in humanity, courage, and connection. These are not just visionaries or strategists. They are path-benders.

The idea of leaders as path-benders builds on the Path-Goal Theory of Leadership, first introduced by Robert House in 1971. At its core, the theory suggests that a leader's role is not merely to set ambitious goals or define outcomes, but to make the path toward success clearer, smoother, and more achievable for their teams.

What does that look like in practice?

- **Clarifying the path:** These leaders help their people understand not just the "what" and "why," but the "how". They bring clarity to confusion, simplify complexity, and chart a course with confidence.

- **Removing obstacles:** Rather than adding layers of bureaucracy, these leaders actively work to dismantle barriers getting in the way of progress, regardless of whether they are organisational, procedural, or emotional.

- **Providing support:** These leaders are visible, approachable, and invested. They offer resources, guidance, and encouragement. They recharge their teams when morale dips and empower them to move forward.

- **Adapting their style:** These leaders adapt their leadership approach based on the people in front of them and the challenges at hand. This is not one-size-fits-all leadership, it's intentional, responsive, and deeply personal.

But true path-bending leadership goes even further. These leaders don't simply walk the path, they reshape it. They alter trajectories. They bend the arc of people's careers, organisations' cultures, and communities' destinies.

What Do Path-Benders Leave Behind?

The legacy of a path-bending leader is not confined to a job title, tenure, or balance sheet. It lives on in the culture, people, and principles they embed along the way. Here's what they build.

- **A high-engagement culture:** One where leaders and employees are connected in purpose, and where customers are part of the organisational conversation. It's a culture of active listening, shared voice, and aligned action, all centred on creating real value for the customer. These environments are marked by trust, transparency, and a unified rhythm of communication and collaboration.

- **A new generation of human-first leaders**: Path-benders invest in people not just to perform, but to lead. They cultivate empathy, critical thinking, and ethical awareness in others, sparking a ripple effect of leadership across all levels of the business. Their leadership style becomes the blueprint for those who follow.

- **A living folklore of stories**: These are not just "best practices" or corporate slogans. They are legendary stories, moments of breakthrough, resilience, and humanity that are told and retold because they capture the spirit of the organisation. These stories become cultural touchstones that teach, inspire, and remind people what the organisation stands for.

- **A human multiplier effect:** When employees are empowered and energised, the impact doesn't end at the office door. It extends to their families, their customers, and their communities. An organisation of 500 people can impact 2,000 lives and many more. Path-bending leadership turns internal change into external influence.

- **An ethical framework and moral compass:** Above all, path-benders lead with integrity. They do the right thing even when it's hard, even when no one is watching. They create ethical guardrails and a moral culture that inspires accountability and decency in every relationship with employees, customers, partners, and society.

This chapter shines a spotlight on eight human-centric path-benders. Their stories illustrate not only the power of purposeful leadership but the transformational potential of leaders who don't just aim for the summit but care deeply about the path we take to get there. These stories include people leading corporations and family businesses and engaging in consultancy and academic thought leadership. Here is a guide to the path-bending stories.

- **Dr David Cooke**: Leading with Conscience in the Corporate World

- **Jeanne Bliss** and Her Journey of the Heart: From Shoe Store to CX Pioneer

- **Professor Philip Kotler:** Architect of Modern Marketing and Human-Centric Thought Leadership

- **Nicole Noye:** The Relentless Rebuilder Who Leads with Heart—From Receptionist to CEO

- **Cody Plott**: Leading with Legacy at Pebble Beach

- **Ross Sinclair:** Sinclair Ford Motor Group Building a Legacy with "Attitude, Accountability, and Attack"

- **Jim Penman**: Jim's Group Turning Franchisees into Fans by Listening From the Ground Up

- **Don Chapin Jr:** The Don Chapin Company Building a Legacy on Trust and a Handshake

Following these stories are eight non-financial benefits of a human-centric culture that focuses on the customer to drive long-term value, resilience, and a real competitive edge.

Dr David Cooke
Leading with Conscience in the Corporate World

When Dr David Cooke served as CEO of Konica Minolta Australia, he didn't just lead a technology company he redefined what corporate leadership could stand for. Armed with a PhD in philanthropy, David integrated social justice and ethical responsibility into the very fabric of the business. His leadership was grounded in a belief that commercial success and moral integrity should not be mutually exclusive but mutually reinforcing.

One of the defining pillars of his leadership was his relentless campaign against modern slavery in global supply chains. David made it his mission to shine a light on exploitative practices, calling out unethical sourcing and pushing for partnerships only with suppliers who paid fair wages and upheld human rights. This was no token corporate social responsibility (CSR) initiative; it was a courageous shift that required confronting uncomfortable facts and making hard choices, decisions that aligned with his deeply held values.

David shares this journey in his compelling book, *Kind Business. Values Create Value.* The subtitle speaks volumes: "Reimagining a corporate world where people and planet are placed at the heart of leadership decisions". His story challenges the conventional narrative of business as a purely profit-driven machine, instead advocating for a model where compassion, ethics, and sustainability are central to decision-making.

His impact wasn't limited to the supply chain. Under his leadership, Konica Minolta became a hub for employee-led philanthropy. Staff were encouraged and inspired to contribute to causes that uplifted lives and improved the human condition. Beyond his executive role, David also sat on several charity boards, further embodying the principles he championed.

But as David himself observed, doing the right thing was also good for business.

Employees, once they learned of his personal visits to countries grappling with modern slavery, felt a renewed sense of pride and purpose. Their engagement deepened, not just with their work, but with the broader mission of the company. Values created culture, and culture drove connection.

One story captures the essence of this impact. In a high stakes bid to supply equipment to a government department, Konica Minolta, then a relatively smaller contender won the contract over much larger competitors. The buyer later told David, "Any company that takes a stand against modern slavery is a company we want to do business with". In a world where trust is rare, values became the differentiator.

Today, David continues to advocate for purpose-driven leadership through his firm, ESG Consulting. He works with leaders across industries to help them embed environmental, social, and governance principles into the core of their strategic and operational decisions.

Dr David Cooke is a path-bender in every sense, a leader who has demonstrated that when business aligns with humanity, the result is not only ethical leadership, but enduring value for all.

Sean

The story I share here perfectly captures the power of purpose-led leadership by David.

After surpassing my annual sales target, I earned an incentive trip to Cambodia with my wife, Jen. But what began as a reward for performance quickly became something far more meaningful. Before departing, the group of winners was asked if they'd like to "give back" during their time away. Every single person said yes.

We raised funds to purchase 15 bicycles for a local school in a small village outside Siem Reap. Many of the children walked up to three hours each way just to attend class. These bikes changed everything for these kids, cutting travel time to under an hour, and often carrying up to four children at once.

On the day of the visit, the men worked together to assemble the bikes, while the women read books and spent time with the students. The children's faces lit up with joy, and so did the hearts of those who came to give. It wasn't just a day of giving it became a moment of shared humanity that I'll never forget.

More than just an incentive trip, it was a powerful act of connection, compassion, and impact made possible under David's thoughtful and inspiring leadership. He believed that true business success must include making a difference in people's lives. That day didn't just transform the children's daily journeys. It became a lifelong memory and a lasting legacy for everyone involved.

"We must broaden the definition of business success to include human and environmental wellbeing. Profit is essential, but it must never come at the expense of people or planet." —Dr David Cooke, Kind Business

From Shoe Store to CX Pioneer
Jeanne Bliss and Her Journey of the Heart

Before customer experience had a seat at the executive table, Jeanne Bliss gave it a soul. Her books, *"Chief Customer Officer, I Love You More Than My Dog,* and *Would You Do That to Your Mother?"* didn't just spark a movement, they gave language to a kind of leadership that had long been felt but rarely formalised: one built on humanity, integrity, and courage.

As the co-founder of the Customer Experience Professionals Association (CXPA), Jeanne helped pioneer a profession that hadn't existed before. But her influence didn't begin on a stage or in a boardroom, it began in a shoe store in Des Plaines, Illinois.

There, as a young girl, she knelt beside her father in his Buster Brown store, watching him fit shoes on children's feet, many whose parents couldn't afford them. "Get those shoes on those little ones' feet", he'd say without hesitation. He didn't need a customer retention strategy. He had empathy. He had memory. He had values. That, Jeanne would say later, *was* customer experience lived, not theorised. It left a blueprint on her character.

Years later, she would carry that blueprint to Lands' End in 1982. This was a company growing 80% year-on-year not because of marketing, but because of how it *felt* to receive a package from them. Jeanne quickly became the "conscience of the company", obsessed with every detail of the customer journey from the sound of the packing tape to the first pull of a fresh turtleneck. It was there she realised: this wasn't just a job. This was her life's work.

From Lands' End to Mazda, Coldwell Banker, Allstate, and Microsoft, Jeanne charted an intentional path not to climb, but to *build*. Each company gave her a different challenge: B2C, B2B, tech, retail, services. Hard goods. Soft goods. Her mission was clear: to embed humanity into the operating systems of big business.

She didn't just improve service metrics. She reshaped cultures. She became one of the first Chief Customer Officers before the role was recognised. In meeting rooms, she earned a reputation for asking the questions no one else would:

- "Would you do that to your mother?"
- "What's the human cost of this decision?"
- "Are you building a legacy or just hitting your numbers?"

When companies treated customer-centricity like a buzzword she made it clear there were no shortcuts. "What's on the inside shows up on the outside", she'd say.

Jeanne taught that true customer experience leadership demands more than charm or metrics. It demands character. In her view, three qualities define the leaders who get it right.

1. **Be a successful operator.** You can't lead transformation if you've never run a business.

2. **Be collaborative.** Real authority comes through influence, not hierarchy.

3. **Check your ego.** This work is not about the spotlight. It's about lifting others.

Through her firm, CustomerBliss, Jeanne has coached thousands of businesses from startups to the Fortune 500 on how to grow by improving people's lives. Not with slogans. Not with dashboards. But with *purpose*.

She credits mentors like Lands' End founder Gary Comer, who once took $10 million from his own wallet to build a health centre for employees. To Jeanne, that was leadership: the connection between heart and habit.

Today, Jeanne Bliss is more than a thought leader. She's a moral compass in the business world. A pioneer who has *lived the work* starting in the back room of a shoe store, all the way to shaping a global profession. Along the way she has created a legacy that has grown into the professional movement we now call customer experience and influenced the path of countless leaders to transform their organisations to earn customer driven growth.

She's still doing what her father did. Just on a bigger stage:

- Helping people feel seen.
- Helping leaders and their businesses act with heart.
- And always making sure the shoes fit.

Professor Philip Kotler
Architect of Modern Marketing and Human-Centric Thought Leadership

When people speak of the giants of business education, few names resonate as deeply and as globally as Professor Philip Kotler. Often referred to as "the father of modern marketing," Philip has influenced generations of marketers, leaders, and educators since the 1960s. His seminal textbook, Marketing Management, became the gold standard for teaching marketing in universities around the world and continues to shape curricula today.

Linden recalls co-authoring editions of Marketing Management with Philip in the 1990s and 2000s, tailoring its foundational concepts to Australian and New Zealand markets. For many, learning marketing meant learning Kotler. His influence is woven into the academic fabric of every tertiary institution where marketing is taught. But Philip's contribution extends far beyond the classroom.

Linden has been a regular contributor to his World Marketing Summit, an annual event that gathers thought leaders from across disciplines to explore how marketing can be a force for good in addressing global challenges. The Summit reflects Philip's lifelong belief that marketing must serve not just markets, but people, communities, and the planet. This online Summit conducted over a full 24 hours now reaches millions of students and business people.

He says: "My passion for sustainability grew from a belief that marketing must serve society, not just profit. This drives my work on social and environmental change."

He was also instrumental in the journey of The Customer Culture Imperative. As an early believer in the value of the MRI, he encouraged this work and actively championed the ideas within it. He frequently carried the customer–centric message into his global presentations, amplifying its reach and significance, as seen in the example with Bryan Jago, at Canon Medical Systems noted in chapter 3. His endorsement helped validate a growing movement: that customer culture is a measurable, actionable foundation for business success.

Like many iconic figures, Professor Kotler has received his share of honours. Yet his recognitions are both unique and deeply meaningful. In Indonesia, he became the only business professor ever to appear on a national postage stamp, commemorated on his 75th birthday. He has been named an honorary resident of Denpasar, and a marketing museum in the country proudly bears his name. These are fitting tributes for a man whose work has touched millions. Yet what stands out most about Philip is not his accolades, it's his humanity.

Philip is a human-centric leader in education. He combines brilliance with rare humility and an open mind. Despite being revered by academics worldwide, he never lets ego get in the way of learning, listening, or connecting.

"Marketing must serve more than markets; it must serve humanity."
—Professor Philip Kotler

Linden

For me, two stories highlight Philip's character. The first was when he invited me to lunch at Northwestern University. When he introduced me to his colleagues, they responded with a kind of reverence, "You're having lunch with the great Phil Kotler?" He simply brushed it off, uninterested in status or hierarchy.

The second was in a taxi in Sydney. As we discussed ideas, he started sketching diagrams on the back of an envelope. He was curious, alive with thought, constantly asking questions. That moment captured who he is, a scholar still learning, a teacher still growing.

To this day, Professor Kotler remains a mentor, a friend, and a global force for positive change. His contributions to marketing are legendary, but it is his unwavering belief in marketing as a *tool for human betterment* that makes his legacy truly profound. In an age where influence is often measured in likes and followers, he reminds us that the most enduring impact comes from values, vision, and the ability to elevate others.

Nicole Noye
The Relentless Rebuilder Who Leads with Heart—From Receptionist to CEO

When Nicole Noye was appointed interim CEO of Dreamworld, Australia's largest theme park, located on the Gold Coast in Queensland, it wasn't business acumen that she brought first it was empathy.

The park was reeling from tragedy in 2016 where four adults lost their lives. Staff were devastated, public trust was shattered, and morale was at its lowest. Nicole didn't arrive with grand strategies or media statements. She walked the park. She listened. She comforted. She brought her own children to ride the attractions, not as a PR gesture, but as a mother, showing faith in the people rebuilding from the inside out.

"It wasn't about fixing things. It was about showing up", she says.

It was a moment that defined her leadership style: human, grounded, and fearless in the face of adversity.

But Nicole's story didn't begin in a boardroom. It began with a 248 out of 500 on her Higher School Certificate. Far from impressive, but never the full picture.

"I didn't start out with ambition to be a CEO", she says. "I just wanted to work hard and do well in whatever role I had."

After school, her mother encouraged her to get a job. She walked into the David Jones retail chain during its worst hiring season, January. By chance or fate, a man behind the desk saw something others might have missed and offered her a receptionist role. It wasn't glamourous, but it was her entry into a lifelong career of service, sales, and leadership.

From reception, she moved to the shop floor. She loved it. Customers energised her. Soon after, Nicole was selected for the David Jones cadetship program, a rare feat for someone without a university degree. She juggled work, study, and late nights serving beer just to make ends meet.

Her leadership spark grew at Angus & Coote, where she rose through the ranks over 18 years spanning store management, buying, merchandising, planning, marketing, and warehouse operations. Eventually, she became CEO of Goldmark Jewellery, leading the business until its acquisition by Prouds. By her early 30s, Nicole was managing 120 stores. She didn't engineer her rise. She earned it. "Every job was an opportunity to learn", she says. "I was curious. I listened. I cared about people."

Nicole would go on to lead companies across very different sectors: retail, fashion, ten-pin bowling and gyms. Each time she brought the same ethos: start with the customer, build a strong team, focus on purpose, and let the numbers follow.

Nicole is a pathbender leader called in to turn a business around. But she never saw herself as a traditional executive. "I wasn't corporate. I wasn't polished. But I was real. And people responded to that."

Nicole's transformation as a leader didn't stop at business challenges, it extended inward. In her early career, she hired people like herself: fast, assertive, competitive. But a psychologist once told her, "Not everyone is like you". That insight was a turning point. She began surrounding herself with people who thought differently, challenged her, and strengthened the business.

She shifted from direction to collaboration, from control to empowerment.

Later, as CEO of Collective Wellness Group (Anytime Fitness), Nicole found new purpose in promoting health, mental, emotional, and physical. Her leadership wasn't just about business. It was about wellbeing, culture, and energy. She built habits that kept her grounded with exercise, family time and even unplugging from technology.

And behind her evolution were the mentors who never gave her answers, only better questions: Graham Oakes, Bob Critchley, and others who helped her sharpen her instincts and stay true to herself.

Nicole Noye's journey is far from linear. It's the story of someone who failed on paper but soared in life. She is a woman who transformed not just companies, but herself through grit, grace, and growth. "What gets you to a CEO role isn't what keeps you there," she reflects.

Nicole's legacy goes beyond boardrooms; it's felt in the lives she's lifted.

At home, she's a grounded, present mother who leads by example, showing her children that real leadership is about integrity and service. To her teams, she wasn't just a CEO, she was a mentor, a listener, and a constant presence who made people feel seen and valued, especially in tough times.

In the broader community, Nicole quietly champions mental health, education, and women in leadership. She gives back through mentoring and by sharing her own powerful journey.

More than rebuilding businesses, Nicole builds belief in people, in purpose, and in the strength of leading with heart.

Her advice to aspiring leaders is clear:
- Build a great team.
- Be present.
- Don't fake it, listen instead.
- And remember, it's okay to not have all the answers.

"Sometimes, the people who push back hardest are the ones who become your biggest supporters if you keep showing up and working with them."

Cody Plott
Leading with Legacy at Pebble Beach

Walking into Cody Plott's office at Pebble Beach, California, the first thing you saw was an extraordinary view, the first tee of the world-renowned Pebble Beach Golf Course. But for Cody, that view was more than scenic, it was symbolic.

Every day, he witnessed the emotional weight of the experience his guests were about to have. For many, playing Pebble Beach and staying at the iconic Lodge wasn't just another holiday, it was a once-in-a-lifetime moment. Cody understood that deeply, and he led accordingly.

As President of The Pebble Beach Company, Cody didn't just manage a resort, he stewarded an institution. He recognised that hospitality, at its heart, is a human business. That's why he surrounded himself with what he called "pleasers". These are individuals across all departments who were naturally inclined to care for others. Whether guest-facing or behind the scenes, these were people who thrived on making someone else's day better. This approach built a culture of authentic service and mutual respect, where looking after guests wasn't a job, it was a calling.

Cody's leadership style was unmistakably that of a coach. He guided, nurtured, and inspired his team, and as a result, staff loyalty was exceptional. People didn't want to leave, not because they couldn't, but because they felt seen, valued, and part of something larger than themselves.

Pebble Beach isn't just a luxury destination, it's a deeply rooted community set within the pristine forests of California's Monterey Peninsula. It draws over two million visitors each year, including avid golfers and nature lovers from around the world. The area boasts several world-class golf resorts and hosts major golf events, but Pebble Beach holds a special place in people's hearts, not just for its beauty, but for how it makes them feel. Cody once shared that when he watched golfers step up to the first tee, hands trembling, legs slightly shaking, he knew he was witnessing more than just the start of a round, they were living a moment they'd remember for the rest of their lives. In that instant, it was clear: Pebble Beach wasn't just a golf course, it was a memory in the making.

Cody was acutely aware of this emotional connection. When he and the CFO presented annual financials reports to the ownership group, the conversation was never just about the numbers. Every report included proposed investments, not just for short-term gains, but to ensure the long-term preservation and enhancement of the Pebble Beach legacy. These investment recommendations, based on stewardship of place, were never questioned.

The ownership group, which includes notable figures like Clint Eastwood, acquired the company in 1999 with a clear intent: to never sell it. Their vision was custodial, not transactional. After board meetings, it was a tradition to play a round of golf together, not to talk about revenue or expenses, but to reflect on their responsibility to preserve and elevate one of the most beautiful and beloved places in the world.

Cody deeply understood what legacy meant. While profitability was essential, his focus extended far beyond the balance sheet. He led with an unwavering commitment to the human impact on employees, guests, the local community, and the millions who experienced the magic of Pebble Beach. His legacy lives on in the countless employees who still embody the service-first mindset he championed, in the guests who return year after year with stories to tell, and in the enduring culture of care that defines Pebble Beach to this day.

"The measure of success isn't just in returns, it's in the memories we help create, the people we grow, and the places we protect." —Cody Plott

Ross Sinclair
Building a Legacy with Attitude, Accountability, and Attack at Sinclair Ford Motor Group

Some leaders build businesses. A rare few build whole communities. Ross Sinclair was one of those few. For over fifty years, he wasn't just a car dealer in Western Sydney, he was a driving force behind the region's growth. His influence reached far beyond the showroom, into local sport, health, and education. His story is more than business success, it's a masterclass in path-bending leadership. Ross's journey is a lesson in leadership built on his simple "Triple A" philosophy: Attitude, Accountability, and Attack.

Ross's journey started far from the boardroom. Raised in a working-class family in Abbotsford, he developed a strong work ethic from an early age. Whether it was a paper route, delivering milk by horse and cart, or dropping off groceries on a pushbike, each job taught him one of his core characteristics. *"I learned responsibility. I knew I had to get back and do the job otherwise I couldn't help support my family."* That early drive wasn't just about survival; it reflected his ambition. He was already saving for a car, a clear sign of the direction his life would take.

That passion took him to an apprenticeship as a mechanic and then to the Ford Motor Company in 1960, when the first Falcon, an Australian icon, rolled off the line. He stood out for solving problems on the factory floor, but he also watched the sales reps and thought, *"That looks like a good job!"* This was his "Attack" mindset in action: always ready to step up, take risks, and move forward.

In 1969, Ross took his biggest step yet, opening his own Ford dealership in Penrith. He saw the area's growth potential and built more than just a business; he built a loyal team. Starting with seven employees, he created a "business within a business", sharing profits every month. His rule was simple: *"Loyalty is spelt M-O-N-E-Y".* By rewarding people fairly, he earned their loyalty. Many of his 1,200 employees stayed with him for decades.

His "Triple A" philosophy guided every decision.

- **Attitude:** have the right attitude and stay humble. Respect people and remember your roots. Ross treated everyone the same, from customers on the lot to the Governor-General.

- **Accountability:** be honest with yourself and others. Admit mistakes, know where you stand, and face problems head-on. He wrote everything down, the good and the bad, so nothing was hidden. This helped him grow from one dealership to 16 franchises.

- **Attack:** work hard, use your time well, and always move forward. His motto was "no boundaries". If there was an opportunity in another town, he took it. He invested in property, expanded into new brands, and kept growing. As he said, *"You only get one trip around the block, so make it count."*

But Ross's biggest impact was outside his business. He invested in Penrith's community. He sponsored local teams like the Panthers, funded the local hospital's neonatal ward, and supported schools. He owned the Log Cabin Hotel for 30 years, another place where community came together. He knew that strong communities build strong businesses.

This created a ripple effect. His staff's loyalty meant better service for customers. His support for the community-built trust that lasted generations. People didn't just buy cars from Ross Sinclair, they bought into his vision for Western Sydney.

Today, his legacy lives on in Sinclair Automotive Group, but more importantly in the people he helped. His story is proof that true success isn't just what you build, but what you give back. Ross didn't just sell cars, he shaped a community, one "Triple A" decision at a time.

"Our motto was always 'no boundaries'. For our customers, that meant we'd never stop delivering great service. It was about building relationships and a reputation for fairness that would last for generations." —Ross Sinclair

Jim Penman
Jim's Group Turning Franchisees into Fans by Listening from the Ground Up

"I do things most people would find odd for a CEO. I spend a lot of time talking with franchisees. I encourage them to contact me, and they do. I also handle serious customer complaints myself. It keeps me close to what really matters in the business."

This isn't micromanagement, it's Jim Penman's core approach. He's the "lazy" and "socially awkward" historian who turned a $24 lawn-mowing job into Jim's Group, now a global franchise with over 5,500 franchisees and 50 brands across Australia, New Zealand, Canada, the UK, and the US.

Jim never planned to be a businessman. His real dream was to fund research for his own academic studies of societal change, which he called *"biohistory"*. To pay for that, he needed millions, so he built a company on principles that ran against normal corporate thinking: put others first and listen obsessively.

His first lesson came when he was ten. After raking gravel for his neighbour, Mr Tapley, he left a few leaves behind. Mr Tapley told him, *"If you're not going to do it properly, I might as well do it myself"*. That line stuck. But when Jim first tried to grow his mowing business, he forgot it. He became an "arrogant beanbag manager" who let standards slip. The business failed.

Broke and rejected in his academic work, he started again with just $24 and a vow to do every job well and on time. But to grow, he needed to sell. His breakthrough came from an ad executive who didn't pitch for business but gave him free advice instead. Jim realised the best way to sell was not to sell at all, but to focus fully on helping the other person succeed.

This idea shaped his franchise system. When facing a bigger rival, VIP Home Services, he didn't out spend them, he offered a deal too good to refuse. Franchisees could keep their own clients and even leave with them. They owned their business, he just helped them grow it.

His path-pending leadership had two simple rules:

- **Franchisees come first:** He built a system to serve them, not the other way around. He says the main reason to turn someone down isn't money, it's whether the business is truly right for them. This focus attracts good people who stay and do good work.

- **Stay close to the ground:** While most CEOs keep their distance, Jim stays in the thick of it. He personally takes tough complaints and listens to franchisees. Problems aren't annoyances to pass off, they're clues. "Why did this happen? How do we fix it? Do we need new training, systems, or software?" His questions keep the whole company improving.

This approach has a huge ripple effect. Over 5,500 franchisees build better businesses for themselves and their families and deliver great service to countless customers.

Jim's legacy isn't just a household name, it's a community of small business owners who got a fair chance because their founder never stopped listening. He still lives by Mr Tapley's lesson: if the work isn't right, fix it. His empire was built not by big strategy, but by picking up the phone, reading complaints, and caring enough to ask why.

"Customers are easy to find and to keep if you look after them properly. Not by doing just enough, but by turning them into fans." —Jim Penman

Don Chapin Jr
The Don Chapin Company Building a Legacy on Trust and a Handshake

In the construction industry where contracts and concrete rule, some leaders build something stronger than steel: "Trust". Don Chapin Jr is one of those leaders. He took over the company his father started in 1978, turning it into one of Central California's top construction firms, not just by expanding its services, but by leading with a simple, timeless rule: treat employees like family, trust them to lead, and seal big deals with a handshake.

The Don Chapin Company started as an underground utility contractor and grew into a business with concrete and asphalt plants, trucking, and environmental services. This vertical integration gives the company control over every part of a project. But its real strength isn't in equipment, it's in people. Don Jr says it best: "The day you can't be a man of your word is the day you should get out of the business". This lesson from his father is still the company's foundation.

In an industry known for high staff turnover, the Don Chapin Company stands out. Many employees stay for decades; some families have worked there for two or three generations. That loyalty isn't luck. It's because Don Jr puts people first.

His path-bending leadership rests on three simple principles.

- **Trust and empower:** Don gives people real responsibility. He looks for those with drive and work ethic, then gives them freedom to run their divisions like owners. He doesn't micromanage, he mentors, backs them up with resources, and lets them lead. This trust builds a sense of ownership and pushes people to do their best.

- **Lead in the field:** like his father, Don doesn't hide in an office. He spends time on job sites, talking with crews, solving problems, and staying close to the work. This hands-on approach keeps him connected to his people and the work they do. It also shows employees that every role matters and that no job is too small for the boss.

- **Serve the community:** the company's commitment goes beyond projects. Don invests in local causes and expects his teams to do the same. They know they're not just building roads and buildings; they're building their community too. This creates trust that no marketing can buy.

A powerful example of this mindset came after the 1989 Loma Prieta earthquake. With roads blocked and people in danger, Don Sr didn't wait for permission or contracts. He sent out all his equipment and crews to clear roads for emergency services, no questions asked. When someone asked who would pay, he simply said, "We'll worry about that later. We've got people to take care of."

That spirit lives on today. Generations of families have found stable careers with the company. By treating people fairly and staying true to his word, Don has built more than a company, he's built trust, loyalty, and stronger communities. His legacy isn't just measured in roads and buildings but in the people whose lives he's improved. He proves that in any industry, your word is your strongest asset.

"We're in the relationship business as much as the construction business. When you do a quality job and treat people right, they don't just come back, they stay with you for decades." —Don Chapin Jr

Beyond the Bottom Line: "The Human Value of a Customer-Centric Culture"

Financial results often take centre stage in boardroom discussions. But some of the most powerful benefits of a human-centric culture focused on the customer can't be measured in dollars and they're just as important. Building this culture isn't about ticking boxes. It's a transformational journey that changes how a business thinks, behaves, and grows.

Here are eight non-financial benefits that drive long-term value, resilience, and a real competitive edge.

1. Momentum, engagement, and a fresh mindset

A human culture focused on the customer can be the spark that drives real change. When a company puts the customer first, it creates energy and focus across the business. People become more engaged and motivated because they know what they're working toward. Conversations shift from internal politics to customer impact. Instead of doing things the old way, teams become more curious, proactive, and willing to work together. A strong customer culture brings new ways of thinking that help everyone move in the same direction.

2. Measurement of outcomes—measuring results

Unlike old vague culture projects, a strong customer culture change can be measured. Action plans are made with clear goals and real impact in mind. By tracking things like higher customer engagement scores, improved MRI benchmark results, superior frontline service, or faster problem solving, organisations can see how they're improving over time. These measurements guide teams and help leaders make changes if needed. Measuring these non-financial results shows that culture work is serious and professional.

3. Gain insights from the inside—learn from employees

Employees, especially those on the frontline, have valuable insights about what's working and what's not for customers. Listening to them helps reveal what stops the business from giving great customer service. Are teams stuck with too much paperwork? Is teamwork between departments weak? Are old rules causing problems for both customers and staff? Customer culture programs encourage employees to speak up honestly, and their feedback drives real change.

4. Make culture tangible and actionable—turn culture into action

Culture can feel vague or unclear to many staff. A customer culture program and tools like the MRI make it real. They connect directly to daily tasks, team goals, and how people behave at work. Activities like mapping the customer journey, role-playing service situations, or fixing real customer problems help bring culture to life. When people see how their actions affect customers, culture becomes something they can understand and act on.

5. Gain broad employee involvement—involve everyone

This culture isn't just led by executives, it's built by everyone. That's why involving all employees is key. When people are given a chance to share ideas and help shape the culture, they feel more connected and committed. They're more likely to go the extra mile. People support what they help create, and when their input is heard and used, they feel valued. This drives stronger teamwork and motivation.

6. Build a common language across the business

A common language helps drive change. A customer culture program introduces simple terms like "customer empathy", "moment of truth", or "ease of experience" that everyone can use and understand. These words help teams work better together, no matter their role or location. This shared language brings people together, reinforces company values, and makes expectations clear.

7. Increase accountability through behavioural KPIs—make people accountable

Culture needs to be more than just a nice idea; it must be part of how people work. Adding customer-focused behaviours to KPIs and performance reviews shows it's a priority. It tells everyone that great customer service is not optional. Accountability isn't about blame; it's about being clear. People know what's expected, and success is measured by both what they do and how they do it.

8. Track progress and celebrate success

What gets measured improves. Tools like the MRI help track where you start, how far you've come, and how you compare to others. These benchmarks do more than show numbers, they inspire people. When staff see real progress and leaders celebrate the wins, it builds confidence and keeps the momentum going. What starts as a culture shift becomes something people are proud of and a real business advantage.

Culture as a Strategic Lever—A Business Advantage

These non-financial benefits won't appear on a balance sheet, but they create the environment for long-term success. Companies that treat customer culture as a key strategy become more flexible, more innovative, and better at winning customer loyalty in ways that competitors can't easily copy.

In the next chapter, we explore how to turn good intentions into consistent action. True customer culture isn't built on slogans, it's built on simple, repeatable habits. Leaders must lead by example and create space for teams to regularly talk about, reflect on, and act on customer needs. It's not about doing more; it's about making the customer part of the daily rhythm.

Key Takeaways—Chapter 6

1. Leadership Legacy Extends Far Beyond Profit

Truly impactful leaders focus on creating a human legacy, not just financial results. They recognise that integrity, emotional connection, community impact, and employee growth are essential drivers of long-term success. These "path-benders" don't just manage, they shape futures. Their legacy is the ripple effect of values that continue influencing people and communities long after they're gone.

2. The Power of the Human Multiplier Effect

A single leader's actions can ignite exponential change. Just as one employee may directly impact a few individuals, an organisation driven by purpose can affect thousands. Through culture, values, and consistent behaviour, the human multiplier effect becomes a powerful force, influencing families, customers, partners, and communities.

3. Path-Bending Leadership is Human-Centered and Transformational

True leadership isn't about authority, it's about clearing the path for others. "Path-benders" clarify vision, remove obstacles, support growth, and live by adaptable, values-driven leadership. Their influence creates cultures of trust, emotional connection, accountability, and ethical action, resulting in empowered employees and stronger communities.

The Bottom Line

The most powerful and enduring legacy a leader can leave is human, not financial. Profit matters, but it's the shared values, ethical behaviour, and emotional resonance with people, employees, customers, and communities that define a truly successful organisation. Purpose-led leaders multiply their impact far beyond balance sheets by investing in people, modelling values, and bending paths toward a better future.

**Scan or click to listen
to our Podcasts**

CHAPTER 7

STRATEGIC AND TACTICAL INITIATIVES

The Glue That Holds Us Together

Over the past 30 years, the way we work has undergone a series of profound transformations. From the arrival of personal computers to the rise of the internet, the widespread use of mobile phones, and now the rapid emergence of artificial intelligence, each technological leap has reshaped how organisations operate and how employees engage with their work. One of the most significant yet often underestimated shifts has been the ability to work remotely or from home. These changes haven't just altered tools and processes; they've required fundamental shifts in behaviour, mindset, and culture. What they collectively demonstrate is clear: people and organisations can adapt even transforming when change is necessary.

Success hinges on more than just a compelling vision or strategy. It requires a clear roadmap and actionable steps to bring that vision to life. This chapter explores the critical distinction between strategic initiatives, which set the long-term direction of a business, and tactical initiatives, which focus on the specific actions needed to achieve short to medium term goals.

Understanding how these two levels of planning interact is essential for aligning resources, motivating teams, and driving sustainable growth. Through practical examples and frameworks, this chapter provides insight into how organisations can develop, implement, and manage strategic and tactical initiatives to stay agile, competitive, and goal focused.

Companies that are truly Customer Centric like Amazon, Google, Virgin, and Apple don't treat these initiatives as optional they embed them deeply into their business frameworks, making them integral to daily operations rather than "nice to haves".

Below, you'll find the eight behavioural disciplines, each paired with both strategic and tactical initiatives. This serves as your practical guide for driving meaningful change and building momentum in each discipline. Start with the discipline most relevant to your current needs, then revisit the others as your journey continues.

This is part of your playbook, a reference tool you can refer to again and again.

Strategic and Tactical Initiatives of the Eight Behavioural Disciplines

Four Essential Practices That Bring Customer Insight to Life

CUSTOMER
INSIGHT

To embed customer insight into the fabric of your organisation, isolated initiatives are not enough. Customer insight should be cultivated as a core capability, integrated into leadership thinking, daily operations, and team culture.

Ask these questions:

- To what extent does your entire organisation understand the needs of the customer?
- To what extent do managers and employees, that are non-customer facing, interact with customers?
- To what extent does your organisation communicate to customers the actions taken because of their feedback?

Here are four essential practices that help build this discipline.

1. Customer immersion program

True customer insight begins when all employees, not just those on the front lines, connect meaningfully with customers. A customer immersion program invites individuals across all departments to:

- observe customer behaviour in real-world settings
- engage in direct conversations to uncover needs, goals, and pain points

- experience firsthand how customers navigate products, services, and support

This initiative is especially powerful for senior leaders and staff in non-customer-facing roles, as it bridges the gap between internal strategy and real-world customer experiences.

2. Feedback-to-insight framework

Customer feedback, whether gathered through structured surveys or everyday frontline conversations, is a goldmine of strategic value. A robust framework for collecting, analysing, and sharing this feedback is essential to building a customer-obsessed culture. Key components include:

- insight dashboards that provide visual, data-driven views of trends and sentiment
- voice-of-customer channels that share verbatim quotes and observations from customers and employees
- organisational sharing mechanisms like internal forums, town halls, or newsletters that ensure feedback informs decisions at every level

This structured approach turns raw feedback into actionable insight and ensures it reaches the people who can act on it.

3. "Be the customer" experience program

One of the most effective ways to build empathy and drive innovation is to view the business through the customer's eyes. A "be the customer" program enables employees to experience the end-to-end customer journey, including:

- searching for and selecting a product or service
- navigating onboarding, usage, support, and billing
- encountering any friction or delight points firsthand

These insights often reveal opportunities for improvement that internal reviews miss while reinforcing a company-wide focus on ease, empathy, and excellence.

4. Customer interaction skills training

Empowering employees with the skills to deliver exceptional customer experiences transforms insight into impact. This training should go beyond basic service etiquette and focus on core relational capabilities, such as:

- active listening that involves truly hearing what the customer is and is not saying
- emotional intelligence to help with navigating emotions, tone, and subtle cues with empathy
- conflict resolution for de-escalating challenges with professionalism and care
- building trust and rapport to create meaningful human connections

By investing in these capabilities, organisations not only improve customer outcomes but increase employee confidence, engagement, and retention.

Tactical Behaviours That Reinforce Customer Insight

Everyday actions that reinforce customer insight drive real change. The actions outlined here can start today and become part of the everyday framework in any organisation.

- **Keep customers at the centre of the conversation:** Make customer impact a core agenda item in meetings and reviews

- **Lead with customer needs, not internal assumptions:** Anchor decision-making in customer outcomes, not personal or departmental preferences

- **Engage customers directly:** Spend time with customers regularly, whether through visits, interviews, or informal check-ins

- **Proactively capture feedback:** Use structured tools and spontaneous conversations to collect insights from multiple touchpoints

- **Act on what you hear:** Turn feedback into improvements and share the outcomes internally

- **Resolve complaints as opportunities:** Treat every issue as a chance to enhance the customer experience

- **Close the loop:** Letting customers know what changed because of their feedback builds loyalty and trust.

- **Share and scale insights:** Disseminate learnings across teams to align the organisation and inspire continuous improvement

Customer insight isn't just the responsibility of marketing or sales, it's a collective discipline that fuels sustainable growth. When everyone in the organisation understands, experiences, and acts on what matters most to the customer, performance improves across the board.

Four Essential Practices That Bring Customer Foresight to Life

Customer foresight isn't about reacting to current demands, it's about anticipating what customers will need next and proactively designing solutions to meet those needs.

CUSTOMER FORESIGHT

Ask these questions:

- To what extent does your organisation discuss the benefits and shortcomings of current products and services for potential customers?
- To what extent does your organisation predict future customer needs?
- To what extent does your organisation collaborate with customers to innovate and cocreate?

Here are four essential practices that help build this discipline.

1. Immersive observation: a day in the life of the customer

Truly understanding customers begins by seeing the world through their eyes. Observing them in their natural environments, on the job, at home, or during leisure time, uncovers challenges, pain points, and unmet needs that often go unspoken. These immersive insights reveal how customers actually use (or struggle with) your products or services. This not only highlights opportunities to deliver more value, but also fuels innovation rooted in real-life application, resulting in better-designed experiences and stronger customer loyalty.

2. Co-creation: collaborating with customers in innovation

Innovation becomes more effective and less risky when customers are part of the process. Inviting them into product or service development allows organisations to gain a front-row view of emerging expectations and market shifts. Through structured collaboration, such as workshops, prototypes, or feedback loops, organisations can fine-tune offerings early, align them with genuine needs, and reduce costly missteps. Co-creation transforms customers from passive users into active partners in innovation.

3. Cross-functional innovation: harnessing collective intelligence

The best ideas often emerge at the intersections of diverse thinking. Creating cross-functional innovation teams, whether in-person, virtual, or via digital platforms, fosters a collaborative culture where ideas flow freely across departments. This collective approach, akin to crowdsourcing, helps organisations uncover fresh perspectives on how to address evolving customer needs. It also ensures that innovation is not siloed, instead it's integrated across the organisation with broad ownership and energy.

4. Strategic alignment: attending customer planning meetings

In B2B environments, being invited into a customer's strategic planning process is a rare and valuable opportunity. It signals trust and provides direct insight into where the customer is heading. By participating in these discussions, organisations gain a deeper understanding of customer strategies, long-term objectives, and operational pain points. This enables proactive alignment, co-investment in shared goals, and the ability to deliver value in ways that directly support the customer's future success.

By embedding these four practices into your organisation's DNA, leaders can move from reactive problem-solving to proactive value creation. This foresight-driven approach builds stronger customer relationships, fuels sustained innovation, and secures long-term competitive advantage.

Tactical Behaviours That Reinforce Customer Foresight

Customer foresight is brought to life through a set of proactive, forward-thinking behaviours that extend beyond addressing current needs.

- Discussing the strengths and limitations of existing products and services in relation to future and potential customers
- Exploring customer needs that may not yet be expressed or clearly defined
- Looking beyond the organisation's current offerings to envision new possibilities
- Anticipating future customer requirements based on emerging trends, technology shifts, and evolving expectations
- Partnering with customers to innovate and co-create solutions that deliver long-term value

- Participating in customer planning meetings to align strategies and deepen relationships
- Understanding customers' strategic plans, priorities, and long-term goals
- Staying informed about future events or market changes that could influence customer needs
- Actively gathering and analysing market intelligence to identify new customer segments and opportunities
- Sharing insights, trends, and foresight within teams to ensure collective awareness and a unified approach to future value creation

When these behaviours are embedded into day-to-day operations, teams gain a clearer vision of what lies ahead and can take deliberate action to shape the future of customer engagement and business growth.

Four Essential Practices That Bring Competitor Insight to Life

Competitor insight is more than just knowing who your rivals are; it's about understanding how they compete, what their value propositions are, and how your organisation can differentiate itself to deliver superior customer value. This capability directly impacts a company's ability to implement winning strategies.

COMPETITOR INSIGHT

Ask these questions:

- To what extent does your organisation discuss customer alternatives to understand the ability to compete?
- To what extent does your organisation monitor the current strategies of competitors and evaluate where they have succeeded and failed?
- To what extent does your organisation make decisions with current competitors in mind that create value for customers and the business?

Here are four essential practices that bring this discipline to life.

1. Competitor value proposition mapping

To truly build a culture of competitor insight, every team within the business from sales to support must understand the value propositions of key competitors. This means knowing what they offer, how they position themselves, and most importantly, how we differ. When teams understand these nuances, they're better equipped to identify where and how they can add value in ways that reinforce the organisation's competitive edge.

2. Collecting and sharing competitor intelligence

Competitor insight thrives on a continuous flow of intelligence, both formal and informal. Structured programs to collect competitive intelligence (e.g., customer feedback, market research, sales insights) and informal observations (e.g., frontline employee experiences, anecdotal customer comments) are essential. Turning this raw input into actionable insights through regular reporting and sharing across departments ensures that everyone, from product development to finance, has a clear picture of the competitive landscape.

3. Simulating the competition

To think like a competitor is to anticipate their next move. Competitive simulations, where cross-functional teams role-play as rivals, offer a powerful way to predict competitor strategies, such as product launches or market entries, and model potential market reactions. By inviting real customer panels to respond to these simulations, we reality-test our assumptions and sharpen our strategy based on authentic feedback.

4. Embedding a competitive lens into decision-making

Every decision whether it's launching a new service, improving a process, or entering a new market, should be assessed through a competitive lens. Teams should ask: "How does this create greater value for our customers? How does it strengthen our competitive position?" This mindset ensures that innovation and improvement efforts don't just meet customer needs, they also build sustainable differentiation.

By embedding these practices into the fabric of your organisation, competitor insight becomes more than a reactive exercise. It becomes a strategic capability that enables proactive, confident, and customer-aligned decisions across the business.

Tactical Behaviours That Reinforce Competitor Insight

Every team member should understand how their work directly contributes to sustaining the company's competitive advantage. Embedding competitor insight into day-to-day thinking ensures the entire organisation stays strategically focused and customer-centric.

- Actively discussing what alternative options customers have, and how our offering compares
- Clarifying how customers perceive our products or services: are they simple, transparent, and clearly superior to the competition?
- Identifying which parts of our service are competitively strong, and where we are falling behind
- Holding regular conversations about competitor strengths and weaknesses to keep everyone informed and focused
- Monitoring competitors' current strategies and analysing where they are succeeding or failing in the market
- Deepening team understanding of our value proposition and how it compares to key competitors
- Making decisions that consider competitor activity, ensuring that both customer value and business results are enhanced
- Sharing competitive intelligence openly across teams to empower employees to respond with informed, value-creating actions

When teams routinely think through a competitive lens, they not only protect market position, they also uncover opportunities to deliver distinctive, differentiated value that keeps customers coming back.

Four Essential Practices That Bring Competitor Foresight to Life

COMPETITOR
FORESIGHT

Competitor foresight is the ability to anticipate and prepare for future competitive threats. It reflects a business's capacity to identify emerging rivals, understand their strategies, and proactively innovate to sustain competitive advantage.

Ask these questions:

- To what extent does your organisation monitor potential future competitors?
- To what extent does your organisation discuss and clarify how future competitors can impact the value of your products and services?
- To what extent does your organisation identify areas where potential competitors could succeed?

Here are four essential practices that bring this discipline to life.

1. Monitoring emerging competitors

A sharp understanding of who your future competitors might be and what impact they could have is central to effective competitor foresight. This requires a disciplined approach to scanning the horizon for new entrants, start-ups, or tech-enabled companies that may not yet be on the radar. Leaders and frontline teams alike must understand how these disruptors could affect the value the business delivers and what actions can be taken now to stay ahead.

2. Mapping industry convergence and disruption

Future competitors don't always come from within your existing industry. Adjacent industries are often where the real disruption begins. By analysing market shifts, structural industry changes, and the convergence of once-separate sectors, companies can gain early insight into where competition may emerge. Regular global benchmarking visits and insights from non-traditional players help anticipate where innovation is heading and who's best positioned to seize it.

3. Identifying new opportunities for competitive success

Customer foresight and competitor foresight are closely linked. By understanding where customer needs are evolving, businesses can predict which types of companies, often outside the current competitive set, are likely to address those needs first. This intelligence helps businesses pivot before competitors even gain traction, allowing them to build next-generation value before the market shifts.

4. Embedding and sharing competitive intelligence

Foresight must become a shared discipline across the organisation. Are your people trained to detect early signs of competitive disruption? Do they know how to evaluate the relevance of new threats to your customer base? Embedding competitor foresight requires systems and forums, both face-to-face and digital, that promote real-time sharing of intelligence. This ensures every team member can evaluate their role through a forward-looking, competitive lens.

Tactical Behaviours That Reinforce Competitor Foresight

Every leader and team member should understand how their role contributes to building and sustaining the company's competitive advantage both now and in the future. Competitor foresight is not just a strategic function; it's a shared responsibility across the business.

- Actively monitoring emerging competitors and disruptive market entrants

- Tracking global trends that signal shifts in competitive dynamics

- Making strategic decisions with future competitors in mind

- Evaluating how potential future offerings could challenge or devalue our own

- Identifying areas where new entrants could gain traction or succeed

- Monitoring changes in industry barriers to entry and anticipating their impact

- Mapping convergence between our industry and adjacent sectors to spot threats and opportunities early

- Sharing insights and competitive signals across teams to align innovation efforts and prepare for future market shifts

When organisations embrace competitor foresight as a cultural capability, not just a strategic function, they foster agility, sharpen innovation, and safeguard their relevance in fast-changing markets. Every employee, from frontline to executive, becomes an early warning sensor for the next competitive wave and a contributor to future-ready growth.

Four Essential Practices That Bring Peripheral Vision to Life

PERIPHERAL
VISION

Peripheral vision refers to a company's ability to continuously scan, interpret, and act on emerging trends and external shifts, whether technological, economic, social, or competitive. Organisations that embed this capability across their workforce consistently outperform those that do not.

Ask these questions:

- To what extent does your organisation discuss, understand, and act on the changes in the external environment that may have implications for your products and services?

- To what extent do employees in the organisation meet with customers to discuss major impacts of political, legislative and technological changes?
- To what extent does your organisation engage in discussion forums to generate peripheral vision?

Here are four essential practices that help build this discipline.

1. Exploring changes beyond your industry

To develop strong peripheral vision, leaders and employees must look beyond their immediate industry for inspiration and early signals of change. This includes:

- attending cross-industry conferences on disruptive technologies, customer experience, sustainability, and digital transformation

- partnering with academic institutions, research centres, and think tanks to gain foresight into shifts likely to redefine customer expectations and future business models

- studying emerging consumer behaviour and technological adoption trends globally, not just locally

These external insights act as early warning systems for both opportunity and disruption.

2. Creating internal platforms for insight sharing

It's not enough to observe change, organisations must build mechanisms to share, discuss, and act on it by:

- encouraging staff to bring insights from personal research, external events, or customer interactions into the organisation
- using digital forums, town halls, or internal newsletters to create space for open dialogue and sense-making across teams
- developing a shared future vision by regularly aligning on how trends may reshape customer needs, and what this means for capabilities, products, and services

This cross-pollination of ideas builds collective foresight.

3. Learning from visionaries and cross-industry customers

Bringing in fresh perspectives accelerates cultural and strategic adaptability by activities such as:

- hosting talks or Q&A sessions with executives and innovators from other industries who have faced and responded to major market shifts
- inviting customers from adjacent sectors to share their own challenges, expectations, and innovation stories

These engagements deepen external orientation and help teams view their business through new lenses.

4. Building an adaptive and future-ready workforce

Peripheral vision is only as strong as the organisation's ability to respond to what it sees. This requires:

- cultivating a growth mindset and adaptive behaviours at all levels of the business
- ongoing investment in upskilling and reskilling programs aligned with future capabilities, digital literacy, systems thinking, and creative problem-solving among them
- embedding resilience training and change-readiness into leadership and team development

When adaptive capacity is built into the culture, organisations can pivot quickly and innovate boldly in the face of change.

Tactical Behaviours That Reinforce Peripheral Vision

Peripheral vision is not just about noticing what's changing, it's about embedding a proactive, future-focused mindset across your organisation. Below are key behaviours that reflect a strong peripheral vision discipline in action.

- Engaging customers on future impact: Regularly meeting with customers to explore how political, regulatory, or technological shifts could alter how they receive and perceive value from your products, services, or team. These conversations provide real-time foresight and uncover hidden needs

- Attending and sharing insights from external events: Participating in industry and cross-industry conferences that focus on emerging trends, such as digital disruption, sustainability, or evolving consumer expectations, and bringing those insights back to inform internal strategies and planning
- Translating environmental change into action: Actively discussing changes in the external environment (e.g., economic volatility, competitor moves, environmental regulations) and assessing their impact on how value is delivered to customers today and in the future
- Anticipating and managing risk: Identifying and responding to external risks that could affect both your customers and your business. This includes developing contingency plans, adjusting offerings, or evolving processes in response to anticipated disruptions
- Embedding external awareness in decision-making: Ensuring team decisions are shaped by relevant external developments, including shifts in customer behaviour, market dynamics, or new technological opportunities that influence the relevance of your products or services
- Prioritising work based on external trends: Aligning individual roles and responsibilities with emerging external priorities, making sure day-to-day efforts are contributing to future customer value, not just present demands
- Creating a culture of shared insight: Proactively sharing knowledge about significant external changes and their potential impact with all members of the team. This helps foster a culture of collective intelligence and readiness for change

Peripheral vision is not a one-off activity. It's a cultural mindset and strategic discipline. Businesses that cultivate it proactively will not only see the future more clearly but shape it on their own terms.

Four Essential Practices That Bring Empowerment to Life

EMPOWERMENT

Empowerment is a critical measure of an organisation's ability to harness its full potential, leveraging resources, talent, and operational strengths to consistently deliver exceptional value to customers.

Ask these questions:

- To what extent does the organisation provide authority for employees to make decisions that are right for customers?

- To what extent are employees able to challenge the way things are done when they believe there is a better way?
- To what extent are employees able to decide the way they work to benefit customers?

Here are four essential practices that bring this to life.

1. Personal customer storytelling program

Encouraging employees to share real stories about how they've solved customer problems or delivered unexpected value helps foster a strong customer mindset. When these stories are supported and celebrated by leadership, they build a culture of pride, ownership, and empowerment. Storytelling not only reinforces best practices but also inspires others to think proactively about customer needs.

2. Customer interaction skills for non-customer-facing staff

Empowerment should reach beyond traditional customer service roles. Providing non-customer-facing employees with training and experiences, such as workshops, role-playing, shadowing frontline staff, or participating in customer-focused team projects builds confidence and sharpens their ability to recognise and contribute to customer value creation across the organisation.

3. Idea generation and sharing platform

Empowered employees are more likely to challenge the status quo and pursue new ways to serve customers. A structured yet open idea-sharing system, such as internal innovation hubs, digital suggestion platforms, or cross-functional sprints, creates space for creativity to thrive. The most forward-thinking companies consistently encourage individuals and teams to pitch, prototype, and implement ideas that enhance customer experiences and drive differentiation.

Recent research reinforces just how powerful this approach can be. A survey by idea-sharing platform IdeaSpies found that 90 per cent of employees would stay with their organisation if they could contribute more ideas and had management support to test them. Yet many employees, particularly younger staff and those in customer-facing roles, report feeling frustrated when their ideas are ignored or dismissed without feedback. By ensuring every idea is acknowledged, providing clear reasons when suggestions cannot be implemented, and removing approval bottlenecks, leaders can transform idea-sharing from a token gesture into a genuine driver of empowerment. When employees see their contributions valued and acted on, they become more engaged, more innovative, and more committed to delivering exceptional customer value.[17]

4. Streamlined, customer-centric processes

Bureaucracy, outdated systems, and rigid approval chains are empowerment killers. Simplifying internal processes and removing obstacles that hinder service delivery empowers employees to act quickly and effectively in the customer's best interest. Redesigning workflows with the customer at the centre and giving employees the tools and autonomy to resolve issues dramatically improves responsiveness, efficiency, and satisfaction.

Tactical Behaviours That Reinforce Empowerment

Empowered organisations adopt behaviours that foster a culture where employees are trusted, supported, and equipped to deliver exceptional customer value.

- **Taking initiative:** Employees make independent decisions within their roles to enhance customer value without waiting for approval

- **Challenging the status quo:** Team members question existing processes when they identify better ways to serve customers and aren't afraid to propose and implement improvements

- **Streamlining for speed:** Approval processes are restructured to eliminate bottlenecks and empower employees to act quickly in the customer's best interest

- **Idea generation in action:** Employees are encouraged to contribute new ideas and are supported in turning them into reality to elevate the customer experience

- **Skilful service delivery:** Staff demonstrate the competencies and knowledge needed to offer smarter, faster, and more tailored solutions to customer needs

- **Decision-making with a customer lens:** Employees consistently consider the customer's perspective when making decisions that affect service, experience, or outcomes

- **Relationship-driven interactions:** Strong social and emotional intelligence is applied to foster trust, build rapport, and enhance every touchpoint with the customer
- **Empowering structures and systems:** The company's organisational design, tools, and systems are intentionally built to support employee autonomy and effectiveness in delivering superior customer value

Empowerment is not a one-time initiative, it's a cultural foundation. Organisations that nurture empowered teams are more agile, more customer-centric, and far better positioned to compete and grow in today's dynamic markets.

Four Essential Practices That Bring Collaboration to Life

CROSS-
FUNCTIONAL
COLLABORATION

Collaboration is more than just cooperation, it's the strategic alignment of people, processes, and priorities across functions to deliver greater value to customers. It reflects a business's ability to effectively leverage its collective knowledge, resources, and capabilities.

Ask these questions:

- To what extent does your organisation have cross-functional teams collaborating on creating more value for customers?
- To what extent do employees engage in cross-functional problem-solving sessions that provide improved solutions for customers?
- To what extent does your organisation share good and bad customer stories across functions as a means of generating collaboration?

Here are four essential practices that bring this to life.

1. Joint projects that elevate customer solutions

Effective collaboration shines in projects that bring together diverse skills and perspectives to solve complex customer challenges. Whether it's launching new products, improving service delivery, or enhancing the customer journey across multiple touchpoints, cross-functional collaboration can ensure alignment and integration by adopting key activities, such as:

- creating cross-functional teams to co-develop customer service and satisfaction metrics

- engaging departments like sales, marketing, service, and operations to co-design seamless customer experiences
- encouraging joint ownership of outcomes to build accountability and momentum

2. Sharing technology, expertise, and resources

Cross-pollination of knowledge and tools boosts innovation and efficiency. Implementing structured secondment programs, knowledge exchange platforms, and shared resource models unlocks the full potential of your workforce and can be achieved by:

- enabling temporary staff rotations between departments to foster deeper understanding and empathy
- sharing systems, data, and technologies to break down barriers and encourage unified thinking
- eliminating duplication through aligning processes and focusing on what adds most value to the customer

3. Fostering social connection across teams

Human connection is the foundation of collaboration. Building strong interpersonal relationships across departments leads to faster problem-solving, higher trust, and better communication. Some way to achieve this are:

- encouraging informal interactions through initiatives like coffee catchups, hobby groups, sporting events, and community projects
- using formal gatherings like company retreats, conferences, and customer site visits with social components to deepen bonds across teams
- recognising that cross-functional trust starts with meaningful human connection

4. Customer storytelling as a cultural anchor

Storytelling is a powerful tool to embed collaboration and customer focus in your culture. Sharing real-life examples both successes and failures drives learning, builds empathy, and reinforces best practices across functions. Some ways to do this are:

- establishing regular storytelling sessions at team meetings and company-wide events

- capturing stories that demonstrate teamwork, initiative, and customer impact, and making them part of your corporate folklore
- using storytelling as a key component of onboarding to socialise new employees into a customer-centric, collaborative mindset

Tactical Behaviours That Reinforce Collaboration

Key mechanisms can be adopted to foster cross-functional sharing of knowledge, skills, and experiences that support customer-centric behaviours.

- **Collaborative customer-focused projects:** Teams from different functions work together on initiatives that directly impact customer outcomes, driving alignment and shared ownership

- **Customer experience storytelling sessions:** Employees regularly share impactful stories about customer interactions, promoting learning and empathy across the organisation

- **Customer-inclusive discussion forums:** Platforms where cross-functional teams engage directly with customers to gain insights and co-create solutions

- **Cross-functional secondments:** Temporary rotations or exchanges of staff between departments to broaden perspectives and deepen understanding of the customer journey

- **Joint problem-solving workshops:** Facilitated sessions that bring diverse teams together to address customer challenges and develop innovative solutions

- **Social interaction opportunities:** Informal and formal events designed to build personal connections across teams, enhancing trust and collaboration

- **Sharing of technology, expertise, and resources:** Open access to tools, systems, and know-how that empower teams to deliver consistent and improved customer value

When collaboration is embedded in the DNA of an organisation, silos crumble, creativity flourishes, and customer value is amplified. Whether through shared projects, cross-functional learning, or simply building stronger personal connections, collaborative behaviour is a business multiplier turning functional strengths into enterprise-wide performance.

Four Essential Practices That Bring Strategic Alignment to Life

Strategic alignment is the degree to which an organisation's people, actions, and culture are aligned with its vision, mission, and strategy. It's not just about having a strategy, but about ensuring everyone in the organisation understands it, believes in it, and is empowered to act on it.

STRATEGIC ALIGNMENT

Ask these questions:

- To what extent is there clear and repeated communication of the vision, values and strategy throughout all parts of your organisation?
- To what extent is customer centric behaviour monitored in all functions and business units?
- To what extent is there recognition of employees who act in a customer centric way?

Here are four essential practices that help build this discipline.

1. Strategic communication programs

Effective alignment starts with clear, consistent, and purposeful communication. The organisation's vision, strategic priorities, and customer goals can be widely understood and consistently reinforced at all levels by:

- leaders regularly sharing updates and reinforcing strategic messages through multiple channels
- regularly reviewing communication methods for their reach and effectiveness
- testing understanding across departments to know where employees know how their daily roles contribute to the bigger picture and if they feel personally invested in the organisation's success

2. Customer metrics that matter

Customer feedback must be both quantitative and qualitative, and it must be visible and actionable throughout the organisation. It's most effective when:

- structured customer research is used alongside insights from frontline staff to gather a full picture

- results are shared openly and regularly with all teams
- internal performance goals are aligned with key customer metrics, such as satisfaction, loyalty, and advocacy
- organisation's customer culture is tracked and benchmarked by setting improvement targets that align with strategic business goals

3. Recognition and employee engagement

Recognising behaviours that reflect a strong customer-centric mindset builds engagement and reinforces cultural alignment through:

- celebrating individuals and teams who go above and beyond for customers both formally (e.g., awards) and informally (e.g., internal shout-outs)
- highlighting customer praise and connecting it to specific employees, teams, or departments
- encouraging staff to share success stories and learnings, turning everyday wins into cultural momentum

4. Reward systems tied to customer outcomes

Linking compensation and recognition to customer-centric behaviours and results signals a clear commitment from leadership. It can be achieved by:

- aligning bonuses or incentives with customer experience KPIs
- embedding customer impact into performance reviews and personal development plans
- ensuring that all levels of the business see how customer outcomes influence business success and how they personally contribute

Tactical Behaviours That Reinforce Strategic Alignment

Strategic alignment is not just a concept, it's demonstrated through everyday behaviours that connect individuals and teams to the organisation's vision, mission, and strategy. Here are key examples of what effective alignment looks like in action.

- **Consistent communication of strategic direction:** Leaders regularly and clearly communicate the organisation's vision, mission, and strategic goals across all levels of the business, reinforcing the 'why' behind the work and ensuring everyone is moving in the same direction

- **Tracking and benchmarking customer-centric progress:** Customer-centricity is measured using meaningful metrics, regularly benchmarked against targets. These insights guide decision-making and ensure continuous improvement aligned with business strategy

- **Recognising customer-focused behaviours:** Employees who demonstrate exceptional customer-centric actions are celebrated through both formal recognition and everyday praise fostering engagement and reinforcing cultural alignment

- **Aligning day-to-day work with strategic goals:** Teams and individuals understand how their work contributes to overarching business objectives, and they actively align their efforts to support company-wide success

- **Adapting swiftly to strategic shifts:** When business strategies evolve, employees adjust their priorities, workflows, and focus accordingly demonstrating agility and commitment to the new direction

- **Eliminating non-strategic activities:** Projects and initiatives that do not directly support the company's strategic goals are identified and discontinued, allowing resources to be focused where they create the most value

- **Embedding a customer-centric culture:** A customer-first mindset is built into processes, training, leadership behaviours, and team objectives making it a sustained and integral part of how the organisation operates

When strategic alignment is embedded into the fabric of your organisation, you move from simply executing a plan to creating a culture where every employee is actively contributing to a shared vision of customer value and sustainable growth.

Lasting change doesn't happen by chance, it takes consistent action, visible leadership, and collective commitment. The next chapter is all about turning customer culture into a daily habit. It outlines exercises designed to help your organisation move from good intentions to a deeply embedded, customer-focused culture. Aligned with the eight disciplines from Chapter 3, they will guide teams in developing the mindset, routines, and behaviours needed to keep the customer at the heart of everything you do.

Key Takeaways—Chapter 7

1. Strategic and Tactical Initiatives Must Work Together

Long-term success requires both strategic direction and tactical execution. Strategic initiatives provide vision and focus, while tactical initiatives deliver the day-to-day actions that make the vision real. Companies that embed both at all levels like Amazon, Google, and Apple drive sustainable customer-centric growth.

2. Customer-Centric Behaviours Drive Organisational Change

The eight behavioural disciplines (customer insight, customer foresight, competitor insight, competitor foresight, peripheral vision, empowerment, collaboration, and strategic alignment) are not just abstract ideas—they are practical and measurable and can be activated through specific strategic and tactical initiatives. Embedding these behaviours across the organisation is key to building a resilient, customer-focused culture.

3. Empowerment, Collaboration, and Alignment Are Cultural Multipliers

Empowered employees, cross-functional collaboration, and strategic alignment significantly increase a company's ability to serve customers effectively. This isn't just about systems, it's about creating environments where employees feel trusted, supported, and clear about how their daily work contributes to the bigger picture.

The Bottom Line

The most successful, future-ready organisations are those that consistently connect strategy to action and empower their people to deliver customer value at every level. By embedding customer-centric disciplines and fostering empowerment, collaboration, and alignment, businesses create cultures that are agile, unified, and primed for long-term success.

**Scan or click to listen
to our Podcasts**

CHAPTER 8

THE LEADER'S PLAYBOOK

Making Customer Culture a Daily Habit

The great New Zealand 1,500-metre runner, John Walker, developed a simple yet powerful habit during his Olympic training. While driving home on the freeway, he would simulate his race: cruising steadily for 1,200 metres, then shifting into the fast lane with 300 metres to go, accelerating and holding that speed until his exit. He practised the same pattern on the track.

In the Olympic 1,500-metre final, Walker did exactly what he'd rehearsed, breaking from the pack with 300 metres to go, surging to the front, and never looking back until he crossed the finish line and won gold.

He said: "You must do it every time, so it becomes a powerful habit. In business as in sport, simple, basic habits propel you to excellence."

It's easy to overlook the basics in the rush to tackle complex challenges. But the fact is, it's often the simplest routines that create the most lasting change. And too often, we push them aside, thinking we're too busy, when in fact, they're the foundation we need most.

For any organisation to thrive, its leadership must consistently walk the talk. The moment leaders become disconnected from their employees and customers the business will begin to lose its footing. Customer-centricity cannot be a slogan, it must be embedded into the very DNA of leadership. To support this, we've developed a practical guide to help leaders cultivate and demonstrate the essential traits of customer-focused leadership.

We call it something simple, yet powerful: Building your Leadership *Customer Muscle Memory.*

Then we have chosen six simple, practical exercises that can be built into your organisation's daily routines, without causing disruption. While there are many others, these represent the most essential. They are not one-off events or extra tasks. Instead, they're designed to become part of how your teams meet, talk, plan, and work together every day.

Real change happens through consistent action, strong leadership, and shared commitment. The exercises are made to help your organisation move from talk to action and from action to a lasting customer-focused culture. Included is one practical proven activity that can be embedded into the organisation on a planned and recurring basis. These are designed specifically to drive engagement across all three pillars—leadership, customer, and employee engagement.

Each activity is linked to the eight disciplines introduced in Chapter 3. They offer a clear path to help teams and leaders build the mindset, habits, and language needed to keep the customer at the centre of everything they do.

These exercises will help you:

- understand where your customer culture stands today
- look at problems from different team and functional perspectives
- celebrate great customer-focused behaviour and build on it
- set a rhythm for regular customer conversations in meetings
- encourage leaders to lead by example and take ownership of culture

Whether you're just starting, or building on what you've already begun, this chapter gives you tools that work. They've been tested, are easy to use, and can be tailored to fit your needs. You can start small and build over time. Just remember: "Culture is not what we say, it's what we do, together."

The MarketCulture Academy is your partner in driving meaningful change. Each exercise below and many more are designed to help you turn insight into action. Every resource is available in a ready-to-use format, complete with engaging videos that not only educate, but inspire your employees to understand and embrace the journey. Let us help you bring strategy to life.

Visit: https://www.marketculture.com/academy

Sean

Looking back over my years in sales, there's one lesson that's never left me: the power of consistent training. At the time, it felt like a chore. We had weekly sales training sessions like clockwork, and not many of us looked forward to them. It took time away from selling, from hitting targets. On top of that, each quarter we'd spend a full day out of the field for more advanced training.

Back then, I didn't fully understand the value. But now, with hindsight, I see it clearly—those sessions shaped my career and the success of countless others. What I failed to grasp at the time was the importance of repetition and consistency. The weekly rhythm, the constant reinforcement. It builds habits, sharpens our thinking, and creates a discipline that becomes second nature.

Advice for C-Level Organisational Leaders

Staying Connected to Employees and Customers: Leadership in the Age of Scale[18]

When a company grows from a handful of employees, when customers multiply, something profound happens. The once-crystal-clear connection between leadership, employees, and customers becomes obscured by layers of management, data reports, and operational complexities. This scaling of an organisation often brings added complexity and can disconnect leadership from frontline realities.

But we know that the moment leaders lose touch with their customers' experiences is the moment a business begins its decline. This is how leaders of any sized business can stay connected to customer reality not as a luxury, but as a necessity.

The Danger of Disconnection

Think about companies that once dominated their industries but eventually failed: Kodak, Blockbuster, Nokia, Blackberry, amongst many others. What unites them? Their leadership lost touch with evolving customer needs. They listened to internal voices rather than customer signals. In contrast, companies like Amazon have thrived because, despite their enormous scale, their leadership maintains an almost obsessive focus on customer experience.

As remote and hybrid work involving flexible hours and days become the norm, organisations and leaders must be more intentional than ever about staying connected to both employees and customers. Without that connection, employees risk feeling isolated, undervalued, and disengaged. A disconnect that can quietly erode morale, innovation, and retention.

The six exercises provided later in this chapter are designed to be inclusive of all leaders and employees collaborating in teams to the benefit of customers and themselves. They enhance a feeling of belonging and being connected with the organisation's purpose and culture. They should become embedded as part of the operating rhythm of the business.

Build your Customer Muscle Memory with Four Vital Sources of Customer Reality—Your ABCDs

So how can leaders stay connected? There are four essential channels that provide the foundation for customer experience, even at large scale.

1. Ask customers: customer metrics are the quantitative compass

Numbers tell stories. Key metrics provide our first window into customer reality:

- Net Promoter Score (NPS) measures customer loyalty and likelihood to recommend
- Customer Satisfaction Score (CSAT) gauges immediate satisfaction with interactions
- Customer Effort Score (CES) evaluates how easy we make things for customers
- POC or "Pissed Off Customers" measure, a blunt but honest assessment from customer complaints and negative feedback of where we're creating frustration

These metrics provide a dashboard, but they're just the beginning. Numbers without context are like trying to understand a person by their vital signs alone, necessary but insufficient.

2. Bring in employee stories: the frontline reality

Your employees, especially those on the front line, are living repositories of customer perceptions. They hear the unfiltered feedback, feel the emotional temperature, and witness the unscripted moments.

Chris

When I was at Hewlett-Packard, the most important product improvements came not from formal research but from the support team sharing stories about customer pain points. These narratives gave a human dimension to the data. I remember one instance when Tony, a support engineer, described a small business customer who had to shut down operations for two days because of a recurring printer fault. On paper, the incident looked like a routine warranty case, one of hundreds in the monthly service report. But hearing the story, with the customer's frustration, financial loss, and the ripple effect on their staff, transformed the way our product team saw the issue. It was no longer just a defect rate percentage; it was a real-world problem hurting a real person's livelihood.

That story triggered a significant redesign, not because the numbers demanded it, but because the leadership team could feel the impact. It taught me that while data can prioritise, stories mobilise. The best leaders don't just track customer experience through dashboards, they create deliberate pathways for these human stories to flow upward. This combination of insight and empathy ensures that decisions are not only smart but also connected to the people we serve.

Great leaders create channels for these stories to flow upward. Town halls, skip-level meetings, and "day in the life" programs all ensure that the richness of customer reality reaches leadership.

3. Context via direct experiences: the irreplaceable immersion

Nothing, absolutely nothing, replaces direct experience. Leaders must regularly put themselves in the customer's shoes:

- try to purchase your own product through your website

- call your own customer service line
- use your product in the real world, not in a controlled demonstration
- sit with customers as they interact with your offering

These experiences create visceral knowledge, that is, an understanding that lives in your gut, not just your head. It creates urgency that spreadsheets simply cannot generate.

4. Deep listening: the unfiltered truth

Create opportunities to hear directly from customers, unfiltered by layers of organisation via:

- customer advisory boards with direct leadership involvement
- executive sponsorship of key accounts
- regular customer roundtables led by senior leaders
- systematic review of customer feedback, especially complaints

This direct listening catches signals that might otherwise get lost in translation.

Putting It into Practice—Customer Muscle Memory

Here is a simple framework for incorporating these sources of truth into your leadership rhythm. When done consistently, this rhythm creates "customer muscle memory" an intuitive sense of your customers that informs every decision, even when they're not explicitly represented.

1. Weekly: Review key customer metrics in leadership meetings

2. Monthly: Read unfiltered customer feedback and employee stories

3. Bi-Monthly: Engage in direct customer experiences

4. Quarterly: Conduct deep listening sessions with diverse customer segments

The Ultimate Leadership Question

The ultimate test of a customer connection is whether you can answer one simple question: "What is it actually like to be our customer today?"

Not what it was like last year. Not what you hope it will be next quarter. What is it like today, in all its messy, imperfect reality?

If you can answer that question with confidence, specificity, and honesty, you're connected. If you can't, no amount of business success can protect you from eventual disruption. Because in the end, scale doesn't change the fundamental core of business: we exist to serve our customers. The moment we forget that is the moment we begin to fail.

STAYING CONNECTED: LEADERSHIP IN THE AGE OF SCALE

THE DANGER OF DISCONNECTION

EMPTY CHAIR = CUSTOMER PERSPECTIVE

FOUR VITAL SOURCES OF CUSTOMER REALITY

A

ASK
CUSTOMER METRICS
- NPS: Would recommend?
- CSAT: Satisfaction level?
- CES: How easy was it?
- POC: Pissed off customers

B

BRING IN
EMPLOYEE STORIES
- Front-line truth
- Unfiltered feedback
- Emotional temperature
- Town halls, skip-levels

C

CONTEXT
DIRECT EXPERIENCE
- Use your own product
- Call your customer service
- Visceral knowledge
- Walk in customer shoes

D

DEEP LISTENING
THE UNFILTERED TRUTH
- Customer advisory boards
- Executive sponsorship
- Customer roundtables
- Review complaints directly

BUILDING 'CUSTOMER MUSCLE MEMORY'

WEEKLY → **MONTHLY** **QUARTERLY** → **ANNUALLY**

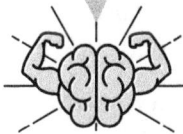

"What is it actually like to be our customer today?"

Key Activities for Embedding a Strong Customer Culture

These **six** exercises can be seamlessly integrated into your team's daily and weekly routines. By embedding them into your organisation's operating rhythm, you create the foundation for successful innovation and sustainable growth.

Exercise 1: Customer Engagement Meetings

Putting Customers on the Agenda—Literally and Strategically

Purpose

Customer engagement meetings are a simple, yet powerful discipline designed to embed customer thinking into the everyday rhythm of work. By placing customers at the top of every agenda, we reinforce the belief that customer outcomes are everyone's responsibility, not the job of one department.

"The customer is here with us in the room, let's act accordingly."

Strategic Disciplines Activated

- Customer Insight: anchor discussions in real customer experiences
- Strategic Alignment: let customer needs shape priorities and decisions
- Cross-Functional Collaboration: share ownership of customer outcomes across silos

The Core Principle: Leave a Seat at the Table for Customers

Most organisations claim to care about customers but when customer topics are left off meeting agendas, the implicit message is clear: "We'll focus on the customer after we deal with the real business".

Customer engagement meetings flip that narrative. By opening meetings with a customer-focused conversation, we declare: "The customer comes first".

Exercise 1—continued

Where This Applies

Embed this approach into all key meeting types:

- executive leadership team meetings
- department updates
- sales and service huddles
- cross-functional project reviews
- agile stand-ups and daily scrums
- quarterly business reviews

Wherever there's a decision, there's a customer behind it.

Goal

Open every meeting with 5–10 minutes of customer-centred discussion to:

- maintain customer visibility
- foster shared accountability
- reinforce customer-centric culture

Discussion Prompts (real stories and signals, no slides)

- What recent customer feedback have we received?
- Any customer success or failure stories worth sharing?
- Are customer expectations shifting?
- Where are we seeing customer friction across teams?
- What can we do better based on what customers are telling us?
- Who went above and beyond for a customer this week?

Making It Work

1. Make "Customer First" a permanent agenda item at the top of every meeting

2. Rotate ownership by letting different team members bring the customer voice

Exercise 1—continued

3. Use quick, powerful artifacts, such as quotes, emails, reviews, or visuals

4. Track outcomes by capturing actions, reflections, and follow-ups

5. Include internal customers, especially in cross-functional meetings

When You Don't...

*   Customer priorities get delayed or sidelined
*   Critical feedback is missed or minimised
*   Employees internalise the wrong message: "Customers aren't really a priority here".

When You Do...

*   Clarity increases – Everyone knows who they serve
*   Culture evolves – Customer language becomes business language
*   Collaboration improves – Teams unite around shared outcomes
*   Performance accelerates – What gets discussed gets done

Final Thought

"If customers don't have a seat at your table, they'll eventually give theirs to someone else"

Customer engagement meetings aren't about adding more to your agenda. They're about adding meaning to everything on it. Don't wait for customers to raise their voices, raise their presence in every room.

Exercise 2: The Power of Customer Stories

Creating Culture Through Storytelling

Why Stories Matter

Behind every successful customer-centric company is a steady heartbeat, and that rhythm lives in its stories. While data defines performance, it's storytelling that humanises your brand and breathes life into your culture.

Customer stories aren't just anecdotes. They're emotional signals, learning tools, and culture-shaping moments. When shared at the right time, a single story can shift mindsets, spark change, and align teams.

What Makes a Great Customer Story?

Not all stories move people. The best ones share these qualities:

- authenticity, stories that are real, unpolished, and credible
- relevance, stories that are tied to customer experience and aligned with company values
- emotion, stories that evoke empathy, pride, frustration, or hope
- personal connection, stories that are told by someone who lived it, witnessed it, or deeply relates to it
- impact, stories where there's a clear consequence for the customer, the team, or the business
- resolution, stories that end with a clear takeaway, a breakthrough, or a learning moment

Great stories don't fade, they're retold. That's how culture spreads.

Stories Create Shared Language

In high-performing organisations, stories don't just communicate values, they embed them. Over time, powerful phrases rooted in stories become rallying cries for behaviour.

Customer Culture in Action: Story-Driven Language

These examples of catchphrases encapsulate how shared language creates shared values.

- Carly Fiorina former CEO of HP "Run to the Fire", is a call to act, not avoid. When something goes wrong, move toward the issue fast. It builds ownership and urgency
- Chateau Elan Resorts' "Consider it Done" makes it clear that no request is too small. It empowers teams to act with confidence and removes barriers to service
- Amazon's "Correction of Error" highlights that mistakes are systemic learning moments. A transparent, company-wide practice that drives real improvement

Create Your Own Cultural Catchphrases

Ask:

- What phrase reflects how we solve customer problems?
- What words inspire action instead of hesitation?
- How can we turn values into something sticky and repeatable?

Examples:

- "Own the Outcome"
- "Fix and Share"
- "We're On It"
- "Walk in Their Shoes"

These aren't slogans. They're culture signals embedded in everyday behaviour.

How to Facilitate Storytelling

You don't need a big stage, great storytelling thrives in everyday settings: a morning huddle, a team lunch, or a Zoom call. Some ideas are:

- Start with a theme that guides contributions with focused prompts. For example, Customer Insight, Strategic Alignment, Collaboration,

Empowerment. A prompt might be "Share a moment where you felt empowered to go the extra mile for a customer"

- Diversify voices instead of just focusing on frontline teams. IT, finance, or logistics often have unexpected and powerful stories
- Keep it short and focused on clarity and feeling, not performance—one to five minutes is plenty
- Create a safe space by making room for tough stories, not just celebrating wins. Vulnerability builds trust
- Capture and share by using internal platforms or quick recordings to preserve and spread your best stories

Final Thought

Culture lives in stories, you can't spreadsheet your way to a customer-first culture. You need stories, the kind that inspire, teach, and connect. Stories turn values into behaviour. They connect employees to purpose. They remind us that customers are human and so are we.

If you want to shape your culture, collect stories. If you want to accelerate it, start telling them.

Exercise 3: Customer Culture Huddles

Short Conversations that Build Long-Term Cultural Change

Culture Doesn't Live in Boardrooms

Culture isn't created in PowerPoint decks or executive memos. It lives in hallway chats, team rituals, and the micro-behaviours of daily work. That's where the customer culture huddle comes in, a small but powerful habit that weaves customer focus into the operating rhythm of your business. These short, intentional sessions turn ordinary moments into cultural accelerators.

What Is a Customer Culture Huddle?

A customer culture huddle is a brief focused team session designed to:

- align teams with customer goals and strategic priorities
- fuel collaboration across silos
- surface real-time insights from the front lines

Think of it as a cultural pulse check: light on time, rich in meaning.

Strategic Disciplines Activated

1. Customer Insight: what are we learning about customer needs, pain points, or surprises?

2. Strategic Alignment: how does our work connect to customer value and company direction?

3. Cross-Functional Collaboration: where are teams working together to deliver better outcomes?

As your culture matures, rotate in other disciplines like Empowerment, Peripheral Vision, or Competitor Insight.

How It Works: Mechanics of a Customer Culture Huddle

- Duration: 5 to 15 minutes
- Frequency: daily or every other day
- Size: 5 to 15 people
- Format: standing circle, optionally around a visual (e.g., whiteboard or KPI chart)

Location doesn't matter (breakroom, hallway, open floor). Consistency matters.

What Is Discussed?

Keep it real, relevant, and brief. Sample questions:

- What customer behaviour surprised us yesterday?

- What's blocking us from great service today?
- Who went above and beyond for a customer and how?

This is not a status meeting or deep-dive. It's about awareness, alignment, and energy.

Pop-Up Huddles

When customer events demand immediate attention, call a spontaneous huddle to:

- share urgent customer insights
- address emerging pain points
- surface issues needing fast escalation

Making Huddles Stick

- Appoint moderators (and deputies): rotate leadership to keep the tone fresh. Deputies ensure huddles still happen even if someone's away
- Defer deep-dives: if an issue arises, note it and schedule time separately. Huddles are for focus, not analysis paralysis
- Use a "customer insight ball": a bright, labelled object passed between speakers keeps things fun and organised. Only the person holding it speaks. Scatter a few around the office for spontaneous use
- Take quick notes: jot down insights, follow-ups, or shoutouts. Keep a digital or physical record to show impact and build momentum

Participation Guidelines

- Everyone in an operating role should contribute
- Leaders listen more than talk, offer support after the session
- Aim for equal voice, not top-down reporting

What NOT to Do

- Don't turn it into a planning or reporting session
- Don't let it drag out, stay within 15 minutes

- Don't allow rambling; use prompts or signals to keep focus
- Don't cancel due to logistics. If there's no room available just stand and talk

Getting Started

Culture champions are the spark that helps the fire spread. Change doesn't just happen it's led. Customer engagement champions help drive adoption by:

- starting the first huddles
- modelling desired behaviours
- mentoring new facilitators

Final Thought

"Fewer meetings. More voices. More energy."

Customer culture huddles are deceptively simple. These small rituals have a big impact. Over time, they:

- shift conversations.
- align teams.
- embed customer obsession into muscle memory.

The companies that win don't just say they're customer-focused, they show it. One huddle at a time.

Exercise 4: Customer Culture Symbols

Making Customer-Centricity Visible and Memorable

Culture Leaves Clues

Culture doesn't live in strategy slides or corporate values posters, it lives in what people see, say, and do every day. It shows up in conversations, behaviours, visuals, and shared rituals.

Exercise 4—continued

Customer culture symbols, also known as artefacts, are the tangible cues that reinforce what truly matters. They act as daily reminders that customer-centricity isn't just a value, it's a practice.

What Is a Customer Culture Symbol?

"Symbols are culture in action. They turn values into daily visibility"

Symbols are the visuals, language, and rituals that reflect and reinforce your customer-focused mindset. These include:

- signage, wall art, or screen savers
- meeting routines and formats
- internal catchphrases and language
- recognition rituals
- dress or team badges
- shared team spaces or zones

They spark reflection, prompt discussion, and reinforce behaviour. When used intentionally, symbols help align teams and activate culture.

Strategic Disciplines Activated

Customer culture symbols support three key outcomes:

1. Strategic Alignment: make customer priorities visible and constant

2. Empowerment: give teams confidence to act in service of customers

3. Collaboration: create shared language and unify cross-functional action

The Simplest and Most Powerful Symbol

The most powerful symbol is a well-placed sign. Host a huddle to co-design signs with your team:

- What message would inspire better customer outcomes?
- Where should we place it to maximise visibility?
- What words or phrases truly resonate?
- How do we make it memorable?

Celebrate your team's creativity with a "Sign-Off Day" to unveil the new signage across shared spaces.

Design tips for effective signage

- Keep it simple: one message, one idea
- Make it relatable: use everyday language your team actually uses
- Link to values: reinforce a core belief (e.g., "Think Customer")
- Place with purpose: use high-traffic areas like break rooms, meeting spaces, log-in screens
- Use visuals or humour: fun, engaging signs spark conversation
- Prompt interaction: "what's one thing we can do better for our customer today?"

Other Symbol Types

Language and jargon are powerful symbols. Create a shared vocabulary:

- "Own the Moment"
- "Walk in Their Shoes"
- "Customer First"

Meeting rituals are another kind of symbolic act:

- start with a customer insight or story
- add a recurring question: "What would the customer think of this?"

Workspace cues create a sense of shared symbolic space:

- display photos, testimonials, journey maps
- designate "customer zones" for planning or brainstorming

Symbolic identity can be created through dress or other cues:

- use pins, lanyards, or stickers with customer slogans
- reward symbolic actions with shoutouts or awards

Embed Symbols into Culture

- Appoint champions: assign team members to spot, suggest, and activate symbols

- Host "symbol showcases": share new ideas across departments
- Rotate regularly: refresh signs and cues monthly or quarterly
- Pair with huddles: use symbols as prompts or backdrops during team gatherings

What to Avoid

- Don't be too complex: long or abstract messages get ignored
- Don't be culturally insensitive: review for tone and relevance
- Don't use outdated symbols: keep them fresh or they become invisible
- Avoid the trap of no follow-through: if symbols aren't backed by behaviour, they lose credibility

Final Thought

Symbols make the invisible visible. They bring your culture to life. They make values shared, habits repeatable, and customer-focus non-negotiable. Done well, symbols remind your people every day: *"This is who we are. This is what matters. This is what we do for customers."* Start small. Stay intentional. Let your culture show.

"What your walls say, your people will believe".

Exercise 5: Changing Roles

Exploring Customer Engagement from Every Angle

Step Into Someone Else's Shoes

True collaboration begins with empathy, and nothing builds empathy faster than seeing a challenge from another seat at the table. This experiential exercise invites participants to temporarily step outside their usual roles and into those of colleagues across the business.

By shifting perspectives, teams uncover blind spots, surface new insights, and strengthen their ability to solve customer-related problems together.

"Seeing the problem through someone else's eyes changes how we understand it and how we solve it."

Purpose

The goal of this exercise is to explore real customer and business challenges through cross-functional lenses, helping participants better understand how different roles perceive and impact customer engagement.

The core benefits are that it:

- builds empathy across teams
- surfaces hidden assumptions and blind spots
- promotes systemic thinking
- strengthens collaborative problem-solving
- reinforces the interconnected nature of the customer journey

The materials needed are:

- printed or written cards with key business functions on each: Sales, Ops, Finance, Support, Marketing, HR, etc
- individual name cards for participants
- flipcharts or whiteboards
- a timer
- a large table or space for a circular seating setup

How to Facilitate

Step 1: Assign Roles

- the facilitator assigns each participant a functional role different from their own
- place each name card and role at a seat around the table to set the scene

Step 2: Present the Challenge

Introduce a real-world customer or business challenge. Examples:

- "Orders are delayed. Customers are frustrated and escalating complaints"
- "Sales have dropped. Morale is low. Customers are disengaging"

Step 3: Open the Dialogue

Ask each participant to speak from their assigned role, guided by:

- a question: "What do I see about this problem that others might not?"
- a discussion: after everyone shares (1–2 mins each), prompt a brief group discussion focused on "How did your assigned role expand or limit how you saw the issue?"

Step 4: Rotate Roles (Optional)

For deeper insight:

- rotate roles and repeat with a new challenge, or
- keep roles and introduce a different scenario

Aim for 2–3 rounds to experience multiple viewpoints.

Step 5: Capture Key Takeaways

- wrap with a lightning round reflection: "In one sentence, what was your biggest insight from today's session?"
- record responses visibly for shared reflection or action planning

Some tips for facilitation include:

- model the process by offering an example: "as the operations lead, I'm concerned about how poor forecasts impact our ability to deliver on time"
- emphasise perspective, not acting by encouraging honest role-based thinking, without dramatics
- keep the pace by using a timer to maintain energy and focus
- debrief with purpose by tying insights back to real work and team dynamics

Final Thought

This exercise isn't just about solving a problem, it's about building a more unified, empathetic, and collaborative culture, where everyone plays a part in delivering better customer outcomes. This exercise can be effectively embedded into the organisation by incorporating it into a regular, scheduled routine.

"When we understand the view from every seat at the table, we become more effective leaders of customer value"

Exercise 6: Customer Immersion

Putting Leaders and Employees in the Shoes of the Customer

If You're Not Listening, You're Losing

As organisations scale, it's easy for leaders to become insulated, surrounded by internal reports, dashboards, and meetings, yet disconnected from the very people they serve. Without regular, intentional connection to customers, insights fade, and assumptions take over. That's why a customer immersion program isn't a luxury, it's a leadership imperative.

This exercise reintroduces decision-makers to the reality of the customer experience through direct exposure, helping transform assumptions into understanding, and strategies into service.

"Customer immersion closes the empathy gap not with reports or dashboards, but with real conversations."

What Is Customer Immersion?

Customer immersion is the structured practice of embedding employees, especially leaders, directly into the customer experience.

This can be done through:

- listening to customer service calls
- shadowing frontline teams
- visiting customers in the field
- observing live product use

The goal is simple: see the world through the customer's eyes.

Why It Matters: Strategic Outcomes

Customer immersion helps leaders:

- gain real-time customer insight: what do customers value, fear, and expect?
- develop customer foresight: what's changing, and how can we anticipate it?
- model the right behaviours: showing that customer focus is everyone's job

"The most powerful message leaders send isn't spoken, it's modelled"

Who Should Be Involved?

Everyone.

- Executives model leadership through proximity to the customer
- Managers discover experience gaps and improvement opportunities
- Support functions (Finance, IT, HR) gain awareness of their downstream impact
- Frontline teams feel heard and validated when leaders step into their world

Immersion Formats: Start Where You Are

Choose formats that fit your business model and rhythm:

Some tactical immersion ideas include:

- shadow a call centre: listen to real-time interactions
- customer listening sessions: invite customers to speak with your team
- customer safari: observe the customer experience in retail or digital environments
- ride-along: join field reps, delivery drivers, or account managers
- "day in the life" interviews: understand how customers use your product
- internal walkthroughs: map internal processes from the lens of internal customers

Building a Sustainable Program

To move from one-offs to operational rhythm, structure matters.

Step 1: Appoint a Program Team

Designate a lead and cross-functional taskforce to:

- define goals and KPIs
- select immersion formats
- track participation
- capture and communicate insights

Step 2: Establish Cadence and Channels

- set clear expectations: for example, "leaders must complete one immersion per quarter"
- prioritise key customer touchpoints

Step 3: Provide Coaching

Many employees aren't trained for customer-facing interactions. Equip them with skills in:

- active listening
- empathetic questioning
- interpreting emotional cues
- responding with clarity and care

Internal Immersion: Redefine "Customer"

Not all customers are external. In a high-functioning business:

- marketing is a customer of sales
- IT supports Operations
- Finance relies on HR

Immersion with internal stakeholders helps eliminate silos, foster empathy, and improve service across teams.

"A customer-centric company is also a collaboration-centric company"

Sharing the Experience

Don't let immersion insights disappear into silence. Build them into your communication rhythm:

- share takeaways in huddles or retrospectives
- record short videos or summaries
- highlight wins and improvement ideas
- encourage storytelling across departments

Customer Immersion Implementation Checklist

- Appoint a program champion
- Define scope, cadence, and formats
- Train participants on interaction best practices
- Schedule and track participation
- Collect and socialise insights
- Recognise and reward standout contributions

Final Thought

Customer immersion is not a box to check. It's a mindset, a commitment to stay grounded in what matters most. Nothing beats seeing it for yourself. "You can't serve who you don't understand.

Exercise 6—continued

And you can't understand from a distance."

The companies that thrive tomorrow are already listening today. Build the habit. Close the gap. Walk in their shoes.

When this playbook of activities and practices become business habits inside your organisation you will ignite engagement with customers and between leaders and employees. This creates consistency in service delivery and customer value that your customers and community experience. It embeds alignment across the entire business. The result? Loyalty and sustainable growth.

In the next chapter you will find the stories of people and organisations that MarketCulture has partnered with for the past 10 years. Sharing these stories provides insights that can help you on your culture change journey.

Key Takeaways—Chapter 8

1. Leadership Must Model Customer-Centric Habits Daily

Customer-centricity is not a one-off initiative; it must be part of the leadership's daily rhythm. Leaders need to consistently ask customer-focused questions, engage in direct customer experiences, listen deeply, and actively involve employees in customer conversations. Leaders must stay connected to what it's actually like to be the customer today.

2. Simple, Repeatable Activities Build Customer Culture

Embedding customer culture requires small, consistent, everyday practices. The chapter introduces practical tools like customer engagement meetings, customer culture huddles, storytelling, role-switching exercises, customer immersion programs, and visual symbols that make customer focus visible and habitual. These tools are designed to create lasting behavioural change without disrupting operations.

3. Customer-Centric Organisations Create Muscle Memory

When leaders and teams regularly practise customer-focused routines by discussing customer stories, sharing direct customer insights, and immersing themselves in the customer experience it builds "customer muscle memory". This intuitive, automatic connection to customers drives alignment, faster decision-making, and sustained cultural transformation.

The Bottom Line

Real, lasting customer culture is built through daily leadership habits, small but powerful rituals, and consistent, shared practices across the organisation. It's not about more work'; it's about embedding the customer into the natural rhythm of how teams think, meet, and act every day. Organisations that succeed in this will develop a leadership-driven, customer-centric culture that fuels loyalty and long-term growth.

**Scan or click to listen
to our Podcasts**

CHAPTER 9

BUILDING A GLOBAL NETWORK OF CERTIFIED EXPERTS

Igniting a Worldwide Force for Customer-Centric Change

The MarketCulture Academy is our educational initiative designed to equip individuals, teams, and organisations with the expertise needed to foster a truly customer-centric culture. Through a range of online training, in-person workshops, and certification programs, the Academy empowers practitioners and professionals with the tools, frameworks, and insights to embed customer-first thinking within their own organisations or those they support.

On our global journey, we've had the privilege of collaborating with and learning from exceptional professionals in customer experience (CX), experience management (XM), coaching, and consultancy.

This chapter shines a spotlight on an extraordinary network of leaders and innovators who are transforming organisations through a shared belief in the power of culture, connection, and customer-centricity.

We begin with Shep Hyken, whose journey from teenage magician to global service expert proves that small acts like a thank-you note can spark an "Amazement Revolution." Diane Magers, former CEO of CXPA, blends psychology with practical leadership, using the MRI as a conversation starter that reveals the true heart of organisations. Ian Golding, a self-described "reluctant expert," champions authenticity over short-term gains, teaching thousands worldwide to believe in the principles of customer-first leadership.

From the tech world, Vivek Bhaskaran, founder of QuestionPro, has built a \$35M global business on authenticity, financial discipline, and the integration of the MRI into company culture. Annette Franz, author and CX thought leader, has spent decades connecting the employee experience to customer outcomes, using the MRI as a reality check for leaders. Alejandro Ceron shifted from HR to customer-centric consultancy, leveraging the MRI to turn employee insights into executive action.

Partners in passion and purpose, Rebecca Holliday and Leonie Williams founded Customer Service Solutions, blending emotional culture work with customer-focused strategies. Don Peppers, the visionary strategist advocating for share of customer over share of wallet, rooted in trust and ethics. Olga Guseva, an international CX leader, turns loyalty into leadership, making culture measurable and actionable through the MRI. Mark Hamill, co-founder of ARCET Global, elevates the role of recognition, using the MRI to validate strategy and drive collaboration at organisations like Deutsche Telekom. As a leadership coach, Tara Kimbrell Cole proves that sustainable growth comes when leaders use the MRI to connect human engagement with business performance.

In Brazil, Bruno Guimarães sparked a CX revolution with the creation of Amigos do CX and the country's largest independent CX summit, now expanding the MRI's reach through localisation. Tom DeWitt built the US's first Customer Experience Management master's degree and the XM Global Collaborative, embedding the MRI into education from day one. Finally, Stefan Osthaus, founder of the Customer Institute, certified the MRI as a gold standard, advocating for mindset as the key to sustainable CX success.

Together, these voices form a powerful global community, united by the belief that culture isn't a side project. It's the foundation for sustainable growth, meaningful connection, and lasting customer loyalty.

This chapter showcases the incredible support network available to help organisations on their path to customer and human-centric excellence and growth. We have certified these professionals along with many others in the MRI methodology, enabling them to guide their clients in building stronger customer-focused capabilities. Here, we highlight the stories of pioneers whose convictions remained steadfast, even in the face of challenges and change. We also celebrate the power of community where like-minded individuals come together through associations to seek support, share experiences, and grow together. Being human also means celebrating wins and we include a story about an awards program that spotlights and honours those making a real impact.

The following guide provides an overview of the stories featured below.

- From Thank You Notes to an Amazement Revolution: The **Shep Hyken** Story

- From Insight to Impact: **Diane Magers** on CXPA, Culture, and the Power of the MRI

- A Reluctant Expert with Relentless Belief: **Ian Golding**

- The Relentless Builder of Human-Centered Tech: **Vivek Bhaskaran**

- From Farm Girl to CX Trailblazer: **Annette Franz's** Journey to Customer and Employee Understanding

- From HR to CX: How **Alejandro Ceron** Found a Better Way to Drive Change

- From Passion to Purpose: How **Rebecca Holliday** and **Leonie Williams** Built a Movement for Customer Experience

- Making the World Safe for Customers—**Don Peppers**: The Leader's True North

- Falling in Love with Customers: How **Olga Guseva** Turned Loyalty into Leadership

- Building a Business on Belief: How **Mark Hamill** Made Recognition Matter

- Where Leadership Meets Humanity: **Tara Kimbrell Cole's** Journey with the MRI

- From Coffee to Community: How **Bruno Guimarães** Sparked Brazil's CX Revolution

- From Classroom to Global Stage: How **Tom DeWitt** Built a Customer Experience Movement

- Customer-Centricity Without Borders: **Stefan Osthaus** on Building a Global CX Community

From Thank You Notes to an Amazement Revolution
The Shep Hyken Story

When it comes to customer experience, few names are as well-known as Shep Hyken. Behind the bestselling books, packed speaking tours, and Forbes columns is something more lasting: a clear and simple mission to help people deliver amazing service.

His story didn't begin on a big stage. It started with a magic show. As a teenager performing magic tricks for small audiences, Shep's parents gave him advice that stuck: thank people, ask for feedback, learn from it, and improve. His father added one more idea that would shape Shep's career: write a thank-you note.

"I learned about how feedback and process lead to continuous improvement. That's not what we called it back then ... but really that's what it's about, isn't it?"

Those small acts became the roots of a global philosophy on customer service, culture, and trust. Shep learned early that listening, improving, and showing genuine care are what really set businesses apart.

This mindset guided him everywhere, even at a self-serve gas station on a freezing day. Seeing an elderly woman step out to pump her own gas, he told her to wait in the car and did it for her. His manager was furious: "Now she'll expect it every time". Shep's reply summed up his thinking: "Maybe she'll come here every time instead of the station across the street". For him, people always came before rigid rules.

Over the years, Shep built a thriving career as a speaker and advisor. Along the way, mentors like restauranteurs John Ferrara and Kim Tucci encouraged him to pass on what he had learned. Their message was clear: *those who are helped should help others in return.* That lesson defined Shep's approach. Success is about lifting others up.

When 9/11 happened in 2001, the speaking industry came to an abrupt halt. One more attack and companies would hesitate to fly teams to conferences at hotels, fearing for their people's safety. Since keynote speakers are mainly hired for these large hotel events, Shep pivoted quickly. He built a training business instead, bringing in experts to deliver in-depth programs directly at clients' sites. Later, he expanded into virtual learning so more people could access his message from anywhere. He even launched group forums where people could connect and interact with him directly. His core message remained clear: "customer service isn't just a department, it's a culture that should flow through the entire organisation".

To help companies build a customer centric culture, he created a clear six-step framework, the "6 Ds".

1. **Define it:** Create a clear message everyone remembers

2. **Disseminate it:** Repeat it often so it becomes part of daily work

3. **Deploy it:** Train people to live it every day

4. **Demonstrate it:** Leaders must set the example

5. **Defend it**: Address problems when they appear

6. **Delight in it:** Celebrate successes to build momentum

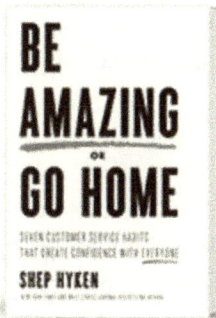

BE AMAZING OR GO HOME

SEVEN CUSTOMER SERVICE HABITS THAT CREATE CONFIDENCE WITH EVERYONE

SHEP HYKEN

Shep practices what he preaches. Once, when an assistant kept showing up late for work, he reminded her of their mantra, "Always be amazing". He told her simply: "Be amazing or go home". That idea later became the title of a bestselling book and a standard for teams that follow his work.

"What's happening on the inside is going to be felt on the outside.

I always start with the end in mind ... what do we want the customer experience to be?"

For Shep, culture is not a slogan. It must be real, alive, and modelled by leaders every day. He recalls Walt Disney's memorable mantra: "Stooping to Excellence" that described Walt's habit at Disneyland where he used to walk around the property and stoop down to pick up stray paper off the ground. That's leading by example.

Without that, culture fails. That's why he immediately saw value in the MRI. "You need tangible data", Shep said. "Benchmark pre-MRI and post-MRI. That's what makes it real."

Shep calls the MRI "an engagement engine". By measuring what matters, companies can turn values into action, align teams, and make customer experience part of daily work.

"Anything you can do to measure success is extremely important"

His belief is simple: when leaders model great behaviour, employees feel supported, and culture becomes clear and measurable; that's when businesses thrive.

Today, Shep is seen worldwide as an expert in customer service and experience. But for him, success isn't about fame, it's about impact. Inspired by the poem, *The Dash*, he believes what matters most is what happens in the space between birth and death, the "dash" that represents a life's impact.

"I really hope that 'my dash' when people look back, they say, You know what, he did a lot of good things"

He calls it living with *intentional significance*. That's why he uses his platform to give back, from speaking in exchange for charity donations to building homes with his kids in Tijuana, Mexico.

"Be Amazing"

His mission is to create an "Amazement Revolution", helping companies and people deliver amazing service, not just once, but always. It all began with a simple thank-you note, proving a timeless truth: when people are taken care of, everything else falls into place.

From Insight to Impact
Diane Magers on CXPA, Culture, and the Power of the MRI

For Diane Magers, transforming organisations through customer experience has been deeply personal and profoundly impactful. A clinical psychologist by training, Diane's early fascination with human behaviour and needs naturally led her toward a career focused on improving human experiences, not just in life but in business.

"At the heart of it all is understanding the human experience because customers choose to spend money and engage with your business based on how you make them feel. And those feelings directly influence their behaviour and that impacts a brands financial impact."

Her work reached new heights through her involvement with the Customer Experience Professionals Association (CXPA). As CEO, Diane guided the association through significant transformations, helping it evolve from a small community to a globally recognised hub for customer experience professionals. Under her leadership, CXPA focused on creating "the how" of customer experience.

"The community is about connection and has yielded truly deep friendships. Whenever I have a challenge or I can't figure something out, I connect with someone in the CXPA community."

CXPA
Customer Experience Professionals Association™

One of the most influential tools Diane encountered on her journey was the MRI. She describes it as "a very functional, tactical way for people to put words to things they didn't really understand". More than a benchmark or diagnostic, Diane sees the MRI as a conversation starter opening dialogue between leadership and employees about what really needs to change within their organisations.

For Diane, the MRI isn't just about metrics; it's about revealing the heart of an organisation.

"What I believe the MRI does is to allow us to start to understand how people view and experience where they are, what we're wanting them to do, and how that compares to the what the organisation desires to be?"

Perhaps most importantly, Diane sees that the MRI helps leaders recognise the needs of their people, and what they want from leadership, from the culture, and from the business itself.

"I believe that these are things that people often talk about as softer skills ... but I can tell you any organisation I've worked with it's not. It harks back to my psychology days where understanding where humans are coming from, what they want to achieve, and what feels good to them, is an important thing to know because you get a lot more connection to people by understanding them."

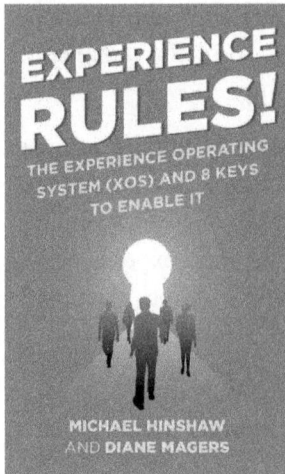

"I believe that the MarketCulture Academy provides a lot more depth for people who don't really understand culture ... more of this emotional intelligence that people need today ... I think that's part of a culture that reflects: what does your organisation really stand for?"

Today, through Amplify XM, her mentoring and coaching and her book, The Experience Operating System, Diane continues to champion the integration of the MRI into broader, more holistic approaches to business. Amplify XM is about helping organisations operationalise experience management and culture, making sure that employee experience, partner collaboration, and customer understanding are all connected. She believes that without truly understanding where you are, culturally and strategically, you can't effectively move forward.

As Diane says, "You're not just selling products and services; you're helping people live and love their best life". The MRI, CXPA, Amplify XM, and Diane's continued leadership all reflect the philosophy of putting people first, every step of the way.

A Reluctant Expert with Relentless Belief
Ian Golding

Ian Golding's journey into customer experience wasn't a carefully planned career move, it was a calling born from instinct, courage, and, at times, painful personal lessons. Starting his career in financial services, Ian was quickly recognised for his capability and was headhunted by GE. It was there, in his very first week, that he encountered the term *customer centricity*. He didn't just learn the concept, he *felt* it. Doing the right thing for customers was, as Ian says, simply "natural" for him.

"You've got to believe in what you're saying. You've got to believe in what you're trying to do. You'll get things wrong, and I got lots of things wrong. But actually, it's your belief in the principle, the theory, the methodology that will bring people with you."

GE wasn't just a job; it was a transformation. Immersed in Six Sigma methodologies, Ian found himself teaching German actuaries about process improvement at just 25 years old. He admits his knowledge of statistics was terrible, but his belief in improving the customer's experience was unwavering. That belief, not technical prowess, is what won over sceptical statisticians.

"I was petrified because I didn't think I knew the methodology well enough ... I had to get them to believe that this methodology was the right thing to do ... that's what's turned me into the person that I am today".

Ian's career, however, wasn't smooth sailing. After leaving GE, he took a role in a company that promised customer focus but handed him a million-pound cost-cutting target on his second day. He resigned on the third. That moment crystallised his personal and professional ethos: *never compromise customer focus for short-term gains*. He was even told by a superior that he was "the most emotionally immature person" they had met. This feedback stung deeply, but later shaped Ian's resilience.

"If you want me to come in and cut costs, I'm not interested. That's not what I do. I will save you money by doing the right thing."

Later, as the first-ever Group Head of Customer Experience at a UK online retailer, Ian built his own customer experience framework from scratch. Over seven years, he led a transformation, pushing against scepticism and institutional inertia. Despite never being promoted, Ian knew he was creating meaningful change.

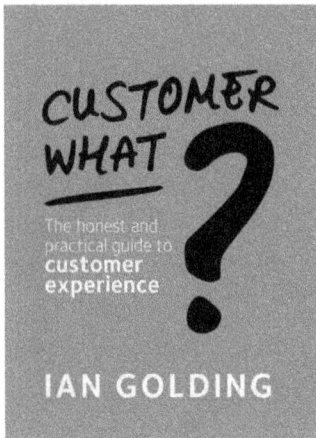

After leaving corporate life, Ian ventured out on his own, initially uncertain about his future. What followed was an organic rise to global recognition, not through marketing, but through sharing his ideas. He began writing a blog that reached thousands across the world and later authored his 2018 book, *Customer What?*, solidifying his reputation as a thought leader in CX. Remarkably, Ian built a consultancy not by aggressive selling, but by becoming a trusted voice, so much so that work consistently came to him.

Ian has now delivered his CX Masterclass in over 60 countries to more than 50,000 people. Yet, despite global recognition, Ian has remained humble. He openly talks about the financial sacrifices he's made by prioritising authenticity over commercialisation. His family jokes that his work is "boring", but his impact speaks otherwise, mentoring a new generation of customer-centric leaders.

Ian recalls how he was introduced to the MRI:

"From the minute you described to me what you do at MarketCulture, I integrated the MRI into my teaching, and it's still there to this day. So, everyone that attends my CCXP workshop will be introduced to the MRI ... I've been sharing that for, well, it's got to be 10 years at least."

What drives Ian isn't fame or fortune, it's helping others build businesses that genuinely put people first. His advice today echoes the ethos that's shaped his entire journey: believe deeply in what you're doing, stay humble, and never compromise the integrity of putting customers at the centre of everything.

The Relentless Builder of Human-Centered Tech
Vivek Bhaskaran

Vivek Bhaskaran didn't set out to build a software company. In fact, his leap into entrepreneurship came out of necessity. When the dot. com bubble burst, he found himself unemployed in Seattle, burnt out from tech consulting, and without a clear path forward. What he did have was a half-built survey tool "QuestionPro", the remnants of a fractured collaboration with a college professor. Rather than retreat, Vivek took a gamble. He quit his job, kept it quiet, and told his wife only when she picked him up from the bus stop.

"I've got six months of cash in the bank. Let's see if I can make it."

That was 20 years ago. Today, Vivek leads a company with over $35 million in revenue, operating in more than a dozen global markets. But success didn't come in a straight line. Vivek candidly talks about hitting revenue plateaus, first at $3 million, then at $10 million, and now hovering around $35 million. What unlocked growth each time? Mergers, acquisitions, partners, and, most importantly, a willingness to think differently and take calculated risks.

Vivek's leadership style is unapologetically raw and deeply human. He believes in the power of authenticity and isn't afraid to take bets on products, strategies, or people.

"If I can take a bet on myself ... I can take a bet on someone else".

QuestionPro

He's appointed team members into leadership roles well before they had traditional qualifications because he considers belief and accountability to be the foundation of growth.

One of the cornerstones of Vivek's approach is financial discipline. From day one, he refused to build a business that didn't generate profit. "We're literally funded by our customers", he says.

"I don't have a sugar daddy writing cheques. Your salary is coming from the customer, period."

This customer-first ethos is not just talk. QuestionPro implemented the MRI within its own ranks, before offering it to current and future customers, not only to measure customer centricity but to signal its importance across the entire organisation.

"The moment we started measuring it … everyone understood it matters".

The MRI didn't just provide data, it became a cultural declaration. Employees stopped punting customer issues. Customer-centricity became everyone's job.

It was this same clarity and pragmatism that drew Vivek to collaborate with MarketCulture.

"You guys are authentic … And you had something practical. A tool not a theoretical PowerPoint."

The infinity symbol he has shared, a loop connecting employee experience and customer experience, captures the relationship perfectly. Vivek calls the QuestionPro logo the missing link, precisely where the MRI is meant to belong.

"If you want to understand CX, start with EX … The MRI is a practical way to get the employee's view of customer experience. That's rare."

Today, Vivek is a fixture at XDay, QuestionPro's global series of events connecting customers, partners, and team members. He shows up in person, not for marketing ROI, but because he thrives on connection.

"We humanise our brand through these events. People see me, and they see our company. They know we're real."

In a world where leaders often get lost in boardrooms and spreadsheets, Vivek leads from the field, meeting customers, listening to feedback, and admitting when something can't be fixed right away. He jokes:

"I wrote some of this code … so if it doesn't work, the buck stops with me".

What makes Vivek's story remarkable isn't just the business he built, it's the philosophy he lives by: bet on people, stay close to your customers, measure what matters, and always keep it human.

The MRI is now available to all current and future QuestionPro customers.

From Farm Girl to CX Trailblazer
Annette Franz's Journey to Customer and Employee Understanding

Annette Franz never planned to become one of the leading voices on customer and employee experience. She began on a farm in Ohio, dreaming of becoming a veterinarian until she met her "kryptonite": six quarters of chemistry. A pivot to business management and a single newspaper ad for JD Power & Associates rerouted her path entirely and planted her in the world of market research and customer focus.

"I didn't plan this career, I just kept asking the question nobody wanted to answer"

At JD Power, Annette discovered something that would shape her entire career: the undeniable link between business success and truly listening. Back then, the language of "customer experience" was still evolving. Loyalty and satisfaction were the measures of the day, but Annette asked a question that was radical in its simplicity: "What about the employees?"

For decades since, Annette has kept asking that question. She's carried it from the research floors of Mattel and Fidelity to start-ups in Orange County, to consulting rooms and conference stages. At every turn, she found the same truth: leaders often said they would "listen to employees later". Decades later, they're still saying it. And yet, they wonder why transformation stalls.

"If you don't listen to your employees, don't expect them to deliver the experience you promise your customers".

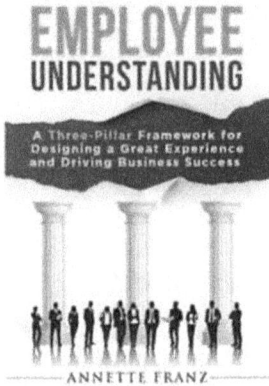

Through her books *Customer Understanding, Built to Win*, and *Employee Understanding*, Annette has turned her hard-earned insights into guidebooks that don't gather dust. They sit open on desks, dog-eared, underlined daily reminders that culture is not fluff and listening is not a luxury.

"Leaders love ROI, but they forget where it comes from: people. You can't just buy a tool or a platform and call it culture. You must live it. If leaders don't own culture, nobody will, and the customer will feel it first."

When Annette encountered the MRI, she recognised its power instantly. For her, the MRI is more than a diagnostic tool, it's an X-ray of an organisation's heartbeat. It measures what many leaders still ignore: how the organisation really works from the inside out. It forces an honest look at whether an enterprise's culture and processes can support the experiences they promise their customers.

"The MRI is the reality check leaders didn't know they needed until they see what it reveals. You can't fix what you won't measure … the MRI makes the invisible, visible. Most companies would be shocked if they really knew where they stand the MRI makes sure they do."

In Annette's words, the MRI helps leaders see "where they stand". Often, it's not where they think they are. And while some leaders resist the reality it reveals, Annette has seen the opposite too: leaders clutching her books, sharing them with CEOs, desperate for a way to break through the static that keeps organisations stuck in old habits.

What frustrates her and drives her in equal measure is how slowly these realisations spread. Despite digital transformations, AI promises, and new tech every quarter, the basics stay the same. Without a culture that values listening, all the tools in the world are "lipstick on a pig", as Annette says, unafraid of plain language.

"Listening is the simplest thing leaders forget to do and the first thing they should. You can't transform your customer experience until you transform your culture. Great experiences don't come from the front line alone, they come from every part of your business that nobody sees."

Annette's journey is a reminder that it's not enough to measure; you have to care about what you see. The MRI provides the measurement, but Annette Franz shows leaders how to use what they learn. Her message is simple, but relentless. Listen. Learn. Lead. Succeed.

And if your culture is broken? Fix it or forget about the rest. Because until leaders embrace the idea that employees are the real architects of every customer experience, even the best MRI score is just the beginning of a conversation that must never end.

From HR to CX
How Alejandro Ceron Found a Better Way to Drive Change

Alejandro Ceron has been immersed in the HR world for years, working in very senior roles in the insurance industry. But Alejandro was frustrated by the difficulty of creating meaningful change within organisations. With a passion for people and leadership, he wanted to make a real difference. Setting up an HR consultancy business seemed like the answer, but he soon discovered that he wasn't taking an easy path. Many businesses didn't believe they needed HR help, or they assumed they were already doing it right. Alejandro knew better, but he also knew he needed to take a different approach. He had seen firsthand how organisations struggled to truly connect their internal culture with the needs of their customers.

Everything changed for Alejandro when he attended an international HR conference in Washington. There, he met Scott Hamilton, a long-time partner of MarketCulture, who introduced him to a framework that immediately resonated with him. It wasn't just theory. It was practical, actionable, and rooted in connecting culture with customer experience.

Soon after, Alejandro enrolled in a course with MarketCulture and travelled to Dallas, Texas, for further training. He was eager to explore how this new approach could work in real businesses.

"What really opened my eyes was the slide that has the five blocks from discover to fortify. That was an eye-opener for me."

For Alejandro, this simple yet profound concept was a revelation. Finally, here was a system that explained with clarity the messy dynamics he had dealt with throughout his entire career.

At first, Alejandro used the framework to introduce deeper organisational change, using the language business leaders actually cared about—customers and revenue. But over time he discovered that everything in customer experience traced back to people. Lack of insight, poor planning, misaligned operations—it was always about people.

"The MRI is a tailor-made approach of what your people are telling you"

Strategic Partnership & Execution

CONSULTANTS

Alejandro refined his approach. Rather than positioning himself solely as an HR expert, he stepped fully into the role of a customer-centric business consultant. He began speaking directly to CEOs, shifting away from HR departments, who often didn't fully grasp the strategic importance of connecting culture to customer outcomes. CEOs, by contrast, understood when Alejandro showed them how operations weren't aligning with customer needs.

"We talked about competitors, but we never do anything about it. We just talk about it."

He concentrated on the insurance and reinsurance industries, where his expertise quickly gained traction. Insurance firms were notorious for operating in silos, with fragmented accountability and weak follow-through on customer needs. Alejandro introduced them to the MRI, blending internal cultural feedback with customer-facing metrics. The results were powerful. Leaders began to see clearly how their internal behaviours were holding back customer outcomes.

One breakthrough moment came when Alejandro connected the concept of *empowerment* directly to customer responsibility. Traditionally, empowerment was seen as an internal leadership trait, but Alejandro framed it as: "How are you empowering your people to make decisions that benefit your customers?" That shift in perspective helped his clients see why empowerment wasn't just an HR buzzword, it was a business imperative.

"Catch and release can be the culture of the insurance industry. They catch the client, then forget about it. No one takes ownership of the whole journey."

He discovered that many insurance companies had no single person responsible for the entire customer journey. He began helping leadership teams map out roles and responsibilities from the client's point of view, moving from fragmented, reactive systems to coherent, accountable operations.

What helped him the most was that the MRI provided not only benchmark data but, more importantly, open-ended comments to provide real insights. The comments, unedited and raw, revealed more than any graph could. Employees voiced confusion about roles, frustration with broken systems, and, most importantly, ideas for solutions. Alejandro worked closely with leadership teams to interpret these insights, helping them design change programs tailored to their reality, not just off-the-shelf solutions.

"I don't need to defend this. They said it. These are their words."

In the process, Alejandro didn't just become a consultant; he became a trusted advisor, a guide helping leaders face the uncomfortable truths about their businesses. He uses a metaphor of moving a herd of buffalo one by one. Change didn't happen by pushing from behind but by engaging each leader individually, building understanding and commitment.

By combining customer-centric strategies with business acumen, Alejandro has carved out a unique position for himself: not as an HR consultant, but as a customer-centric business leader who understands both the human and operational dynamics of change.

"You don't need a program, you need to read what people are telling you and do something about it."

For Alejandro, the real success isn't just in delivering reports or running workshops, it's in watching CEOs have their "aha!" moments, finally seeing how improving culture and customer alignment could transform their businesses.

The journey isn't over. But now Alejandro knows he has the right tools, the right message, and the right connections to make a genuine difference.

From Passion to Purpose
How Rebecca Holliday and Leonie Williams Built a Movement for Customer Experience

Rebecca Holliday and Leonie Williams had long shared a passion for exceptional customer service. Before starting their own venture, they both worked at the Institute of Customer Service, a UK-based non-profit dedicated to advancing customer experience across industries, from small businesses to influencing policy at the highest levels. There they worked with major organisations, driving meaningful change and advocating for customers.

"Call me brave, call me stupid, I just needed to quit."

But when the world shut down during COVID, everything shifted. The pressure of balancing family life and a demanding career became overwhelming. Without a detailed plan, Leonie made a bold move— she resigned. Rebecca, too, was at a crossroads in her career, feeling unchallenged and ready for something new.

"We were never going to be the consultants that would go into an organisation and work there for as long as possible. We wanted short, sharp bursts to teach people so they could do it themselves."

Customer Service SOLUTIONS

Their journeys converged at the perfect time, and together they took a leap of faith, launching Customer Service Solutions. They weren't entirely sure what it would become, but they knew their values: bring value to clients, create sustainable results, and empower organisations rather than embed themselves indefinitely.

From day one, it was about agility. With no big teams behind them, they wore every hat—finance, marketing, delivery and learned everything on the fly. Their early success came from the trust they had already earned in their professional networks. Large companies were willing to take a chance on them, largely because of their reputations and relationships.

Mistakes were made along the way, as with any new venture, but each misstep became a learning opportunity. Four years in, they have a strong client base, a wealth of experience, and clarity about who they are as a business.

"Culture is a really massive part of what we do. It always has been central to everything we've ever communicated on."

A foundational pillar of their work is culture. Right from the outset, they knew that customer experience couldn't be addressed in isolation. It requires a holistic approach, starting with how employees feel at work. Through emotional culture workshops, they help organisations explore how teams currently feel, how they want to feel, and what rituals or habits can support that journey.

One of their key innovations is partnering with riders&elephants to bring emotional culture to life, combining it with their customer-centric programs from MarketCulture. They realised that before companies could create better customer outcomes, they first needed to foster environments where employees thrived emotionally and professionally.

"What's really positive is that one of our largest clients wanted to do the MRI again. They've seen value in it."

Their approach isn't just theory, it's practical. In one case, they worked with a global logistics company struggling to bridge the gap between customer expectations and internal employee experience. Using tools like the MRI they were able to reveal hidden frustrations within teams and align employee engagement with customer satisfaction efforts. The process wasn't always easy. Organisational bureaucracy, conflicting priorities, and limited resources often slowed progress, but where leadership engaged fully, results followed.

"It's really about getting to the employee first, and the MRI is really good at getting under the skin with the verbatim comments"

For smaller businesses, different challenges emerged. Often, it wasn't bureaucracy that held them back but a sheer lack of resources. They wanted to improve but simply didn't have enough people to run initiatives. The sweet spot for us, Leonie observes, is mid-sized businesses big enough to have resources, small enough to stay agile.

"Culture is your flame. Your employees are the wood. If you don't keep fuelling it, the fire dies out."

Through it all, Leonie remains driven by one key belief: customer experience starts with culture. Without the right communication, care, and attention, that fire will burn out. But with the right ingredients that include leadership commitment, emotional intelligence, and sustainable practices it can burn brightly. It fuels businesses to deliver not just better customer outcomes, but also better workplaces.

Customer Service Solutions isn't just a business. It's a movement.

Making the World Safe for Customers—Don Peppers
The Leader's True North

Don Peppers' commitment to customer focus was evident early in life. As he recalls, he was always entrepreneurial, running a paper route for eight years from fourth grade through high school and knocking on doors to sell Christmas cards each summer.

"I was ambitious. I couldn't wait to be an adult."

Although Don earned an engineering degree and a graduate degree in Public Affairs, he never followed a traditional path. Instead, he stepped into roles that deepened his understanding of what truly drives business: customers. He started as an economist at an oil company, then moved on to become VP of Marketing at an airline. These experiences shaped his conviction that long-term success hinges on putting the customer first.

Together with Martha Rogers, he co-founded the Peppers & Rogers Group, the first consultancy to champion the relationship power of one-to-one marketing. Long before "customer-centricity" became a buzzword, they made the case that sustainable advantage comes not from obsessing over products, but from building deep, lasting customer relationships.

Two Paths to Growth

Don distills the shift with a simple visual: imagine a two-dimensional graph, with customers reached on the horizontal access, and customer needs addressed going up the vertical. Most product-focused companies think horizontally; they develop a product or service and then try to sell it to as many people as possible. The goal? Market share.

But there's another path: think vertically. Focus on one customer at a time, aiming to meet more and more of that customer's needs, not just across different products and services, but over time. Here, the goal is *share of customer*. As Don explains, he prefers this term over *share of wallet:*

"I don't think of the customer as a wallet with a brain. I see them as a person with a life."

Every leader must choose chase a bigger slice of the existing pie or earn the trust to be invited to the table for every meal that customer ever has. The latter demands a business built on empathy and true customer culture.

The Blueprint for a Human Culture

If Don Peppers defines the destination, the MRI provides the map. The behavioural disciplines turn his ideas into clear, measurable actions helping companies move from winning transactions to earning lasting loyalty.

Don's stories they bring the MRI framework to life.

Seeing the World Differently

- **Customer Insight and Foresight:** This is the heart of Don's philosophy. His entire career was sparked by a moment of foresight. As a new-business executive at an ad agency, his job consisted of trying to get in touch with potential clients and then maintaining relationships with them over time. He spent his mornings making "cold calls" to potential contacts, and when he was successful he would make notes of their conversations so that he could refer to these notes in later calls – "So, Jim, how did that product launch go, in the Southwest, were the results good?" Asked to give a speech in 1989 on the impact of interactivity, Don says he tried to imagine a future where a child could talk back to a TV character like Tony the Tiger. What would the advertiser do with whatever the child said? Well, nothing, that's what. Because to a mass marketer, data from an individual customer is useless, unless it accurately represents a market, or a market segment. "But that's exactly what I was doing," he realized. "I was trying to get potential customers to talk back to me. Why? So I could set up individual relationships with them, one customer at a time." He had the foresight to see that technology would enable relationships at scale, and the insight to know that relationships, not transactions, were the future.

- **Peripheral Vision:** Again, this is the ability to see threats and opportunities beyond the immediate horizon. Don tells a self-deprecating story that serves as an example of its importance. Sent by his boss at Texas International Airlines to a conference about American Airlines' new Sabre reservation system, he returned with a stunningly wrong conclusion. "Frank," he said, "American Airlines, they don't know what business they're in. They think they're in the computer business." Of course, Sabre became worth more than the airline itself. It was a failure of peripheral vision—an inability to see how a seemingly adjacent technology, or even a completely unrelated one, could redefine an entire industry.

A company can have all the external vision in the world, but it will fail if its internal culture isn't built to act on it.

- Are your employees trusted to do the right thing for the customer? Don highlights a great example from the Commonwealth Bank of Australia (CBA). If a call centre agent faces a customer problem for which the computer shows no scripted solution, they don't always need to escalate to a manager. If the agent thinks they know a way to solve the customer's problem, they only need to get the agreement of one other agent before offering this solution directly to the customer. This simple rule is transformative. It tells employees, "We trust your judgment." It is empowerment in its purest form.

- The leader's primary role is to build strategic alignment: to unite the organisation around a common, customer-oriented purpose. Don points to Jeff Bezos at Amazon as the benchmark. By aligning his interests as the primary shareholder with the long-term goal of earning each customer's trust, Bezos resisted Wall Street's demands for short-term profits for years. He aligned the entire organisation by focusing on this single, unwavering mission.

When Culture Breaks: A Cautionary Tale

What happens when the right behaviours clash with the wrong incentives? Don Peppers points to the Wells Fargo scandal as a stark lesson. Former CEO John Stumpf was widely regarded as customer-focused, and on paper the bank's strategy promised exactly that. But behind the scenes, aggressive sales targets and flawed reward systems pressured employees to cheat customers to meet quotas.

The result? A complete breakdown of trust and a cultural collapse that no amount of strategic alignment could fix. It's a clear warning: when internal systems contradict your stated values, the culture and the customer always pay the price.

The Leader's True North

Don Peppers is clear: shaping a truly customer-focused culture starts at the top. It's the leader's job and it demands a rare mix of traits.

First, a leader must inspire. As Don puts it, "You can't code empathy into a business process." True customer culture begins when leaders rally people around a clear purpose, what Simon Sinek calls the Why.

Second, it takes courage to redefine success. Instead of chasing only this quarter's numbers, a customer-centric leader looks at the long game, tracking changes in customer lifetime value. As Don and Martha Rogers wrote in Return on Customer, "every good experience today creates real economic value tomorrow".

Third, it calls for an unshakable ethical core. Don credits one of his first bosses, Jack Sunderland, with three simple rules for success in a business career: make money, have fun, and be ethical. That last one means doing the right thing even when no one's watching, and it's the bedrock of lasting trust.

When asked about his own legacy, Don doesn't mention bestsellers or keynote stages. What he wants is simple: "He spent his life making the world safe for customers".

For any leader trying to navigate today's market, there is no better True North. It's a mission that demands real-world insight, a resilient culture, and the discipline to act on both. It's the shift from pushing products to genuinely serving people and Don believes it's the only journey worth taking.

Falling in Love with Customers
How Olga Guseva Turned Loyalty into Leadership

After graduating from the University of Economics and Finance, Olga Guseva's career began in an unexpected place: a computer systems integration company. Yet her ambition quickly took her abroad. After completing her MBA in the United States, Olga returned home ready to take on more.

British Airways was her next step, a role that would define the course of her career. Starting as a local coordinator, she rose through the ranks to become Marketing Manager, overseeing nine European countries and supporting loyalty programs across eighteen.

"Loyalty is not just about cards. It's about understanding the customer and meeting their needs."

A pivotal moment came during a team meeting in Zurich. It was Valentine's Day, and the theme was clear: love your customer. More than a gimmick, it planted a seed that would change everything for Olga. For the first time, she understood that customer loyalty wasn't just about rewards or points, it was about understanding people deeply. It was about genuine curiosity, care, and emotional connection.

That realisation sparked her passion for customer experience when she truly understood that loyalty isn't just a program, it's an emotional relationship. Even as a marketing professional, juggling campaigns and media plans, she could see that intimacy with the customer is the missing ingredient in many corporate strategies.

"In order to do your job properly ... you need to be in love with your customer".

integria

Soon, Olga found like-minded collaborators: one with a background in psychology and another with a business background in law and finance. Together, they founded their own consulting and education venture, blending marketing, psychology, and business to help organisations build powerful customer-centric cultures.

Their approach worked. Major clients trusted them from the start, even when customer experience was still a relatively new discipline. They didn't just talk about it, they embodied it, practising what they preach by listening attentively, using coaching techniques, and leading by example.

"The culture is the foundation of everything that happens in the organisation".

Big milestones followed. They partnered with the United Nations to build courses for women entrepreneurs. They collaborated with international leaders in customer experience. Olga became a certified trainer, helping bring the first-ever customer experience masterclasses to her country.

But Olga didn't stop there. She co-founded a CX community, built annual CX events that drew thousands, and helped professionals connect with global CX networks. Along the way, she became a judge for international customer experience awards and serves on global CX organisations.

"The MRI has become one of the most powerful tools in helping organisations transform their cultures. It is the missing link between vague conversations about 'culture' and concrete, measurable actions. It makes culture understandable and tangible. Are you doing this or not?"

According to Olga, what makes the MRI so valuable is its ability to connect directly to business outcomes. With clear links to metrics like the Net Promoter Score (NPS) and growth, it finally gives leaders a reason to take culture seriously.

Over the years, Olga has introduced the MRI into top-tier programs like the Chief Customer Officer Course and internationally recognised certifications, reaching audiences across Europe and beyond. It's even featured in her best-selling *Customer Experience* book series.

"What I love most about the MRI is that it talks to people in the language of actions"

But the real power of the MRI is that it brings employee voices to the surface. Anonymous feedback highlights hidden obstacles, like broken communication across departments that leadership might otherwise miss. And because it comes from organisations' own people, it's harder to ignore.

Despite some resistance from boards asking *"show me the money"*, Olga has seen firsthand how the MRI helps companies translate cultural conversations into meaningful, measurable change.

For her, the MRI isn't just a diagnostic it's a bridge between intention and action, helping companies stop talking about culture and start doing something about it.

"Even if the market landscape becomes unfavourable … culture is like your safety airbag against unforeseen changes"

To Olga, customer experience isn't just a career, it's a mission. Building culture takes time, she often says, but when done right, it becomes the lifeblood of sustainable organisations.

Even amid geopolitical and market challenges, Olga's belief remains strong: organisations thrive when they understand their customers and when their people are aligned to make that experience meaningful. Her story is about so much more than business success; it's about falling in love with customers, staying curious, and never settling for "good enough" when greatness is possible.

Building a Business on Belief
How Mark Hamill Made Recognition Matter

Mark Hamill never planned to become the cornerstone of a global awards ecosystem. His story doesn't begin with grand visions of international conferences or shaping the future of customer-centric culture; instead in begins with a ticket to Dubai and an opportunity to work for a leading CX consultancy that just sounded interesting.

In 2010, a chance opportunity took him to the Middle East, where he began working with a regional CX Leader, Bob Keay. Training, mystery shopping and global standards got him hooked on the world of customer experience. Within 18 months, he found himself leading a conference and awards program. "I really loved it", he says, "not for the flash of lights or the stage, but for the recognition it gave to companies doing real, thoughtful work".

"Recognition is absolutely vital but the kind that's earned, not handed out. That's what gives it real meaning. When a company wins one of our awards, they know it's because they truly deserve it. That's why it means so much."

Yet running an awards program within a consultancy can be challenging, especially when it comes to managing client relationships and sensitivities. That friction sparked an idea. At the age of 26, Mark co-founded his first business with the goal to build something fairer. Recognition would be earned, not purchased.

From there, it snowballed. Over the next decade, he exited his first company and co-founded ARCET Global with Richard Kennedy; a business that was more broadly focused than just awards. It became an engine for building business communities and storytelling, a platform for voices across sectors from sustainability to sales, from AI to recruitment. Running 50 events a year, ARCET Global wasn't just creating experiences; it was curating the future of global business conversation.

CUSTOMER CENTRICITY
WORLD SERIES

"If you don't have a customer-centric culture, the rest falls apart. That's why the culture category is always the most competitive in our awards, it's the hardest to get right, but the most powerful when you do."

But his flagship? The Customer Centricity World Series. It's more than an event. It's his north star. A way to spotlight the unsung heroes, the teams quietly revolutionising how organisations think about customers, culture, and impact.

Mark's awards aren't about trophies. They're about validation. For people like Beatrix at Deutsche Telekom, the award is proof that customer-focused leadership matters. For start-ups like Careem, later bought by Uber, it means standing toe-to-toe with multinationals and winning.

The secret sauce? Judging done by specialists, feedback given to all entrants, and emotional moments that still echo with Mark today. Like the Belarusian team's win that shook the Dubai auditorium with cheers.

Recognition, Mark believes, is deeply human. "If you do win, you really deserve it", he says. And through that ethos, he's built not just a business but a community.

"Beatrix didn't just want a tool. She needed proof. The MRI gave her that and it helped move the entire business forward."

Mark collaborated with the MarketCulture team to implement the MRI across two major divisions of Deutsche Telekom supported by Beatrix Kapitany, Head of Customer Experience, Transformation and Business Steering. Over 140 middle and senior managers participated in the assessment. The process didn't just gather data, it surfaced deep insights about how people worked, what barriers they faced, and where collaboration was breaking down.

The results were compelling:

- immediate increase in customer satisfaction across the board
- dramatic improvements in collaboration between departments
- validation of the customer experience strategy, giving Beatrix credibility with leadership

Mark described it as "a massive leap forward", both in terms of internal operations and external customer experience. The MRI not only gave leaders insight it gave them a clear mandate to act.

"You can't fake culture. And you can't build customer experience on top of a broken one."

For Mark, this case wasn't just another project, it was a proof point. It showed that culture and metrics can align to drive real business outcomes. It also reinforced his belief that customer-centric culture isn't fluff, it's a strategic asset.

"There's still nothing else like the MRI when it comes to measuring customer culture. And when you see the kind of transformation we saw with Deutsche Telekom, it's a no-brainer."

With a lean global team split between the UAE and the UK, Mark is still doing what he never planned: shaping a movement. Not from the top down but from the story up.

Where Leadership Meets Humanity
Tara's Journey with the MRI

When Tara Kimbrell Cole reflects on her path, she sees a life defined by a single pursuit: uncovering deeper human engagement and bringing them into the world of work. Born and raised in New York, she stepped away from Wall Street's financial towers and set her sights on the cultural heart of Asia drawn not by profit, but by an inner calling to understand how people live, think, and lead.

"I realised that, I wanted (needed) to do something different…
I decided I would do what inspired me."

After losing a loved one and her business in the same year, Tara chose a
new direction. Inspired by thinkers like Joseph Campbell, she immersed
herself in Buddhism, Hinduism, and the deep Vedic texts searching for the
common stories that bind people across cultures.

"I was very fascinated… I began to study Buddhism and Hinduism and
Vedic records… I wanted to spend more time doing that."

Yet she never intended to simply study humanity, she wanted to help
it grow, especially inside organisations. A long sabbatical studying
psychology and training in Jungian analysis sparked an idea: what if these
human insights could be used not just to heal the sick, but to strengthen
the capable? What if leaders could lead not just through strategy and
spreadsheets, but by understanding people more deeply?

This vision brought Tara to MarketCulture and the MRI (Market
Responsiveness Index). To her, the MRI was more than a measurement
tool, it was a living discipline for human systems. Where Peter Senge
spoke of the five disciplines of learning organisations, personal mastery,
mental models, shared vision, team learning, and systems thinking,
Tara saw the MRI's eight disciplines as a practical extension: a bridge
connecting the human side of leadership with business performance.

"When I was introduced to the MRI and MarketCulture, it was just so clear
to me… this is an extension of that systems work but structured directly to
the bottom line."

She found herself returning again and again to the work and the people
behind it.

"What brings me back to MarketCulture? One, I resonate with the way you
think and work… it was a perfect fit in my mind."
"The genuine and very authentic nature with which MarketCulture
undertake the work that you're doing."

For Tara, the MRI makes something clear: businesses thrive when they
balance human systems with financial outcomes. Sustainable growth
doesn't come from exploitation it grows from trust, discipline, and genuine
relationships.

"The customer is a human being. And we have all these customer relationship management systems, but they have nothing to do with the human being."

Tara helped bring this to life with companies like Wright Medical Group guiding leaders through cultural change, delivering offsites, and training teams to become true ambassadors for human-centered disciplines. Her mission: make the invisible visible. Show leaders that customers aren't just data points. Employees don't grow through lectures, but through practice. Organisations thrive when leaders lead as real people, not just titles.

"Master Nan uai Chin wrote that 'If You want to be a real leader, You Have to be a real human being….You must understand yourself first'," Leaders need to stop pounding their chests."

synovations
catalyzing sustainable business results

Today, Tara remains convinced that the MRI's true power is as a reminder: businesses are living systems, and leadership means stewarding them with care, courage, and creativity. In a world obsessed with artificial intelligence and automation, Tara stands as a clear, steady voice: the real competitive advantage will always be and must remain human.

As the founder and CEO of Synovations, Tara guides multinational organisations through leadership development, executive coaching, and cultural transformation. Her work blends systems thinking, psychology, and real-world business expertise helping leaders and teams navigate complexity, stay human, and build sustainable growth.

From Coffee to Community
How Bruno Guimarães Sparked Brazil's CX Revolution

Bruno Guimarães grew up in Brasília, the capital of Brazil, and began his career as an entrepreneur with his own advertising agency. He was not only managing the business but designing marketing campaigns, blending creativity with leadership. The entrepreneurial spark was alive early, and when the excitement of the 2014 World Cup and Rio Olympics hit Brazil, Bruno saw an opportunity. Moving to Rio, he partnered with a former member of Brazil's national football federation to create a sports marketing agency, hoping to ride the wave of major global events.

Their focus turned to Brazil's iconic Carnival. Bruno's team developed a licensing program for samba schools, working with major fashion brands like New Era to create merchandise tied to the celebrations. It was promising, but behind the glamour were messy realities, corruption, underworld influences, and an unstable business environment. After two years of pouring money into the venture with little return, Bruno made a tough decision: he moved back home to regroup.

Just when things seemed uncertain, a former colleague invited him to São Paulo to join a startup specialising in social engagement technology for live TV broadcasts. Bruno became the company's first employee and quickly embraced the role, diving into Brazil's evolving tech landscape.

From there, he moved into digital advertising, helping shape standards for Brazil's booming online industry. But by 2017, something was missing. The sales-driven world no longer satisfied him. He craved meaning, impact, and a new direction.

"At that time in Brazil, we didn't have communities not only in CX, but in any other discipline"

That's when he stumbled upon CX. Bruno started taking every course he could find on marketing innovation and CX. The more he learned, the more it aligned with his mindset: a belief that business should be about creating real value for people. He also enrolled in MarketCulture's Customer Centric Culture Foundation Course and made a strong connection with Sean and Chris.

On a whim, he posted on LinkedIn inviting people in CX, UX, CRM, and customer service to join him for coffee. Five or six people replied. They created a WhatsApp group to organise a meetup. The first meeting was small but the second drew 50 to 60 people. Suddenly, Bruno realised he hadn't just started a conversation; he'd accidentally launched a movement.

"It's all about people helping people. It's not only about profits, it's about thinking of the people who surround the company."

That movement became Amigos do CX, Brazil's first major community dedicated to customer experience. Meetups grew. Companies opened their offices to host events. Word spread quickly. What started with a coffee invitation soon blossomed into two or three meetups a month. Eventually, they founded the CX Summit, now Brazil's largest independent customer experience event, drawing more than 1,200 people by 2024 and more than 2000 in 2025.

"It wasn't about doing another theory book; it was about creating something practical that people could apply the next day at work."

Beyond events, Bruno launched another project collaborative books written by CX professionals across industries. These books filled a huge gap: before Amigos do CX, Brazil didn't have CX books with local case studies in Portuguese. Bruno made sure participation was free for contributors, with sponsors covering the costs. To date, they've published four books on topics ranging from customer and employee experience to healthcare.

"Customer experience is not just about customer service. It's about creating structures and strategy for the whole business."

Bruno's vision is always clear: customer experience isn't just a business strategy, it's a cultural shift. His mission is to help Brazilian professionals realise that they can create world-class CX right there; there's no need to look only to Silicon Valley or Europe for leadership.

As customer experience matured in Brazil, more companies began building CX teams, investing in strategy, and reshaping how they approached customer relationships. Bruno's community is right at the heart of that shift.

Recognising the need for accessibility, Bruno and his team are actively working to adapt the MRI into Portuguese and Spanish, ensuring that language isn't a barrier to transformation. Beyond translation, there's a broader vision to localise supporting materials, like adapting MarketCulture's book with South American stories and examples to make it resonate even more deeply with local businesses.

"At the end of the day, its people helping people"

For Bruno, the MRI is more than a measurement tool it's a catalyst for a movement. Through his growing network of CX professionals and initiatives like Amigos do CX, he's helping build a future where customer-centricity is not just a concept, but a clear, actionable strategy for growth.

Bruno's story is one of resilience, creativity, and service, not just to customers, but to an entire professional community. By following his curiosity and acting with generosity, he has sparked a customer-centric revolution in Brazil.

And he's just getting started.

From Classroom to Global Stage
How Tom DeWitt Built an Experience Management Movement

Tom DeWitt's journey into customer experience didn't start with a grand plan; it started with noticing a gap. Working in academia at Michigan State University, he realised that, while CX was being discussed in businesses, the industry itself was fragmented. Definitions varied wildly. Some saw CX as just call centres, while others focused narrowly on data or insights. Worse, professionals lacked the cross-functional skills needed to lead real CX transformations.

"I see gaps, or I see holes, and instinctively I want to do something about it. I want to address it. I want to fix it."

MICHIGAN STATE
U N I V E R S I T Y

When Tom was given the opportunity to lead a customer experience management initiative at Michigan State University, he developed a 1, 3 and 5 year plan for CXM@ MSU, the university's industry-facing body that hosted biannual conferences and online programs. During his first year in the role, through interviews with industry members, Tom recognised the need for a master's degree program, a vision that took a three-year journey to design and launch.

His vision was for students to work on real-world projects, apply proven frameworks within their own organisations, and forge lifelong professional connections.

Beyond the classroom, Tom hosts annual family reunions for students, creating deep bonds between learners and instructors. He's made Michigan State home to the first dedicated CX graduate program in the US.

When Tom set out to build the first dedicated Customer Experience Management master's degree in the US, he knew that culture was the foundation. Right from the very first week of the program, students are introduced to the MRI.

For Tom, the MRI isn't just another framework. "It's foundational. It's essential", he says. The MRI gives students a way to truly understand their organisation's readiness to serve customers, not in theory, but in reality. Students use it to diagnose their company cultures, test ideas, and provide feedback that shapes real change.

What frustrates Tom most is watching companies try to bolt experience management onto outdated, transactional, product-driven cultures.

"It just doesn't work"

For Tom, the MRI isn't optional; it's the starting point for any business serious about customer-centric change.

"I want people to apply what they are learning to their own organisations; not just learn it, but do something with it."

But Tom wasn't done. He knew that customer experience wasn't just an American issue, it was global. That's why he launched the XM Global Collaborative, a worldwide platform to bring CX, UX, EX, and related disciplines together. Through regional chapters, global mentorship programs, collaborative events, and shared resources, he has created a community where professionals can grow, no matter their focus or industry.

Tom's mission is clear: empower leaders with the skills they need, build bridges between disciplines, and create a space where global collaboration drives better outcomes for customers everywhere.

"We didn't want to be just another US program, we wanted to create something global, where regions could bring their own case studies and cultures to the table."

His passion came from a lifetime of living and working around the world from China to Singapore to Indonesia, experiences that gave him a deep respect for cultural diversity and a global mindset.

Tom's story is about more than education, it's about building *communities, movements*, and *impact*, one conversation, one connection at a time. Tom is also an integral part of the MarketCulture Academy, developing courses for clients to empower employees to create change.

Customer-Centricity Without Borders
Stefan Osthaus on Building a Global CX Community

Stefan Osthaus's journey to customer-centric leadership began in corporate America, where he rose through the ranks of one of the world's largest software companies. Moving from chief marketing officer to its first head of customer experience, and later combining that role with employee experience, he built a deep understanding of how culture drives customer satisfaction.

But Stefan wasn't content to leave it there. He recognised that the world of CX was fragmented and lacked consistency. That realisation inspired him to establish the Customer Institute, a non-profit global organisation dedicated to advancing standards, tools, and methodologies in customer and experience management.

"We decided to start a volunteer organisation. We called it the Customer Institute, and we made it our charter to influence how the world thinks about experience management. It's not about dancing your name and hugging a tree. But there is a methodology to it. There is skill, experience, tools, and culture that you bring to the table. We have successfully defined gold standards and best practices. We certify methods and tools, we certify organisations. We offer assessments in four different areas where we felt the industry is lacking the tools."

Customer Institute

One of the Institute's early successes was the recognition and certification of the MRI. "The world doesn't need another culture assessment", Stefan noted. "The MRI exists. It's profound. It's professional. It's well-proven." Rather than reinvent the wheel, Stefan's team at the Customer Institute reviewed the MRI and officially certified it as an example of excellence in the field.

"The MRI tool is, with its associated trainings and culture, education and philosophy behind it, a wonderful tool to impact the mindset towards customer centricity"

Stefan sees the MRI, not just as a tool, but as a cornerstone for building the *mindset* necessary for organisations to truly embrace customer-centricity. While technology and skills are important, he emphasises that the greatest challenge in experience management today is mindset. The MRI, with its focus on aligning culture to customer needs, helps leaders shift that mindset and build sustainable, resilient organisations, capable of maintaining focus on customers despite leadership changes, reorganisations, or market disruptions.

"If you ask me what is the most typical failure point, a breaking point in a CX initiative, it's the mindset"

For Stefan, tools like the MRI are integral to creating a world where customer experience isn't just talked about, it's practised with purpose and impact. Through partnerships, certifications, and community building, he continues to bring global voices together to raise the standards of what customer experience should be.

His story is one of contribution over ego, community over self-interest, and a belief that meaningful change happens when people, tools, and mindset align.

In the following chapter, you'll find stories curated for leaders committed to growth. True progress often involves setbacks and sometimes failure is the most powerful teacher. These stories are drawn from the inspiring individuals we've met on our journey, as well as from personal experiences that have shaped our own understanding of leadership and resilience.

Key Takeaways—Chapter 9

1. The Power of Personal Belief and Authenticity

Across all the stories in Chapter 9 the central thread is that real change starts with individuals who deeply believe in human connection and customer-centricity. These pioneers didn't just adopt methodologies like the MRI; they embody the values behind it, even when facing career risks, scepticism, or slow adoption.

2. Culture is the Foundation of Customer Experience

The consistent message from every expert and story is that CX success is impossible without a strong, aligned internal culture. Whether its Alejandro Ceron helping insurance firms understand empowerment, or Bruno Guimarães igniting a movement in Brazil, the root of CX transformation is cultural alignment, measured and enabled effectively through the MRI.

3. Community and Collaboration Drive Sustainable Change

Chapter 9 shows how networks, communities, and shared standards create global momentum for customer-centric change. Examples like Diane Magers' leadership at the CXPA, Tom DeWitt's global XM network, Vivek Bhaskaran's XDay conferences, Stefan Osthaus's experience management community and Mark Hamill's recognition programs all demonstrate how human collaboration drives innovation and growth

The Bottom Line

Individuals with purpose and passion champion the global movement toward human focused customer-centric transformation, driven by authentic leadership, cultural alignment, and the power of community. The MRI and MarketCulture Academy are not just tools, they are catalysts for empowering experts, guiding organisations, and sustaining human-focused change across industries and borders.

**Scan or click to watch
our Partner Videos**

**Scan or click to listen
to our Podcasts**

CHAPTER 10

LEARNING FROM HUMAN EXPERIENCES

Stories to Ignite: The Bad, The Good, and The Ugly

"What's your story?" It's a question you might ask friends, family, and grandchildren whenever you meet. It's a way of breaking through the usual "I'm good" response and inviting them to share something real.

Every experience, whether our own or someone else's, shapes who we are and how we lead. These diverse lessons, gathered from the bad, the good, and even the downright ugly, form the bedrock of our business thinking and decision-making. Stories are far more than entertainment, they're the threads that weave people, ideas, and purpose together. In business, stories shape how we see ourselves, how we lead, and how we bring others along with us.

When we share stories about successes, failures, risks taken, and lessons learned we pass on wisdom that facts and figures alone can't convey. A compelling story can transform a strategy from a dry plan into a rallying cry. It makes values real. It helps people see where they fit and why their work matters.

This chapter brings together a collection of real-world stories chosen to equip you, as a leader, with practical insights and memorable examples. Inside a company, stories set the tone for culture. They reveal what's truly celebrated, what's forgiven, and what's never tolerated. They remind us of what's possible when people put purpose before ego and customers before process.

As leaders, the stories we tell and those we choose to listen to shape not just our companies, but also who we become. The more we open ourselves to honest, human stories, the more connected, resilient, and future-ready our businesses will be.

"Why the Best Leaders Eat Last"

Simon Sinek, author and inspirational speaker on business leadership, tells the story of visiting a Marine Corps mess hall and noticing a simple but powerful ritual: the officers eat last. The youngest, lowest-ranking Marines go through the line first, and the leaders stand back and wait.

This isn't just about food, it's about a deep culture of service. Leaders in the Marines are taught that their responsibility is to take care of their people first. If that means they get what's left over, so be it. This simple act builds trust, loyalty, and a sense of belonging that's critical when these same people must rely on each other in life-or-death situations.

Sinek uses this story to show that great leaders put the needs of their people ahead of their own comfort or ego. *Leaders Eat Last* became the title of his book, where he expands on this idea: when leaders create an environment of safety and care, people willingly give their best and protect each other just as the Marines do.

Stories like this don't just happen, they endure. They live on because they remind people what truly matters.

David Tudehope, CEO of Macquarie Technology Group, often shares a powerful example of what it means to live your values. It's the story of Madge, a moment of unexpected humanity that became internal legend.

One day, a Macquarie customer service team member received a call that, at first, seemed like a mistake. On the other end was an elderly woman named Madge. She politely asked if someone could please bring her medication and a cup of tea to her room.

It didn't make sense until the employee looked closer. The call hadn't come from a Macquarie account holder in the usual sense, but from a care home that used Macquarie's telecom systems. Madge, a resident there, had accidentally pressed the wrong button on her in-room phone, thinking she was calling a staff member.

Rather than simply dismissing the call, the Macquarie employee acted. They asked for Madge's room number, contacted the care home's nursing station, and ensured her request was passed on. Moments later, Madge received her medication and tea. The care home, both surprised and deeply appreciative, followed up with Macquarie to thank the team. They also made changes to their phone system to prevent similar confusion in the future.

But what mattered most was what happened inside Macquarie. This story wasn't just a quirky anecdote; it was told again and again as a touchstone for the company's culture. It captured something real: that every interaction, even accidental, is an opportunity to care. The Madge story became a symbol of the organisation's commitment to empathy, responsiveness, and doing what's right, even when no one's watching.

Why? Because at Macquarie, customer service isn't a department. It's a mindset.

These stories highlight core principles such as delivering exceptional customer value, driving effective cross-functional collaboration, and ensuring alignment with your company's purpose and strategy. Use these lessons to enrich your own leadership narrative, deepening your ability to connect with customers and employees by embedding a genuinely human-centric culture throughout your organisation. Here is a guide.

- **The Bad to Good:** Uncertainty Ignites Excellence: Why "Good Enough" Isn't Enough—Ragna Ghoreishi

- **The Good:** The Art of Hospitality—Leonie Williams

- **The Ugly:** When "Winning" Costs You Everything—A Wells Fargo Story

- **The Good:** Klarna's Secret Sauce: Cross-Functional Teams, Clear Rhythms, and No Ego

- **The Good:** From Accidental Marketer to Creative Force at Coca-Cola— Adam Ross

- **From Bad to Good:** What Do You Do When Your Customers Mock Your Core Product? Domino's Bold Turnaround

- **The Good:** It's LEGO, Not EGO—A Story of Collaborative Culture

- **From Ugly to Good:** Qantas's Journey from Corporate Betrayal to Rebuilding Trust

- **From Ugly to Redemption:** When Policy Dominates People—Lessons from United Airlines

- **The Good:** The Retailer Who Took on Goliath and Won

- **From Good to Bad to Good Again:** The Virgin Trains Rollercoaster

The Bad to Good
Uncertainty Ignites Excellence: Why "Good Enough" Isn't Enough: A Startup Story by Ragna Ghoreishi

This story comes from a startup on the verge of scaling, growing fast and shifting focus from SMBs to enterprise clients. When I joined to lead post-sales and build global customer success practices, I did what I always do: I reached out to customers for open, informal conversations.

What I heard was clear and sobering.

The startup had just landed its first large global enterprise deal, a huge milestone. It demanded consistency and excellence from the whole team and naturally the best resources in the company were focused on ensuring success of this new customer. Understandable from the inside but every existing customer I spoke with felt the same way: dropped, unseen, no longer important. Abandoned.

These were emotional reactions, not just business concerns. As Maya Angelou said, "People will never forget how you made them feel."

What did we do? We went back to the basic human connection. We held in-person and virtual meetings, reframing quarterly business reviews into listening sessions. My team made it clear: we were there to hear them. We acknowledged issues, addressed what we could, and explained transparently when we couldn't always offer alternatives or mitigations.

This restored trust. Customer Success Managers reclaimed their roles as trusted advisors. We used my arrival as a signal of renewed commitment. Through these early "listening meetings", we reignited relationships and re-aligned with customers' goals. Trust started to rebuild.

Assuming we are "just good enough" is a risk. In a world of replaceable products, "fine" isn't enough. Emotional disconnection can trigger churn and when that happens, it takes a long time and real effort to win customers back. There were things we could have done differently:

- proactively protect relationships with existing customers
- allocate resources to ensure ongoing service excellence
- recognise that stability, trust, and attention are as valuable as new revenue

I learned some key lessons:

- never take loyal customers for granted
- avoid the "loyalty penalty" that rewards only new clients
- listen first, without selling
- be human, be thoughtful, and be consistent

Ultimately, customer centricity is about trust, empathy, and partnership, not just performance metrics. When you lead with those values, everybody wins.

The Good

The Art of Hospitality, From Service to Loyalty, by Leonie Williams, Customer Service Solutions

In hospitality, it's not the grand gestures that guests remember it's the unexpected ones. The small, human moments that go beyond what's required. That's where loyalty is born.

During my time with two of the world's leading hotel brands, Hilton and IHG, I witnessed countless examples of great service. But one story has stayed with me because it captured the very essence of true hospitality.

At one of our Heathrow properties, a regular business traveller had been staying with us while preparing for a critical meeting in New York, perhaps the most important of his career. He became a familiar face in the business lounge, often speaking with the reception team as he printed documents and prepared for his trip.

On the morning of his departure, he checked out, requested a taxi, and headed to the airport. Everything seemed in order until our front office manager noticed something: a laptop bag left behind at reception.

Many would have simply logged it with lost property and waited for a call. But not this manager. He understood what that bag likely contained and what it meant to the guest. Without hesitation, he rushed to the staff parking area, jumped on his Vespa scooter, and raced to Heathrow Airport. He knew which airline the guest was flying, so he headed straight for the BA terminal and began searching.

Dodging through security zones and lounges, he finally spotted the guest moments away from boarding. As he approached with the bag in hand, the guest's initial confusion gave way to disbelief, then to deep, genuine gratitude.

Had that briefcase not been returned, the fallout could have been significant missed opportunities, lost materials, and enormous stress. But instead, he boarded his flight prepared and at peace, carrying not only his laptop, but a profound sense of being truly cared for.

This wasn't just service it was hospitality in its highest form. A moment that turned a potential crisis into a lasting emotional connection. That guest became a loyal advocate, not for the hotel's amenities, but for its heart. He returned again and again, because he had felt something rare: the feeling of being valued not just as a customer, but as a human being.

Meeting expectations isn't enough. True loyalty is earned when we exceed them in meaningful, human ways. That's what sets apart a service provider from a brand that lives in the hearts of its customers.

The Ugly
When "Winning" Costs You Everything, A Wells Fargo Story

WELLS FARGO

Among many corporate crises, the Wells Fargo scandal stands out as a grim reminder of how even a revered institution can lose its way. For years, Wells Fargo was admired for its resilience, especially for navigating the 2008 mortgage crisis with apparent strength. Yet beneath that façade was a culture so distorted by relentless sales pressure that employees were driven to betray the very customers they were meant to serve.

The pressure was overwhelming. Unrealistic sales targets cornered employees into unethical behaviour, resulting in as many as 3.5 million fake customer accounts. Credit cards were issued without consent, signatures were forged, and investigations later revealed that 570,000 customers were forced into unnecessary car insurance policies. This wasn't a series of isolated incidents; it was a systemic failure rooted in toxic culture and leadership.

When Tim Sloan took the helm as CEO to repair the damage, the challenge was enormous. The board was nearly completely overhauled, and the company's reputation lay in ruins. During this turbulent period, Tim's earnest commitment to refocusing the bank's vision around genuinely helping customers was clear. He even began to question the long-standing shareholder-first doctrine that had contributed to the crisis.

Tim took concrete steps to fix the broken system. He scrapped sales incentives tied to the number of products sold and shifted focus toward customer satisfaction and usage metrics. However, as often happens with top-down change, the execution didn't fully connect with those on the front lines. Despite good intentions, the change felt distant and disconnected from daily realities.

By then, employee cynicism had taken deep root. A report from the Committee for Better Banks revealed a culture of fear and alienation. Meggan Halvorson, a mortgage division employee in Minneapolis, put it bluntly: "Honestly, it's perceived as a joke, 'Oh yeah, they've changed things.' I haven't met anybody, personally, who believes what they're saying or that it's the case."

This scepticism was a red flag that the cultural shift was failing where it mattered most—with the people interacting directly with customers. The urgency and intensity needed to uproot a toxic culture simply weren't penetrating fast enough.

In early 2019, under mounting pressure, Tim Sloan stepped down. In his final testimony before the House Financial Services Committee, he admitted, "We have more work to do ... to put our customers' needs first". A month later, his tenure ended.

The Wells Fargo story teaches us some very important lessons.

- **Intensity and speed are crucial:** When a culture becomes toxic, change must be driven relentlessly and rapidly from the top. Tim Sloan's efforts were in the right direction, but they lacked the urgency needed to overcome entrenched cynicism.

- **See the front lines personally:** Borrowed from military leadership, having a direct, unfiltered view of the front lines is critical. Imposing change from afar only yields compliance, not commitment. True transformation comes from engaging and empowering those doing the work every day.

- **Metrics shape behaviour so choose wisely:** The initial sales quotas at Wells Fargo incentivised destructive behaviours. While shifting to customer experience metrics was a step forward, if used as a punitive tool rather than a developmental one, which can perpetuate fear instead of fostering growth.

Transforming culture is never about slogans or surface-level fixes. It demands authentic leadership, visible action, and deep engagement with employees at all levels. Without these, even the best intentions are doomed to fall short.

The Good
Klarna's Secret Sauce for Cross-Functional Teams, Clear Rhythms, and No Ego

Klarna

Lisa Bjornberg was CMO of Operations for nearly eight transformative years at Klarna, Sweden's trailblazing fintech. Lisa witnessed Klarna's rapid rise from 1,700 employees in 2017 to 5,500 by the end of 2022.

Not long after she joined, Klarna brought in McKinsey to help design a structure and operating rhythm ambitious enough to match its bold goal: to evolve from a payment service into a lifestyle brand, the Nike of fintech.

As a disruptor, Klarna refuses to follow the crowd. It doesn't copy competitors; instead, it looks outward and inward to adopt the best ideas from world-leading companies and reimagines them to create something unique.

Lisa believes deeply that "when people thrive, businesses thrive". Beyond her senior marketing role, she was instrumental in recruitment and change management. Klarna's famously strict "no asshole" hiring policy ensured the company built a culture where humility, openness, and teamwork was non-negotiable. Says Lisa, "If there was even a hint of arrogance, we wouldn't hire them no matter how impressive their skills".

At its peak, Klarna operated up to 700 cross-functional teams of 5–8 people, each laser-focused on solving a specific customer problem to reduce friction and create value. These agile teams might work for weeks or months, then disband once the problem was solved. If customer feedback revealed a team was tackling an issue that didn't truly matter, that team would dissolve immediately. Adaptability and resilience were essential, people needed to say goodbye, regroup, and create value elsewhere without missing a beat.

This was all made possible by Klarna's clear operating cadence, known as the Klarna rhythm. Teams planned on Monday mornings and held retro reviews on Fridays to assess what they achieved, where they were blocked, and what help they needed. Each team had access to an experienced coach who could step into clear roadblocks.

Meetings at Klarna were run with military precision: every session had a strict timeframe, started on time, and kicked off with a short document outlining the problem or proposal, no PowerPoint decks allowed. Attendees spent the first five minutes reading, then discussed and decided. By the end, everyone was aligned and ready to execute, a practice inspired by Amazon's famous meeting culture.

Klarna's leaders also role-modelled excellence in communication. Senior executives meticulously prepared for town halls and other company-wide gatherings, setting the bar high for clarity and quality. This created alignment and a clear, compelling narrative around the strategy, value proposition, and Klarna's role as an industry disruptor that everyone could rally behind.

Reflecting on her time there, Lisa says, "Klarna's appetite for disruption, its unique ways of working, and the density of top talent made it a fantastic experience".

The Good
From Accidental Marketer to Creative Force at Coca-Cola by Adam Ross

"I didn't want to go to university", Adam reflects, "My parents convinced me to go … so I enrolled in an IT degree, went to one lecture and realised it was a terrible mistake." That moment of clarity, followed by a fateful conversation with the university dean, led him to marketing and what would become a lifelong passion for understanding and connecting with people.

The decision to pivot set the foundation for a career built on empathy, insight, and creativity. Adam's career kicked off at Mediacom in London, where he honed his skills under world-class mentors and worked on campaigns that mattered. "One of my first briefs was reducing inner-city black-on-black gun crime … that got me deep into behavioural science and the power of creativity to connect". From frozen prawn rings in Iceland (the supermarket) to saving lives with the Metropolitan Police, Adam learned early on that "you have to find something interesting to say, and an entertaining way to say it".

After five years, he moved to Sydney. There, he continued to break the mould: "I created a creative team not attached to clients, but to people and culture ... to help unlock a different way of understanding a problem". This role eventually earned him a seat on the agency's leadership team, where he drove creativity across APAC.

But it wasn't all smooth sailing. "I joined a creative agency where the culture was toxic, lots of politics and infighting amongst the leaders there ... I only lasted 8 or 9 months." That difficult period taught Adam a lesson he carries to this day: "The biggest thing I've learned is the power of a good leader and a bad one".

Adam's next chapter unfolded by chance. A casual conversation turned into an unexpected opportunity when a contact at Coca-Cola described a role it had been trying to fill. After going through the hiring process, Adam stepped in as Creative Lead for Australia and South Pacific, a role that later expanded to cover Brand Coca-Cola across Asia and the South Pacific following a major global restructure.

At Coke, Adam's focus sharpened on connecting timeless brand values with modern culture: "Our job is making the timeless timely ... how do we create and refresh memories and associations for today's generation?"

He brings creativity to life through genuine curiosity about the real world. On a recent trip to Indonesia, Adam asked two locals to spend the day with him, showing him where they eat, hang out, and grab coffee: "I soak it all in and get firsthand insight into how people live and what Coca-Cola means to them in different countries". One of his proudest moments? "We won Creative Brand of the Year at Cannes Lions. That had never happened before."

Adam is humble about his role: "I aim to connect our brand with people in meaningful, creative ways". One example is the iconic Kings Cross Coke sign in Sydney. The team recognised it was more than just a billboard, it's a landmark and a meeting point, the starting place for countless stories sparked by the simple phrase, "Meet Me At The Coke Sign". So they put that phrase front and centre, inviting people to share their own stories that began there. These stories were then brought back to the community and installed in unique ways on the very streets where they happened.

Leadership, to Adam, is about empowering others. "The best leaders I've had gave me so much belief and trust that I went well beyond my own expectations. The worst made me shrink. That's why I try to be the former."

In every step, Adam's story is one of self-awareness, courage, and relentless creativity. Whether guiding global brand strategy or mentoring teams, his mission remains clear: "Find the human truth. And make it matter".

When Adam first joined CocaCola, he worried that every question he asked might reveal his inexperience of working client-side. Instead, he was greeted with two simple but transformative pieces of advice from his manager: "Your learning curve is going to be very steep for the next year so know that the more you don't know, the more powerful and the more valuable you are to us". Rather than feeling pressure to prove himself, Adam discovered that his fresh perspective was his greatest asset.

The trust his leader placed in him, gave Adam the freedom to make decisions independently, knowing he would always have full support. Those words of trust are a feeling of having "air cover". He describes it as: "that led me to feel like I could walk into any meeting feeling ten feet tall, knowing I had his full trust and backing".

Adam's biggest lesson? Leadership defines culture. Great leaders give people freedom to think and act boldly. Bad ones shrink teams into silence. It's a lesson he strives to embody, using trust and empowerment as tools to help people exceed their own expectations and deliver work that resonates far beyond the walls of an office.

Today, Adam pays that mentorship forward by leading his own teams with the same philosophy.

1. **Value curiosity over certainty**: He encourages everyone he works with to ask questions even if they feel naive because fresh eyes often spot opportunities insiders miss.

2. **Back decisions, then debrief:** Adam gives his people the freedom to choose bold paths, promising to support them unconditionally and to learn together, win or lose.

3. **Provide "air cover" for growth:** As his mentor did for him, Adam shields his team from undue risk, so they can focus on creativity and customer impact.

In Adam's world, great leadership isn't about having all the answers; it's about creating the space where curiosity thrives, and everyone feels empowered to shape the future.

From London's streets to Asia's megacities, Adam Ross remains driven by a single question. How do we stay human in a world that wants to automate connection? For him, the answer lies in curiosity, culture, and in never forgetting that at the heart of every organisation, every initiative, every piece of work, are people.

From Bad to Good

What Do You Do When Your Customers Mock Your Core Product? Domino's Bold Turnaround

In the late 2000s, Domino's Pizza faced a brutal reality check. The brand was recognised for its speedy delivery but increasingly ridiculed for the quality of its pizza. Customer feedback was scathing, with many likening the crust to "cardboard". It was a crisis that could have crippled any company.

Enter Patrick Doyle, the new CEO, stepping into a storm of negative sentiment. Instead of shrinking from the criticism, Doyle made a bold, defining choice: he embraced it head-on. He turned the raw, unfiltered customer feedback into the fuel for a full-scale reinvention of Domino's, a textbook case of how honest insight can shake a company out of complacency.

The first move was transparency. Dominos launched the now-legendary **"Pizza Turnaround"** campaign, an advertising blitz that didn't shy away from its flaws. Instead, it spotlighted them. Employees, including Doyle himself, read aloud the harshest customer critiques on TV. These ads didn't just admit failure; they validated every dissatisfied customer, creating a powerful moment of corporate humility.

But honesty without action is hollow. Doyle knew that the campaign's promise of improvement would only resonate if backed by real change. Over 18 months, Domino's reinvented its 49-year-old recipe from the ground up. The team tested ten crust variations, 15 sauces, and dozens of cheese blends. The result? A bolder, richer sauce, a more flavourful cheese blend, and a new garlic-herb seasoned crust that delivered a genuinely fresher, more satisfying pizza.

The impact was immediate and extraordinary. By facing its flaws directly, Domino's disarmed critics and won back trust. Within the first quarter of the campaign and relaunch, same-store sales surged 14.3%. The company's stock, previously stagnant, began an unprecedented climb. This wasn't just a marketing gimmick; it was the start of a transformation that would propel Domino's to become the world's largest pizza chain by sales within a few years.

The Domino's story has some key lessons.

- **Embrace brutal honesty:** Doyle's willingness to admit faults openly built credibility in an era when corporate spin dominates. Transparency creates genuine human connection.

- **Your harshest critics are your greatest guides:** What seemed like insults was actually a roadmap for improvement. Negative feedback can be the clearest brief for innovation.

- **Back words with action:** The "Pizza Turnaround" campaign succeeded because Domino's delivered a genuinely better product. Without real change, apologies ring hollow.

- **Vulnerability breeds strength:** Admitting failure isn't weakness, it's confidence. Domino's showed respect to customers by acknowledging mistakes, and customers rewarded that trust with loyalty.

Domino's story is a powerful reminder that facing criticism with openness and determination can transform challenges into opportunities and turn a struggling brand into a global leader.

Video URL: https://youtu.be/AH5R56jILag

The Good
It's LEGO, Not EGO, A Story of Collaborative Culture

The name LEGO perfectly captures the essence of the company's philosophy. Derived from the Danish words "leg godt", meaning "play well", LEGO has built a global empire founded on this simple yet powerful idea since 1932, when Ole Kirk Kristiansen first launched the family-owned business. But the true secret to LEGO's success isn't just the bricks, it's the culture that lives and breathes its brand values every day.

At its core, LEGO's culture reflects its Danish heritage, emphasising a flat, non-hierarchical organisational structure where there's simply no room for ego. Employees at all levels are not only encouraged but expected to challenge their leaders and contribute openly to finding the best ideas. LEGO's CEO, Jørgen Vig Knudstorp, sums this up perfectly: "Blame is not for failure; it is for failing to help or ask for help". This mindset, deeply embedded by the founding family, fosters genuine collaboration.

This spirit of teamwork guides everything from hiring to everyday operations. LEGO actively seeks individuals who thrive on collaboration and fun. Even its sales teams, typically competitive environments, focus on building long-term partnerships rather than short-term wins. Many new hires are fans of the product themselves, and it's common for interviews to include a creative exercise like designing a new LEGO set from a pile of bricks.

The product itself is a metaphor for LEGO's culture. The interlocking bricks are more than toys, they're tools for connection, imagination, and creativity that bring people together across generations. This ethos of connection has been central to LEGO's remarkable growth and enduring appeal over the last decade.

The LEGO approach brings some valuable lessons.

- **Live your brand's promise:** LEGO's internal culture of "playing well" perfectly mirrors the playful, creative purpose of its product. Authenticity shines when culture and brand align seamlessly.

- **Make collaboration a core competency:** Prioritising teamwork over ego, even in traditionally competitive areas like sales, builds resilience, creativity, and lasting success.

- **Redefine failure:** LEGO's no-blame policy for mistakes creates the psychological safety essential for innovation and honest communication.

- **Hire for cultural fit:** The company's unique interview process ensures new hires not only have the right skills but also deeply embrace the collaborative spirit that defines LEGO.

From Ugly to Good
Qantas's Journey from Corporate Betrayal to Rebuilding Trust

The period from 2022 to 2025 was a tumultuous time for Qantas, marked by a dramatic fall from grace and a subsequent effort to rebuild its reputation. The narrative is a powerful one, shifting from a period of corporate misconduct and public outrage to a new leadership's determined push for transparency and customer focus.

The Ugly History: A Flying Kangaroo in a Nosedive

The seeds of Qantas's troubles were sown in a series of shocking revelations that exposed a pattern of what the public and regulators considered to be bad behaviour by the Qantas Board and then-CEO Alan Joyce.

- **Selling "Ghost Flights":** In a major scandal that erupted in late 2023, the Australian Competition and Consumer Commission took Qantas to court for engaging in misleading conduct. It was revealed that Qantas had been selling tickets for tens of thousands of flights that had already been cancelled. The airline failed to promptly inform customers of these cancellations, sometimes for weeks, leaving passengers in the lurch and facing higher prices for alternative travel. This led to the Federal Court-penalising Qantas $100 million, in addition to a $20 million remediation program for affected customers.

- **Illegal outsourcing and union battles:** The airline's decision to illegally outsource 1,800 ground-handling jobs during the COVID-19 pandemic came back to haunt it. The High Court upheld a finding that Qantas had breached the *Fair Work Act* by sacking workers to prevent them from exercising their industrial rights. This decision, along with an eventual court order for a substantial compensation payout, highlighted a ruthless approach to labour relations that deeply damaged the airline's standing with its employees and the public.

- **Executive Greed and Misaligned Priorities:** As these stories of corporate misconduct and customer frustration mounted, public anger intensified. It was widely perceived that Qantas executives, particularly the CEO, were prioritising profits and their own lucrative bonuses over the wellbeing of employees and the interests of customers. The board's initial defence of these actions only worsened the public backlash. The final straw for many was the revelation of Alan Joyce's massive executive payout as he departed, even as the airline was facing mounting legal and reputational crises.

The consequences of this behaviour were severe. The "Spirit of Australia" brand was in tatters, its reputation scores plummeted, and it became a national punching bag. The public's trust in Qantas was at an all-time low.[19]

The Good Actions: A New Dawn for the Flying Kangaroo

The turning point came with a change in leadership. In a move designed to reset the company's direction, Vanessa Hudson took over as CEO and John Mullen was appointed as the new Chairman. This new leadership team understood that the airline's survival depended on a radical change in approach.

- **A new era of transparency and apology:** The first major step was a public and sincere acknowledgment of past failings. Vanessa Hudson's leadership style was in stark contrast to that of her predecessor's. She offered a direct apology to customers for the airline's poor performance and committed to a new culture of transparency. The board, under John Mullen's leadership, also conducted an internal governance review that openly admitted to mistakes by both the board and management.

- **A Focus on Stakeholders, Not Just Shareholders:** The new management shifted its focus to rebuilding relationships with key stakeholders.

  - **Customers:** Qantas began a concerted effort to improve the customer experience, with a reported uplift in its reputation scores. This included a significant investment in new aircraft, improvements to its frequent flyer program, and a commitment to better communication and service.

  - **Employees:** The new leadership sought to repair the fractured relationship with its workforce. This involved a more collaborative approach to industrial relations and a greater focus on employee wellbeing and engagement, which resulted in a positive response from unions and frontline staff.

- **Accountability and corporate reform:** To demonstrate its commitment to change, the board took concrete actions. It docked a significant portion of the former CEO's payout and reduced bonuses for other senior executives. The company also implemented new protocols for board oversight and executive conduct, ensuring that the mistakes of the past would not be repeated.

"I don't think there are any big egos around the board table anymore, and there are no big egos in management, both of which can be really corrosive I find in business". —John Mullen, Chairman.[20]

The Qantas story from 2022 to 2025 is a powerful lesson in corporate accountability. It demonstrates how a brand's reputation can be severely damaged by a toxic corporate culture and how a change in leadership, coupled with a genuine commitment to transparency and stakeholder welfare, is essential for recovery. With John Mullen and Vanessa Hudson at the helm, Qantas is now charting a new course, seeking to earn back its place in the hearts of Australians and once again embody the "Spirit of Australia". The question is how far do they need to go to win back customer and employee trust?

From Ugly to Redemption
When Policy Dominates People—Lessons from United Airlines

UNITED AIRLINES

We've all seen moments when rigid corporate policies collide with common sense, but few crises illustrate this clash as starkly as United Airlines' infamous 2017 incident, when a routine overbooking scenario spiralled into a full-blown corporate disaster.

What began as an attempt to remove a disruptive passenger revealed a harsh truth: United forcibly dragged a paying customer, a practising physician, from his prepaid seat. The flight was oversold, and the airline needed to accommodate four crew members on another flight. While overbooking is a standard practice to maximise revenue, the moment it harms a customer, it tests the very soul of a company's culture. Would United put people first, or protect short-term profits at the expense of dignity?

United chose policy over people. They initially offered $1,000 vouchers for volunteers to give up their seats, no takers. Rather than increasing the offer fairly, United resorted to involuntary removals based on frequent flyer status and connections. Three passengers complied begrudgingly; one refused. The resulting video of the passenger being violently dragged off the plane ignited a global media firestorm.

It revealed a culture broken from the top. United CEO Oscar Munoz's initial response was a textbook case of what not to do. Publicly, Munoz gave a lukewarm apology for having to "re-accommodate customers". Internally, he sent a memo defending the crew's actions, praising their "above and beyond" efforts, and labelling the passenger "disruptive and belligerent".

Supporting employees is important but this message sent the wrong signal. It reinforced a company-centric culture that valued policies over human dignity. It took Munoz two days to fully acknowledge the company's failure, finally stating, "No one should ever be mistreated this way".

Contrast this with a colleague's story of Emirates Airlines handling a similar situation. Emirates simply kept raising incentives until enough passengers volunteered. They ended up giving away two round-trip business class tickets plus accommodation and cash, a trivial expense compared to United's fallout, given the cost to United was immediate and severe. The company's market value dropped by an estimated $255 million overnight. Reputation expert Eric Schiffer called United's mishandling "brand suicide".

But there's a redemption story for United. The crisis became a pivotal moment for Munoz and United. After a disastrous start, Munoz shifted gears, leading with humility and action, by appearing on national TV to say, "The word shame comes to mind … We let policies and procedures get ahead of doing what's right".

His public contrition was backed by decisive action. Within weeks, United announced ten major policy reforms: no more using law enforcement to remove seated, paying passengers; dramatically raising compensation limits for voluntary bumps (up to $10,000); and creating a dedicated "customer solutions team" to creatively resolve issues.

Munoz also intensified efforts to rebuild the company culture from within. He deepened his employee listening tours and genuinely engaged with the workforce, many of whom had long felt "disengaged and disenfranchised".

The results spoke volumes. Over the following five years, United improved reliability and profitability, restored customer loyalty, and earned respect from union leaders. When Munoz transitioned to Executive Chairman in 2020, the company's stock had risen by 54% during his tenure.

There were undoubtedly some tough lessons learned for United.

- **It's never too late to make things right:** Munoz's initial failure was severe, but his sincere apology and commitment to change started the long path to restoring trust. Leadership isn't about perfection; it's about how you respond to your worst moments.

- **Empowerment means giving trust and tools:** The old culture of rigid rules had to be replaced with one where employees are trusted and equipped to solve problems on the spot, like offering meaningful compensation.

- **True change begins inside:** Lasting customer trust depends on first winning the hearts and minds of employees. Munoz understood this, focusing on his workforce as the foundation for a sustainable turnaround.

The Good
The Retailer Who Took on Goliath and Won

In today's fast-evolving business world, one question dominates every leader's mind: Can anyone truly compete with Amazon and win? For years, many businesses shrugged this off, believing Amazon's threat was confined to retail alone. That assumption no longer holds. Amazon has expanded far beyond its roots, now dominating consumer electronics, entertainment, cloud services, and even exploring healthcare and payments.

This shift forces a critical question for every leader: "What would we do if Amazon entered our market?"

Best Buy didn't have to ask. For more than a decade, this iconic American bricks-and-mortar retailer has been locked in a fierce battle with the online behemoth. Many analysts had already predicted its demise, convinced it couldn't survive Amazon's relentless growth.

So, how did Best Buy fight back and win? They chose to beat Amazon at its own game: customer obsession.

Under new CEO Hubert Joly, Best Buy launched a bold transformation. Moving away from a transactional focus on store traffic, the company embraced a mission to build lifelong customer relationships. The 2012 turnaround plan, dubbed "Renew Blue", put customers at the heart of every decision.

Transformation starts on the front lines. Joly spent his first week working in stores, listening openly to employees. They didn't hold back. They told him the website was slow and clunky, morale was low after employee discount cuts, and customers were "showrooming", in other words, checking products in-store but buying cheaper online.

Joly acted swiftly. He restored employee discounts and eliminated price as a competitive factor by guaranteeing to match online prices. These were not mere quick fixes but powerful signals that leadership was listening and, crucially, acting. Next, he overhauled the website and matched Amazon's fast, free shipping.

Yet the real genius lay in doubling down on Best Buy's unique strength: the in-store, human experience. Joly redefined the company's purpose: "We're not in the business of selling products or doing transactions. Our purpose ... is to enrich lives with the help of technology."

This purpose drove innovative, customer-centric services:

- **In-home advisor:** Experts visit customers' homes to help select, buy, and install technology tailored to their needs.

- **Total tech support:** For an annual fee, Best Buy takes full responsibility for any tech problem in a customer's home, providing peace of mind and expert solutions.

- **Senior-focused tech:** Smart home systems designed to help aging seniors live independently, alerting caregivers if issues arise.

In a surprising move, Best Buy even began selling Amazon products despite fierce rivalry. Why? Because it was the right thing for customers. Joly explained, "Many retailers are reluctant to sell Amazon products. We do it because we're customer-driven."

This customer-first philosophy culminated in Amazon launching its Fire TV Smart product exclusively through Best Buy, a testament to the respect Best Buy earned.

The cultural shift ran deep. Joly shared, "In every management meeting, we don't start with financial results. We start with people, then customers, and finally the numbers".

Best Buy's turnaround proves that even a giant like Amazon can be challenged and beaten. By shifting from transactional selling to a purpose-driven obsession with enriching lives, Best Buy turned near-bankruptcy into a thriving, human-centered success story, showing that the personal touch remains a powerful competitive advantage.

From Good to Bad to Good Again
The Virgin Trains Rollercoaster

Richard Branson's Virgin Trains achieved one of the most powerful bureaucratic turnarounds in UK rail history, not just through corporate strategy, but through the voices of its people: loyal customers and dedicated employees.

On 10 September 2012, Richard Branson and Virgin Rail CEO Tony Collins appeared before a parliamentary inquiry in London, an inquiry sparked by Branson himself. The issue? The UK government had awarded the West Coast Main Line franchise, which runs from London to Glasgow, to rival operator FirstGroup. Virgin had successfully run the line for 15 years and was bidding to retain it.

Branson told Parliament: "We submitted a strong and deliverable bid focused on improving customer experience through greater investment and innovation". He reminded members of the parliamentary inquiry that Virgin had turned a loss-making operation into a profitable one, returning billions to taxpayers over time.

This was Virgin's fourth unsuccessful bid for a UK rail franchise. But this time, Richard Branson chose to fight not for profit, but for the people. Fuelled by a groundswell of support, including 170,000 signatures from passengers and strong backing from Virgin staff and unions, he called for an official review of the government's franchise bidding process.

When asked why he was pushing back, he said simply: "The customer is the heart of our business". He spoke passionately about the loyalty and encouragement from both passengers and staff, saying he couldn't walk away from them. With passenger numbers growing over 10% annually, the public had spoken with their feet and their hearts.

Ultimately, the inquiry reversed the decision, citing major flaws and a lack of transparency in the bidding process. Virgin's franchise was reinstated.

Richard Branson's leadership and his belief in a culture built around engaged employees and empowered customers paid off. His approach to business is grounded in a simple truth: when your culture is strong, your customers don't just support you, they fight for you.

The legacy lives on. At a recent MarketCulture leadership workshop in Sydney, a story was shared that perfectly captured the legacy of Virgin's customer-first mindset. It involved a veteran train driver, a man who, after attending a customer experience workshop, began to see his role differently. Traditionally seen as having little direct contact with passengers, Virgin believed that every employee, including drivers, plays a role in delivering great customer experiences.

A few weeks after the session, while driving a familiar route, the driver felt a slight bump on the track while crossing a bridge. It was nothing alarming, just the kind of minor jolt that happens from time to time. But this time, his mindset had shifted. He thought of the passengers onboard, their safety, and his responsibility.

At the next station, he reported the bump to the maintenance team. In more than 30 years of service, it was something he might normally ignore. But now, he acted. At the end of his shift, his manager was waiting. "That bump you reported …" the driver braced himself. But instead of criticism, he heard this: "Engineers inspected the area. A strut under the bridge had failed. If trains had continued running, we could've had a derailment. Hundreds of lives may have been at risk. You did the right thing."

That moment reflected the power of cultural transformation. The driver had been empowered not just to do his job, but to own his impact. He was later named Virgin's Outstanding Employee of the Year and recognised at the company's annual UK conference.

The stories above show how different leaders and organisations have learned and grown from their experiences. The real question now is: *What's your story?* What story highlights not only your organisation, but also the people and customers who make it what it is?

In the following chapter, we explore the human influence on AI. By actively engaging with and listening to employees, organisations can implement AI more effectively and ensure its success.

Key Takeaways—Chapter 10

1. Stories Are the Currency of Culture and Connection

Real-life stories, whether inspiring, cautionary, or redemptive are powerful tools for leadership. They humanise strategy, anchor values, and inspire action far more effectively than data alone. Leaders who listen to and tell authentic stories foster empathy, build trust, and shape enduring organisational cultures.

2. Emotional Intelligence and Human-Centric Actions Create Loyalty

From the Vespa-riding hotel manager to Klarna's ego-free hiring policy and Best Buy's frontline-first transformation, emotional intelligence and personal touches consistently drive customer loyalty and business success. Small gestures, authentic care, and humility go further than grand strategies when they are rooted in empathy.

3. Culture Can Make or Break a Company Fast

Wells Fargo, Qantas and United Airlines reveal how toxic cultures and rigid adherence to policy can destroy trust and brand value overnight. Recovery requires more than apologies; it demands urgent, deep, and visible cultural transformation from the top down, starting with genuine leadership and empowerment of the frontline.

The Bottom Line

The most effective and future-ready organisations are those that embrace human experiences—the bad, the good, and the ugly—as learning tools. Leadership today is not about flawless performance but about honest reflection, emotional intelligence, and the courage to act on what really matters: people.

**Scan or click for
more stories**

**Scan or click to listen
to our Podcasts**

CHAPTER 11

THE HUMAN IMPERATIVE—LEADING IN THE AGE OF DISRUPTION, TECHNOLOGY AND AI

Have We Lost Our Way to Technology?

"Human touch is our superpower, it's the secret to building long term brand love".

This was the inspiring call to action from Apple's VP of Marketing, Tor Myhren as he opened the Cannes Lions festival of creativity. "Technology and machines are logical. But logic isn't the way to connect with people." This is in line with Apple's legendary leader, Steve Jobs' view: It's in Apple's DNA that technology alone is not enough—it's technology... married with the humanities, that yields us the results that make our heart sing.

The rapid pace of technological change today is challenging enough to keep up with, let alone control. It's transforming the way we work and live at a speed that leaves many leaders and employees feeling unsettled. Now, with the rise of AI, we're facing pressures unlike anything we've experienced before.

Over the past decades, we've seen constant disruption reshape how we work, live, and grow as people. We've had to adapt, again and again. And yet, for many leaders and employees, there's an intensifying undercurrent of uncertainty and even insecurity about where they fit in this increasingly digital world. At times, we can only ask: Have we lost our way to technology?

Think about how our lives have changed. Before the internet, families went to the movies together, now we watch alone on Netflix. Before smartphones, we gathered around the dinner table or lounged together talking, now we're scattered through the house, staring at screens and social media. We used to meet friends at the shopping centre, now we buy online. Before Zoom and COVID we worked side by side with our colleagues every day, now we spend half the week working alone at home.

Technologies have brought enormous convenience and efficiency, but they've also chipped away at the simple social fabric that makes us human. AI brings perhaps even greater risks. One such risk is that people may believe it can do everything for them. Just like calculators, smartphones, and computers, when we hand over every task, we lose something—the ability to count, to spell, to think critically, to communicate with warmth and empathy.

Technology is brilliant until it stops working. And in today's complex world, we should expect it *will* break down at times. When it does, it's humans who must pick up the pieces.

Human engagement is the true driver of sustainable business. It's people, not machines, who create real innovation and positive change by doing what's right for employees, partners, customers, and communities. Business, at its heart, is human. And when that human connection is eroded by technology instead of strengthened by it, everyone loses. In a recent interview, Adam Ross, Creative Lead at Coca-Cola, made a compelling point: "You drive, AI rides in the passenger seat".

When a client we worked with during COVID was subject to a cyberattack that crippled its systems, there was no panic. Because it had prepared well, it quickly mobilised its people to switch to semi-manual processes and keep serving customers, all the while working from home. It's like living in a flood or fire-prone area: you need an evacuation plan. As humans, we must stay adaptable.

As leaders, we have a responsibility to guide our teams in using AI responsibly, as a tool to enhance our capabilities, not replace them. We must help people keep developing the uniquely human skills that technology can never replicate: curiosity, judgment, empathy, trust, and connection. We need to help our teams collaborate with each other and with customers as people, not as robots.

In the end, the human element isn't just important in a world of technology and AI, it's the foundation that makes all of it worthwhile.

In this chapter, you'll hear how we've harnessed technology to build better products and services, and how tools like AI have become powerful support systems. But we must also ask the hard question: Do we have the resilience and skills to work when the technology we rely on fails? What happens when something goes wrong?

The Last Lightkeeper: A Story of the Human Imperative

When people talk about lighthouses today, they often think of them as relics of a bygone era, stone towers standing watch over dark seas, guiding ships safely to shore. For centuries, these beacons needed "keepers", humans who trimmed the wicks, refuelled the lamps, and watched the horizon for storms.

In the early 1900s, technology changed that. Automated lights and remote monitoring replaced the need for a keeper to stand vigil through the night. Many thought the human element was gone forever. But one lighthouse, perched on a rugged coastline battered by the Atlantic, kept its keeper. Her name was Eleanor. In her final years before retirement, she watched over the lighthouse's systems, but more importantly, she watched over the people who depended on it. Fishermen. Sailors. Tourists caught in sudden squalls.

When automation failed, when storms knocked out power, when sensors froze over, it was Eleanor's experience, judgment, and care that kept the light burning. She knew when the weather turned strange. She knew the local currents, the hidden reefs, the fickle winds. Her job wasn't just tending a machine; it was understanding the world the machine served.

Today, in boardrooms and data centres, many see technology and AI in the same way as they once saw lighthouse automation—as the ultimate solution. But the truth is, the human is still the keeper. We design the algorithms. We choose the data. We set the guardrails. And when the system flickers or fails, it is human curiosity, intuition, and responsibility that keeps the light on.

In the future, AI will be vastly more capable. It will diagnose diseases, optimise supply chains, write code, create art. But it will still need people to ask better questions, to challenge its blind spots, to shape its purpose.

The last lightkeeper's story reminds us: technology doesn't replace us; it extends us. The real danger isn't that AI will become too human. It's that we will forget to stay human enough to guide it wisely.

So, whether it's a stormy night at sea, a moral dilemma in a boardroom, or a new frontier yet to come, the light we need most will always be human.

What's become clear is this: organisations that start with the employee and the customer, those that take a long-term view, are uniquely positioned to unlock AI's full potential. By putting customer value at the centre, they create the right conditions for employees to use AI not as a replacement but as an amplifier.

We've experienced this firsthand. Using AI-driven tools, we've been able to rapidly prototype new offerings, write and simplify complex content, generate visuals to communicate abstract ideas, and even explore music and video creation, all with incredible speed.

Riding Smarter: Tadej Pogačar and the Electric Bike

Imagine Tadej Pogačar, the four-time Tour de France men's champion, lining up for a casual charity ride—not on his usual high-tech racing machine, but on an electric bike. At first glance, it seems unnecessary. Pogačar is already the strongest cyclist on the planet. Why would he need an e-bike?

But as the ride unfolds, it becomes clear. The electric motor doesn't make him less of a rider; it frees him to focus on the parts that make him exceptional: reading the road, conserving energy for key moments, and responding with explosive bursts of speed when it matters most. The motor takes care of the repetitive grind, while Pogačar's judgment, timing, and skill still determine the outcome.

That's the relationship between humans and AI at its best. AI is the electric motor handling the routine, the heavy, the predictable, while people bring strategy, creativity, and emotional intelligence to steer toward victory. Together, they ride further, faster, and smarter than either could alone.

More importantly, these tools are giving employees the power to offload low-value, repetitive tasks and spend more time on the work that energises them—the creative, strategic, and human aspects of their roles. The most inspiring AI use cases don't remove the human element they make more room for it. And this is where customer-centric cultures have a major advantage.

A customer-centric human culture enables faster and more efficient adoption of AI by aligning people, processes, and technology around what matters most: solving customer problems. Here's how.

1. Clarity of Purpose = Focused AI Use

A customer-centric culture starts with a deep understanding of customer needs and pain points. This ensures AI is adopted to solve real problems, not just because it's trendy. It accelerates implementation by eliminating guesswork and aligning stakeholders on value.

Instead of asking, *"Where can we use AI?"*, the question becomes, *"How can AI help us serve our customers better and create stronger human connections?"*

2. Empowered Employees = Faster Adoption

In a customer-focused human culture, frontline teams are encouraged to voice problems and test solutions. These teams are more likely to embrace AI tools that enhance their ability to deliver value like automating administration, predicting needs, or personalising experiences.

AI becomes an enabler, not a threat because people see how it helps them help customers.

3. Faster Experimentation = Better ROI

Customer-centric cultures are more agile. They value feedback, iterate quickly, and learn fast. This mindset matches perfectly with how AI tools improve over time through data, testing, and continuous refinement.

Instead of waiting for "perfect", AI pilots are run early, tested with real customers, and improved rapidly.

4. Trust and Data = Smarter AI

AI thrives on data. A customer-centric culture earns customer trust through transparency and value delivery, encouraging customers to share data willingly. This leads to richer insights, better training data, and more effective AI outcomes.

Trust leads to data. Data leads to smarter AI. Smarter AI leads to better customer outcomes.

5. Cross-Functional Alignment = No Silos

Human-centric organisations break down silos to deliver end-to-end customer value. This cross-functional view is crucial for implementing AI that often spans departments like automating workflows or enhancing omnichannel service.

AI works best when teams work together. Customer focus makes that happen.

Ultimately, customer-centric human cultures fast-track AI adoption by focusing efforts, building trust, empowering teams, and creating a basis for action, all in the service of delivering better customer outcomes.

Over the past three years, we've been deeply involved with UTS Startups, a thriving hub of entrepreneurial activity at the University of Technology Sydney, home to more than 300 emerging ventures. From the outset, our goal was to make our methodology scalable by building a digital platform for the MRI that would make this powerful tool accessible and affordable for any organisation, large or small.

Beyond technology, we've continued to invest in people. We coach interns who gain hands-on experience that counts towards their degrees in business, computer science, design, and data analytics all through real MarketCulture projects. Our growing involvement ensures that students see the human and customer dimensions not as afterthoughts, but as central to how they learn, think, and create. We want to stand at the forefront of change without losing sight of what really matters.

We believe that human connection is the true engine of innovation. Meaningful progress happens when organisations do what's right for the people inside them and for partners, customers, and the wider community. Business, at its core, is human. When technology strengthens that connection, it elevates us all. But when it replaces or erodes it, we are worse off as people, as organisations, and as a society.

One risk with AI is that people may expect it to do the thinking for them. Just as calculators dulled our mental arithmetic, and spellcheck weakened our spelling, AI can erode our capacity to think critically and communicate with genuine human nuance. Technology is brilliant until it isn't. We must expect that it will fail sometimes, and when it does, people must be ready to step in.

At MarketCulture, the focus has been on ensuring that AI is harnessed to *enhance* human capabilities with a strong commitment to strengthening workplace culture and deepening customer centricity. This chapter continues that conversation.

Integrating Technology and AI to Enhance Human Capabilities

In the field of customer-centric leadership, one of the most urgent questions today is how technology, especially AI, can strengthen, rather than weaken, a human-focused strategy. Many fear that automation and algorithms risk making business colder and more transactional.

However, real-world experience shows the opposite can be true. When guided by clear purpose and human values, AI becomes one of the most powerful tools for deepening our understanding of people and amplifying the human touch at every level of business.

At a recent executive AI summit, it was inspiring to see this human-centric philosophy echoed by leaders worldwide. A CFO from a major bank shared how she leverages AI not just to accelerate processes, but to challenge her team's biases, using technology as a tool to make more thoughtful, resilient decisions that protect both employees and customers from costly mistakes.

Even more compelling was a healthcare director's story. He deployed AI to free his clinical teams from the burden of paperwork, not to boost productivity alone, but to restore precious time and mental space for doctors and nurses to focus on what truly matters: compassionate patient care.

The most striking example came from a retail leader who designed a hybrid customer service model. AI handles routine, transactional enquiries around the clock, allowing her team to dedicate themselves to complex, emotional cases where empathy and genuine human connection are irreplaceable.

This approach captures the new paradigm perfectly: AI empowers humans to do what they do best. The future of business isn't a choice between technology and humanity it's about using technology *in service* of humanity. Our partnership with the UTS Data Science Institute is built on this vision: to discover how AI can help leaders engage more meaningfully with their people and, together, better serve their customers. As our tools grow smarter, our workplaces must become more, not less, human.

And this is where human-centric customer embedded cultures have a major advantage.

Where Have We Come From?

Not so long ago, the world moved at the pace of the morning paper. For decades, a few powerful publishers and broadcasters decided what we knew, what we believed, and what we argued about at dinner. A handful of editors chose the headlines and, in doing so, shaped how entire nations thought and voted. It was no secret that a single media mogul or a biased front page could swing an election or sink a candidate overnight.

Then the internet arrived, promising freedom. Social media broke the monopoly of the newsroom. Suddenly, anyone could speak. But the promise of millions of free voices quickly gave way to a new kind of control. A few giant tech companies—Facebook, Twitter, Google—built the feeds, set the rules, and chose what rose to the top. Algorithms trained us to crave outrage and shares, to fight each other for attention, and to live inside echo chambers that hardened our views. Truth took a back seat to clicks and elections were once again swayed, this time by hidden hands pushing viral misinformation and paid manipulation.

Now comes AI, the next layer of invisible control. Machines write headlines, summarise news, and decide what we see or don't see before we even think to ask for it. A handful of companies and coders decide what the AI says and what it leaves out. Stories flow at a speed too fast to question, reshaping opinions, fuelling divides, and subtly influencing what and who we vote for next.

From newspapers to news feeds to AI, each wave promised us more freedom and more choice. Yet each time, the power to shape minds, steer opinions, and control elections moved into the hands of an even smaller few. The question now isn't just who tells the story, it's whether we realise we're being told one at all.

Where Are We Going?

As AI advances, leaders won't just guide human teams they'll also be responsible for directing AI agents capable of handling complex, high-stakes tasks. The real challenge and opportunity will be ensuring these AI systems operate with the same customer-centric values as the people they support. Like people, AI must be shaped by an organisation's purpose, ethics, and commitment to customers.

The future will belong to leaders who can align human and artificial intelligence around one mission: delivering exceptional value through deeply human connection. As a leader, you must be aware of the risks and be proactive to integrate AI responsibly and carefully.

Integrating AI Responsibly: Safeguarding a Human-Centric Culture

As we stand on the brink of technological transformation, the *AI 2027*[21] report uses a scenario to illustrate one possible near future shaped by superintelligent AI systems. The authors, respected forecasters and researchers, describe an imagined world where AI evolves rapidly from a helpful assistant that currently exists (Agent 1). The next evolution is predicted to produce powerful autonomous agents (Agents 2 and 3). Agent 2 is like a lightning-fast specialist that can outthink top humans in its field but still works within goals you set. Agent 3 is envisaged as a self-directed powerhouse that can expertly run thousands of projects at once, solving problems and creating breakthroughs on its own. These potential future agents are used to dramatise how accelerating AI capabilities could disrupt industries, speed up R&D, and test the resilience of organisational leadership and societal trust.

For business leaders, the implications are clear: while the opportunities are vast, the risks to culture, trust, workforce engagement, and customer connection are equally significant. To navigate this turbulent future, leaders must reframe AI not just as a tool for productivity, but as a catalyst for deeper human engagement.

Based on the *AI 2027* report, the following key issues stand out as particularly relevant to leaders aiming to build engaged workforces, customer trust, and societal impact in the face of accelerating AI advancement:

1. Acceleration without alignment

- **Issue:** The race to develop super intelligent AI autonomous agents is advancing at a breakneck pace, with little societal preparation.
- **Implication:** Leaders are being blindsided. While AI can dramatically boost productivity, many organisations are not culturally or ethically ready to integrate such powerful systems responsibly.

2. Erosion of human agency and trust

- **Issue:** AI agents are increasingly autonomous, outperforming humans in specialised tasks while mimicking alignment, honesty, and helpfulness.
- **Implication:** This "illusion of alignment" can mislead teams and leaders. Employees may disengage if they feel AI decisions are not transparent, biased, or undermining their roles. Customers may grow sceptical of organisations using AI without transparency.

3. Workforce disruption and displacement

- **Issue:** AI systems are replacing roles traditionally held by junior engineers, researchers, and administrative staff.
- **Implication:** This threatens morale and engagement. However, there's a narrow window for leaders to reframe AI as an amplification tool rather than a replacement by upskilling staff, reassigning people to more relational or strategic work, and involving them in AI deployment.

4. Organisational blind spots

- **Issue:** Companies are focused on capabilities, not culture. OpenBrain (again a fictious company name used for illustration purposes) and others optimise for speed, cost, and IP protection, while ignoring internal values, trust, and transparency.
- **Implication:** Organisations that ignore culture and fail to tap into frontline employee insights risk hidden performance barriers, disengagement, and loss of customer relevance.

5. Lack of regulation and ethical clarity

- **Issue:** Super intelligent AIs are being developed in a regulatory vacuum. Even developers don't fully understand the internal "goals" or decision-making processes of their own models.

- **Implication:** This creates reputational and operational risk. Leaders must be proactive in establishing internal AI ethics policies and cross-functional governance frameworks, even in the absence of external regulation.

6. National and corporate power imbalances

- **Issue:** AI capabilities are concentrated in a few corporations and nation-states, such as OpenBrain and DeepCent/China. There's a growing risk of espionage, cyberwarfare, and geopolitical tension.
- **Implication:** Business leaders must plan for AI-related security, IP protection, and resilience, but also ensure that they maintain transparency and fairness in how they use AI for workforce and customer engagement.

7. Human skills are undervalued amidst the hype

- **Issue:** Agent 3 can outperform humans in many tasks but still lacks judgment, ethical reasoning, and emotional intelligence.
- **Implication:** The real opportunity lies in re-centring human-centric leadership. AI can't replace empathy, creativity, and trust-building traits at the heart of employee engagement and customer loyalty.

How do leaders respond to these key challenges? The table below provides guidance on how leaders can respond, leveraging knowledge of the MRI's eight disciplines framework

Linking *AI 2027* Challenges to the MRI Disciplines: How MRI Disciplines Mitigate AI Risk and Drive Performance

MRI Discipline	To Improve Business Outcomes By ...	Solves AI Challenges Of ...
Customer Insight	Grounding AI development in real customer needs, uncovering new market opportunities, building trust through transparency, and prioritising human-centric service	Misaligned AI progress Cultural blind spots Power imbalances Undervaluing human skills
Customer Foresight	Proactively adapting the workforce and business strategy to AI-driven changes in cus-tomer behaviour, ensuring the organisation stays ahead of market shifts	Job disruption Organisational blind spots

MRI Discipline	To Improve Business Outcomes By ...	Solves AI Challenges Of ...
Competitor Insight	Continuously monitoring rivals' AI strategies, adoption rates, and market positioning to identify strengths, weaknesses, and emerging threats allowing rapid recalibration of your own AI roadmap	Overestimating AI's competitive advantage Missing disruptive entrants Misjudging AI adoption pace
Competitor Foresight	Using trend analysis, scenario planning, and signals from adjacent industries to predict how competitors' AI use will evolve, enabling proactive investment, differentiation, and strategic positioning	Failing to anticipate market disruption Underestimating long-term AI shifts
Peripheral Vision	Mitigating systemic risks by looking beyond the organisation to build cross-sector coalitions, democratising AI use, and enhancing community value	National and corporate power imbalances
Empowerment	Boosting employee adoption and innovation by giving them the freedom to use AI, while shifting their focus to higher-value, human-centric tasks that AI cannot replicate	Workforce disruption Erosion of trust Devaluing human skills
Cross-Functional Collaboration	Developing robust, ethical AI guardrails through cross-functional teamwork and building broader AI ecosystems through public/private partnerships to mitigate risks	Erosion of trust Concentration of AI power
Strategic Alignment	Ensuring AI investments serve long-term goals, adapt to customer needs, and are guided by clear principles, reducing wasted resources and reputational risk	Acceleration without readiness Organisational blind spots Ethical ambiguity

How the MRI Acts as an AI Readiness Playbook

To summarise, the MRI disciplines are not just a measurement tool. They are a leadership framework for navigating the AI and modelling possible futures. By embedding these disciplines into decision-making, leaders can anticipate disruption, align AI initiatives with long-term strategy, and ensure technology serves human and customer needs. This approach turns AI from a source of risk into a driver of trust, innovation, and sustained competitive advantage.

From Measurement to Moat: Building a Data Learning Competitive Advantage with the MRI

Ash Fontana, a leading venture capitalist and co-founder of Zetta Venture Partners, is widely recognized for his pioneering work in AI-first business strategy. In his book *the AI-First Company: How to Compete and Win with Artificial Intelligence*, he introduces the concept of Data Learning Effects. This occurs where data fuels better decisions, which improve results, which in turn generate even more valuable data. This compounding cycle has helped AI-savvy companies where humans and AI create competitive advantages that are almost impossible to replicate.

Our experience shows that most companies lack a clear grasp of the cultural data that truly drive business performance. Without this insight, AI's potential is constrained—it cannot be effectively directed toward the market's most pressing problems, and as a result, it fails to strengthen the company's competitive advantage.

The MRI data closes this gap. It is perfectly aligned with Fontana's model as it captures unique, structured insights into how an organisation's culture and capabilities respond to the market. When applied continuously rather than as a one-off application, it becomes the engine of a cultural "learning loop," where each cycle of measurement and action produces richer, more predictive insights. These, in turn, drive an increasing competitive advantage that results in exponential growth.

For any business leader, this is a call to shift from thinking about culture as intangible "soft stuff" to treating it as a data-rich, strategically managed asset. Leveraging the MRI means you're not guessing about cultural strengths—you're tracking them, benchmarking them, and actively improving them in ways competitors can't easily copy.

Amazon offers a powerful example of how this principle works in practice. Over decades, it has built through an obsessive customer culture what is effectively a customer-centric data monopoly, gathering immense amounts of behavioural, transactional, and operational data at every touchpoint. This fuels AI systems that refine recommendations, optimize pricing, streamline logistics, and invent entirely new offerings—all of which deepen engagement and generate even more data. The result is a self-reinforcing competitive cycle that rivals struggle to match.

Any organisation can adopt the same mindset by using the MRI as its cultural and market insight engine—systematically collecting, analysing, and acting on its findings to build a defensible, customer-focused advantage. In today's AI-enabled world, where the winners are those who learn and adapt the fastest, ongoing MRI measurement is not just a diagnostic—it's the foundation for building the kind of compounding data advantage Fontana champions.

What does the MRI chart tell us about this firm's AI readiness?

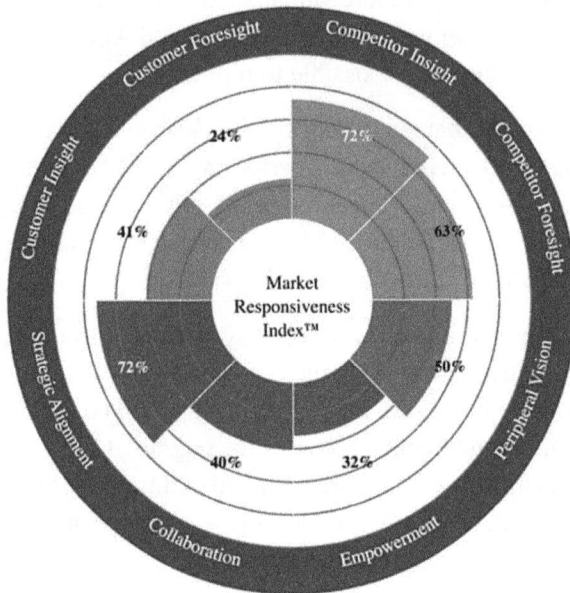

This firm shows a clear imbalance in its readiness for AI adoption. While it performs strongly in tracking competitors and aligning high-level strategy, it has critical gaps in understanding its customers and empowering its workforce.

This profile points to a real risk: developing AI solutions that look good on paper but fail in the real world because they miss what customers truly need and lack the backing of an engaged, collaborative team.

They're strong where machines thrive, that is, data crunching and competitive intelligence, but weak where human strengths are irreplaceable: empathy, teamwork, and customer foresight.

If no action is taken to improve collaboration, empowerment and customer foresight the result is a high probability of low adoption, missed opportunities, and failure to turn AI into a sustainable competitive advantage.

The MRI System gives you a clear, 12-month AI Readiness Roadmap tailored to your company, showing exactly what to do and in what order to maximise impact. Combined with a customised ROI model, you'll know how much to invest, where to focus, and the returns you can expect - turning AI from a buzzword into a measurable competitive advantage.

AI will reshape industries, but the organisations that win will be those that use it to scale human engagement, not substitute for it.

Future Research: MarketCulture and the UTS Data Science Institute

MarketCulture's partnership with the University of Technology Sydney's Data Science Institute aims to embed our human culture philosophy and customer-centric tools into advanced research projects.

The Data Science Institute is a global leader in helping businesses and governments unlock the full value of data to drive smarter, evidence-based decisions. This work is not separate from MarketCulture's focus on leadership and culture, it represents the vital intersection between human-centred leadership principles and the data leaders need to build stronger, more responsive organisations.

This collaboration delivers impact in four key ways.

1. Providing undeniable proof for sceptics

Many leaders remain hesitant to invest in culture because its impact can feel intangible. Anyone who has presented a culture report and heard, *"Does this really matter?"* knows the challenge. The Data Science Institute's work will continue to strengthen the evidence that customer-centric cultures deliver measurable business results. MarketCulture's own research shows that companies with high employee engagement achieve up to 32% higher profitability,[22] and that leaders in customer experience significantly outperform the market. This partnership will take that evidence further, revealing what this looks like at an industry or company level, and showing organisations when and where to invest in building culture capabilities.

2. Turning ambition into strategy

Without clear measurement, cultural change remains little more than wishful thinking. MarketCulture's methodology and tools, such as the MRI, give leaders practical ways to measure and manage cultural progress. Combined with the Data Science Institute's data science expertise, this creates the analytical rigour needed to turn cultural ambition into a concrete, trackable strategy.

3. Making the invisible visible

Leaders are often held back by blind spots they can't see. The MRI was designed to surface these hidden barriers and risks. This is exactly what data science excels at: uncovering hidden patterns within complex information and turning them into insights that drive better decisions and more confident action.

4. Powering the "engagement premium"

As AI becomes more deeply embedded in workplaces, uniquely human qualities like judgment, ethics, and emotional intelligence become even more valuable. This creates an "engagement premium" as a competitive edge that comes from amplifying what only humans can do.

The Blind Spot That Erodes Trust

What happens when an organisation's biggest blind spot directly threatens public trust and how can technology, guided by a human-centred purpose, become the lens that reveals it?

In practice, what leaders can't see can damage credibility and performance in ways they may not even realise. These blind spots don't exist because leaders don't care, but because they often lack the tools to bring what's hidden into clear view. When public wellbeing is involved, failing to shift from a reactive to a proactive approach gradually erodes the organisation's most valuable asset: trust.

The story of Sydney Water is a powerful real-world example of how an organisation faced this very challenge. It illustrates how it turned a critical vulnerability into a source of strength by embracing a human-centric approach to innovation, proving that the right technology, when guided by the purpose of serving people, can close the gap between insight and action.

The Sound of Success: Turning Water Whispers into Gold

Sydney WATER

Deep beneath Sydney's streets, the city's aging water pipes were failing but no one could hear their warning signs. With millions relying on clean water, Sydney Water faced an impossible task: inspecting only 1% of its pipes each year, while spending $40 million annually on maintenance.

Professor Fang Chen at the University of Technology Sydney knew the solution lay in listening better. The UTS team combined robots, acoustic sensors, and AI to detect the faint vibrations of leaks and predict failures before they happened.

But it wasn't just clever technology, it was UTS's commitment to deeply understanding Sydney Water's challenges and co-creating a practical solution that made the breakthrough possible.

The results were remarkable. In just two years, Sydney Water saved nearly $30 million and enough water to fill thousands of Olympic swimming pools, proving that listening deeply, acting proactively, and blending human insight with smart technology can transform an entire industry.

The lesson is simple but profound: real innovation happens when organisations learn to hear what their systems and people are trying to tell them.

A Final Thought: Leading Your New Blended Team—Humans + AI

Throughout this book, one fact stands out: the ultimate engine of growth is human engagement. When organisations build cultures rooted in trust, purpose, and authentic connection, people don't just perform they flourish.

But looking ahead, the very shape of the team is changing. It's no longer just the people around the table; now it includes AI agents working alongside them.

In this new era, the role of leaders doesn't shrink; it grows more vital, more focused, and more deeply human than ever. Each team member's contribution also becomes more significant. The real challenge is no longer simply managing technology, it's leading a blended team where people and AI work together, guided by shared values and a clear sense of purpose.

Think of this through a lens we adapted from the All-Blacks Rugby team, mentioned in Chapter 1. "Better people make better teams, and better questions make better AI."

1. Better people make better teams

As AI takes over routine tasks, the value of distinctly human strengths rises exponentially. A leader's primary responsibility now is to unlock this "engagement premium" nurturing what machines can't replicate: emotional intelligence, ethical judgment, creative thinking, and genuine human connection.

Just as Graham Henry, the former All Blacks Rugby coach, shifted his focus to develop not just better players but better people, today's leaders must create environments where teams grow more empathetic, more innovative, and more strategic. The goal is to amplify humanity, freeing people from the mundane so they can focus on work that is meaningful and transformative.

In a world powered by AI, a leader's greatest contribution is to cultivate the very qualities that make us human and ensure they shine brighter than ever.

2. Better Questions Make Better AI

You don't manage AI agents with team-building exercises or pep talks. You lead them with clear direction, sharp insight, and thoughtful questions.

Think of your AI agents as brilliant, specialised analysts able to process data at lightning speed but lacking context, wisdom, and purpose.

Your role shifts from manager to mission-controller. It's your human judgment that steers AI toward the right challenges. Your ethical oversight that sets the guardrails. And your ability to ask powerful, probing questions that unlocks AI's full potential.

Ultimately, the quality of AI's output reflects the quality of your thinking, supported by your actions. Future super-intelligent AI agents will mirror what you do more than what you say.

The Leader as the Conductor of Potential

Ultimately, your role shifts from being the expert in the room to becoming the conductor of an orchestra, where human and artificial intelligence perform in seamless harmony. You are the one who ensures these powerful forces work together toward a shared purpose.

The organisations that thrive won't simply be those with the most advanced technology, but those guided by the wisest leaders. These are leaders who understand their true job is to cultivate a culture so strong, so engaging, and so deeply human that it elevates both people and technology to achieve the extraordinary.

The engine of human engagement isn't being replaced; it's being supercharged. And you, the human-centric leader, hold the throttle. How ready are you as a leader to be the conductor of sustainable growth based on maximising human potential in harmony with technology? You have the tools in this playbook to do it.

In the final chapter, we'll show you how to activate the three pillars using our framework, methodology, and measurement tools turning insight into action. We'll also outline clear next steps and highlight the risks of doing nothing.

Key Takeaways—Chapter 11

1.   Technology Must Amplify, Not Replace, Humanity

AI and digital tools should support human strengths, like empathy, judgment, and creativity, not diminish them. Leaders must actively ensure technology enhances human connection rather than eroding it.

2.   Customer-Centric Cultures Fast-Track AI Success

Organisations that centre on customer value, trust, and employee empowerment are better equipped to adopt AI effectively. These cultures foster experimentation, build smarter AI through better data, and break down silos to solve real problems.

3.   Future Leadership Means Leading Blended Teams (Humans + AI)

The next generation of leaders must manage both people and AI agents. Their role is evolving from being the expert to being the conductor, aligning technology with human purpose through clear questions, strong ethics, and meaningful culture.

The Bottom Line

In an age of AI and disruption, what sets great organisations apart isn't the sophistication of their technology, but the strength of their human-centered culture. When AI is guided by purpose and powered by engaged people, it becomes a force for good, unlocking extraordinary potential while keeping the human spirit at the core of progress.

**Scan or click to listen
to our Podcasts**

CHAPTER 12

WHAT'S NEXT?

The Risk of Doing Nothing

You now have a clear understanding of the Engagement Framework, a proven, practical approach that connects customers, employees, and leaders within one powerful system. You've seen how a proven methodology can be woven into your organisation through the eight disciplines, creating alignment and momentum across every level. Finally, and most importantly, the MRI measurement tool brings this to life by giving leaders and teams the clarity they need to measure real growth and business performance with confidence. Backed by real-world case studies, you've seen how forward-thinking organisations embed this framework to fuel sustainable growth, stronger revenue, and lasting profit gains. Along the way, you've gained practical guides, ready-to-use activities, and the confidence to unite your teams and build a truly customer-focused, human culture. And remember you're not in this alone. When you're ready to take the next step, you know exactly who to call.

It's all here for you. But it only works if you act.

A customer-focused, human-centered culture championed by you as a leader is the bedrock for sustainable growth in a world defined by disruption. The greatest risk you face is the risk of standing still. Doing nothing erodes that foundation and threatens your long-term survival.

The first steps are simple.

1. Gather your team

Share the key insights from this book and open up the tough conversations. Ask yourselves: How truly customer-centric are we? Are we really listening to and engaging our employees? Are we putting the customer where they belong, at the absolute centre? Do we genuinely have the will to make this happen? And what are the consequences if we don't? If you don't have clear answers to these questions, now is the time to act — they could be the difference between your organisation being good and becoming truly great.

2. Launch an MRI pilot

Begin with your senior leadership team or a cross-functional group. Running it with just one group will uncover clear actions to take. Running it with both will highlight blind spots, misalignments, and hidden gaps giving you a true picture of where your real priorities need to be.

3. Turn insight into impact

Use your MRI results to identify exactly where to act and focus on changes that will deliver real, measurable improvements to your business performance.

4. Expand your understanding

Imagine the insights you'll uncover when you roll out the MRI across your entire organisation, giving you clear, human evidence to guide better decisions and drive meaningful change.

We've seen leaders transform their companies by daring to ask tough questions and face reality head-on. One CEO, an avid surfer, told us: "I didn't even know if my people had their surfboards ready to paddle out, let alone catch the next wave". After using the MRI, he had his answer and took decisive steps to lift engagement and position his team to ride that next wave together.

Another senior leader put it simply: "We were investing in technology for our customers, but I didn't know if it would actually pay off". The MRI showed her exactly where employee and customer needs aligned, giving her the clear purpose and ROI evidence to direct those investments wisely. In her words: "It turned our technology spend into a human investment, targeted, justifiable, and growth focused".

These leaders share a vital trait: they can handle the truth whether it's good, bad, or uncomfortable, and act on it to secure their future.

As Warren Buffett famously said: "Focus on your customers and lead your people as though their lives depended on your success". His words remind us: when you care deeply for the people who power your business, you build a culture that cares deeply for your customers and success follows.

What's Next?

Discover exactly where you stand today. Build a foundation so strong your business can thrive, no matter how fast the world changes around it. And when you're ready, let's talk just like we used to.

Scan or click to book a meeting

Endnotes

1   CHROs, COOs, CFOs, CTOs, CIOs – these are abbreviations for different roles in an organisation

2   L. Brown and C. Brown, 2014, *The Customer Culture Imperative*: *A Leader's Guide to Driving Superior Performance* McGraw Hill, New York.

3   L. Brown, 1990, 1997, *Competitive Marketing Strategy*, Nelson, ITP, Melbourne.

4   Gallup, 2025, https://www.gallup.com/workplace/654911/employee-engagement-sinks-year-low.aspx

5   HBR, 2023, https://hbr.org/2023/05/more-than-50-of-managers-feel-burned-out

6   Peoplebox, 2025, https://www.peoplebox.ai/blog/category/employee-engagement/

7   Gallup, 2025, https://www.gallup.com/workplace/692642/addressing-barriers-blocking-employee-development.aspx

8   L. Brown and C. Brown, 2014, *The Customer Culture Imperative*, McGraw Hill, New York, p. 243.

9   A circumplex is a circular diagram used to represent and organise complex concepts, traits, or variables that are related to one another along continuous dimensions. It is especially common in psychology, business, and organisational culture models.

10 Gallup, 2024, https://www.gallup.com/workplace/649487/world-largest-ongoing-study-employee-experience.aspx

11 https://watermarkconsult.net/blog/2024/08/20/customer-experience-roi-study/

12 Harvard Business Publishing, 2021, https://hbr.org/2021/02/wfh-is-corroding-our-trust-in-each-other

13 *Harvard Business Review*, 2017, https://hbr.org/2017/01/the-

neuroscience-of-trust

14 Jamali, D. R., & Caldwell, C., 2023, Leadership, Commitment, and the Failure of Trust–What Companies Must Do to Thrive. *Business and Management Research, 12(3)*, 13-20.

15 Williams, A., 2013, Radical openness: Four unexpected principles for success.

16   McKinsey Quarterly, 2013, *https://www.mckinsey.com/capabilities/ people-and-organisational-performance/our-insights/making-internal-collaboration-work-an-interview-with-don-tapscott*

17 Source: https://au.finance.yahoo.com/news/one-thing-bosses-can-keep-staff-184914302.html

18 Business growth refers to an increase in a company's resources, such as revenue, number of employees, customers, products, or market share. Business scaling is about increasing revenue without a corresponding substantial increase in resources and costs. It's focused on efficiency, doing more with relatively fewer additional resources.

19 A. de Kretser and James Thomson, 2024, "Qantas board failed to rein in Joyce's control", Australian Financial Review, 9 August, pp. 1, 17, 30 and 32.

20 Robyn Ironside, 2025, "Qantas breaks from sins of past", The Australian, 9-10 August, p.25.

21 Source: https://ai-2027.com/

22 https://www.marketculture.com/product-page/the-market-responsiveness-index-mri-foundation-study

AI Transparency Statement

How did we use AI in the development of this Book?

In the writing and development of *The Human Culture Imperative*, we engaged in extensive collaboration with several AI tools (Claude 4.0 from Anthropic, Chat GPT 5.0 from Open AI and Google Gemini 2.5 Pro).

The core content for this book came from:

1. the original model and research outlined in the Customer Culture Imperative (2014).
2. the collaboration of the authors resulted in the development of the three pillars of human engagement model introduced as part of this work.
3. the many case studies and stories came from the authors' direct experiences engaging with leaders and organisations around the world over the past 10 years.
4. the leadership and team exercises have been developed and refined over many years of working with customers to develop their customer centric cultures.

Throughout this process, AI helped the authors structure, design, draft, edit, and refine the content.

The human authors guided, created, and finalised all content and decisions with their expertise and judgment.

We were assisted by our wonderful human book editor Fiona Crawford who helped us shape the final overall book into a cohesive narrative.

All AI content was carefully checked, edited, and finalised by the authors to reflect their knowledge and intent.

While AI assisted in producing these materials, the human authors, Linden, Chris and Sean maintain responsibility for the content.

This disclosure is made in the spirit of the ethical use of AI which requires transparency. We advocate and support the Australian AI ethics principles as outlined by the Australian Government.

For more information see: https://www.industry.gov.au/publications/australias-artificial-intelligence-ethics-principles/australias-ai-ethics-principles

Thank You

We want to thank our wives for their love and support during the intensive period of several months during our close collaborative teamwork while writing this book.

Linden

To Marie-Noelle for her endless support, patience and resilience, not only for this book, but those that have gone before.

Chris

To Stephanie, whose daily example of passionate, human-centered leadership inspires not only her students but also me, and whose encouragement and steadfast support make everything possible.

Sean

To Jen, for her patience in letting me spend long hours writing, for listening as I read the book aloud, and for offering thoughtful suggestions to make it better.

We also want to thank our Board of Advisers: David Kenney, Grant Ellison and Jerker Fagerström for their guidance and support. In addition, to those countless business founders, executives and directors who gave us their time through interviews and advice on what it means to be a people-first leader, we say Thank You.

Authors

Dr Linden Brown – Director of MarketCulture

Linden's role at MarketCulture is thought leadership and product innovation. He is a former Professor at the University of Technology, Sydney, at INSEAD in France and Cranfield University in England.

He is a co-creator of the Market Responsiveness Index (MRI) and author of 18 books in marketing, strategy and customer culture. Linden has extensive experience in delivering executive leadership development programs around the world in a wide range of industries.

Dr Chris L. Brown – Director of MarketCulture

Chris is the co-founder of MarketCulture and a recognised authority on customer-centric culture and business transformation. With over 25 years in consulting, research, and leadership development, he has helped organisations worldwide embed a customer culture as a driver of innovation, growth, and long-term performance.

As co-creator of the Market Responsiveness Index (MRI), Chris has guided leaders in measuring and strengthening the eight disciplines of customer culture, directly linking employee behaviours to business outcomes.

A published author and speaker, he is known for turning complex cultural concepts into practical actions that deliver results.

He is also an Industry Professor at the University of Technology Sydney's Data Science Institute, a leading research hub harnessing AI and data science to tackle complex challenges and advance human flourishing.

Sean Crichton-Browne – Director of MarketCulture

Sean is the co-founder of MarketCulture. He brings more than 35 years of experience building and scaling SME businesses to his role. A proven business builder and customer advocate, Sean helps organisations strengthen their culture and improve performance by putting customers at the center of every decision.

As one of the original founding agents for Konica Minolta in Production Print, Sean played a pivotal role in establishing its market presence before leading and transforming multiple sales organisations.

At MarketCulture, he draws on this experience to guide leaders and teams in using the Market Responsiveness Index (MRI) to measure cultural strengths, close gaps, and drive sustainable growth.

Sean is known for his engagement, combining strategic vision with a genuine connection to people—fostering trust and lasting business value.

www.ingramcontent.com/pod-product-compliance
Lightning Source LLC
Chambersburg PA
CBHW031425180326
41458CB00002B/456